Python 3 Text Processing with NLTK 3 Cookbook

Over 80 practical recipes on natural language processing techniques using Python's NLTK 3.0

Jacob Perkins

[PACKT] open source✳
PUBLISHING   community experience distilled

BIRMINGHAM - MUMBAI

Python 3 Text Processing with NLTK 3 Cookbook

First published: November 2010

Second edition: August 2014

Production reference: 1200814

Published by Packt Publishing Ltd.
Livery Place
35 Livery Street
Birmingham B3 2PB, UK.

ISBN 978-1-78216-785-3

www.packtpub.com

Cover image by Faiz Fattohi (faizfattohi@gmail.com)

Credits

Author

Jacob Perkins

Reviewers

Patrick Chan

Mohit Goenka

Lihang Li

Maurice HT Ling

Jing (Dave) Tian

Commissioning Editor

Kevin Colaco

Acquisition Editor

Kevin Colaco

Content Development Editor

Amey Varangaonkar

Technical Editor

Humera Shaikh

Copy Editors

Deepa Nambiar

Laxmi Subramanian

Project Coordinator

Leena Purkait

Proofreaders

Simran Bhogal

Paul Hindle

Indexers

Hemangini Bari

Mariammal Chettiyar

Tejal Soni

Priya Subramani

Graphics

Ronak Dhruv

Disha Haria

Yuvraj Mannari

Abhinash Sahu

Production Coordinators

Pooja Chiplunkar

Conidon Miranda

Nilesh R. Mohite

Cover Work

Pooja Chiplunkar

About the Author

Jacob Perkins is the cofounder and CTO of Weotta, a local search company. Weotta uses NLP and machine learning to create powerful and easy-to-use natural language search for what to do and where to go.

He is the author of *Python Text Processing with NLTK 2.0 Cookbook, Packt Publishing*, and has contributed a chapter to the *Bad Data Handbook, O'Reilly Media*. He writes about NLTK, Python, and other technology topics at `http://streamhacker.com`.

To demonstrate the capabilities of NLTK and natural language processing, he developed `http://text-processing.com`, which provides simple demos and NLP APIs for commercial use. He has contributed to various open source projects, including NLTK, and created NLTK-Trainer to simplify the process of training NLTK models. For more information, visit `https://github.com/japerk/nltk-trainer`.

I would like to thank my friends and family for their part in making this book possible. And thanks to the editors and reviewers at Packt Publishing for their helpful feedback and suggestions. Finally, this book wouldn't be possible without the fantastic NLTK project and team: `http://www.nltk.org/`.

About the Reviewers

Patrick Chan is an avid Python programmer and uses Python extensively for data processing.

> I would like to thank my beautiful wife, Thanh Tuyen, for her endless patience and understanding in putting up with my various late night hacking sessions.

Mohit Goenka is a software developer in the Yahoo Mail team. Earlier, he graduated from the University of Southern California (USC) with a Master's degree in Computer Science. His thesis focused on Game Theory and Human Behavior concepts as applied in real world coourity games. He also received an award for academic excellence from the Office of International Services at the University of Southern California. He has showcased his presence in various realms of computers including artificial intelligence, machine learning, path planning, multiagent systems, neural networks, computer vision, computer networks, and operating systems.

During his tenure as a student, he won multiple competitions cracking codes and presented his work on Detection of Untouched UFOs to a wide range of audience. Not only is he a software developer by profession, but coding is also his hobby. He spends most of his free time learning about new technology and developing his skills.

What adds feather to his cap is his poetic skills. Some of his works are part of the University of Southern California Libraries archive under the cover of The Lewis Carroll collection. In addition to this, he has made significant contributions by volunteering his time to serve the community.

Lihang Li received his BE degree in Mechanical Engineering from Huazhong University of Science and Technology (HUST), China, in 2012, and now is pursuing his MS degree in Computer Vision at National Laboratory of Pattern Recognition (NLPR) from the Institute of Automation, Chinese Academy of Sciences (IACAS).

As a graduate student, he is focusing on Computer Vision and specially on vision-based SLAM algorithms. In his free time, he likes to take part in open source activities and is now the President of the Open Source Club, Chinese Academy of Sciences. Also, building a multicopter is his hobby and he is with a team called OpenDrone from BLUG (Beijing Linux User Group).

His interests include Linux, open source, cloud computing, virtualization, computer vision, operating systems, machine learning, data mining, and a variety of programming languages.

You can find him by visiting his personal website `http://hustcalm.me`.

Many thanks to my girlfriend Jingjing Shao, who is always with me. Also, I must thank the entire team at Packt Publishing, I would like to thank Kartik who is a very good Project Coordinator. I would also like to thank the other reviewers; though we haven't met, I'm really happy working with you.

Maurice HT Ling completed his PhD in Bioinformatics and BSc (Hons) in Molecular and Cell Biology from The University of Melbourne. He is currently a Research Fellow in Nanyang Technological University, Singapore, and an Honorary Fellow in The University of Melbourne, Australia. He co-edits *The Python Papers* and co-founded the Python User Group (Singapore), where he has been serving as the executive committee member since 2010. His research interests lie in life—biological life, and artificial life and artificial intelligence—and in using computer science and statistics as tools to understand life and its numerous aspects. His personal website is `http://maurice.vodien.com`.

Jing (Dave) Tian is now a graduate research fellow and a PhD student in the Computer and Information Science and Engineering (CISE) department at the University of Florida. His research direction involves system security, embedded system security, trusted computing, and static analysis for security and virtualization. He is interested in Linux kernel hacking and compilers. He also spent a year on AI and machine learning directions and taught classes on *Intro to Problem Solving using Python* and *Operating System* in the Computer Science department at the University of Oregon. Before that, he worked as a software developer in the Linux Control Platform (LCP) group in Alcatel-Lucent (former Lucent Technologies) R&D for around 4 years. He has got BS and ME degrees of EE in China. His website is `http://davejingtian.org`.

I would like to thank the author of the book, who has made a good job for both Python and NLTK. I would also like to thank to the editors of the book, who made this book perfect and offered me the opportunity to review such a nice book.

www.PacktPub.com

Support files, eBooks, discount offers, and more

You might want to visit www.PacktPub.com for support files and downloads related to your book.

Did you know that Packt offers eBook versions of every book published, with PDF and ePub files available? You can upgrade to the eBook version at www.PacktPub.com and as a print book customer, you are entitled to a discount on the eBook copy. Get in touch with us at service@packtpub.com for more details.

At www.PacktPub.com, you can also read a collection of free technical articles, sign up for a range of free newsletters and receive exclusive discounts and offers on Packt books and eBooks.

http://PacktLib.PacktPub.com

Do you need instant solutions to your IT questions? PacktLib is Packt's online digital book library. Here, you can access, read and search across Packt's entire library of books.

Why Subscribe?

- ▸ Fully searchable across every book published by Packt
- ▸ Copy and paste, print and bookmark content
- ▸ On demand and accessible via web browser

Free Access for Packt account holders

If you have an account with Packt at www.PacktPub.com, you can use this to access PacktLib today and view nine entirely free books. Simply use your login credentials for immediate access.

Table of Contents

Preface

Natural language processing is used everywhere, from search engines such as Google or Weotta, to voice interfaces such as Siri or Dragon NaturallySpeaking. Python's Natural Language Toolkit (NLTK) is a suite of libraries that has become one of the best tools for prototyping and building natural language processing systems.

Python 3 Text Processing with NLTK 3 Cookbook is your handy and illustrative guide, which will walk you through many natural language processing techniques in a step-by-step manner. It will demystify the dark arts of text mining and language processing using the comprehensive Natural Language Toolkit.

This book cuts short the preamble, ignores pedagogy, and lets you dive right into the techniques of text processing with a practical hands-on approach.

Get started by learning how to tokenize text into words and sentences, then explore the WordNet lexical dictionary. Learn the basics of stemming and lemmatization. Discover various ways to replace words and perform spelling corrections. Create your own corpora and custom corpus readers, including a MongoDB-based corpus reader. Use part-of-speech taggers to annotate words. Create and transform chunked phrase trees and named entities using partial parsing and chunk transformations. Dig into feature extraction and text classification for sentiment analysis. Learn how to process large amount of text with distributed processing and NoSQL databases.

This book will teach you all that and more, in a hands-on learn-by-doing manner. Become an expert in using NLTK for Natural Language Processing with this useful companion.

What this book covers

Chapter 1, Tokenizing Text and WordNet Basics, covers how to tokenize text into sentences and words, then look up those words in the WordNet lexical dictionary.

Chapter 2, Replacing and Correcting Words, demonstrates various word replacement and correction techniques, including stemming, lemmatization, and using the Enchant spelling dictionary.

Chapter 3, Creating Custom Corpora, explains how to use corpus readers and create custom corpora. It also covers how to use some of the corpora that come with NLTK.

Chapter 4, Part-of-speech Tagging, shows how to annotate a sentence of words with part-of-speech tags, and how to train your own custom part-of-speech tagger.

Chapter 5, Extracting Chunks, covers the chunking process, also known as partial parsing, which can identify phrases and named entities in a sentence. It also explains how to train your own custom chunker and create specific named entity recognizers.

Chapter 6, Transforming Chunks and Trees, demonstrates how to transform chunk phrases and parse trees in various ways.

Chapter 7, Text Classification, shows how to transform text into feature dictionaries, and how to train a text classifier for sentiment analysis. It also covers multi-label classification and classifier evaluation metrics.

Chapter 8, Distributed Processing and Handling Large Datasets, discusses how to use execnet for distributed natural language processing and how to use Redis for storing large datasets.

Chapter 9, Parsing Specific Data Types, covers various Python modules that are useful for parsing specific kinds of data, such as datetimes and HTML.

Appendix, Penn Treebank Part-of-speech Tags, shows a table of Treebank part-of-speech tags, that is a useful reference for *Chapter 3, Creating Custom Corpora*, and *Chapter 4, Part-of-speech Tagging*.

What you need for this book

You will need Python 3 and the listed Python packages. For this book, I used Python 3.3.5. To install the packages, you can use pip (`https://pypi.python.org/pypi/pip/`). The following is the list of the packages in requirements format with the version number used while writing this book:

- NLTK>=3.0a4
- pyenchant>=1.6.5
- lockfile>=0.9.1
- numpy>=1.8.0
- scipy>=0.13.0
- scikit-learn>=0.14.1
- execnet>=1.1
- pymongo>=2.6.3
- redis>=2.8.0

- ▶ lxml>=3.2.3
- ▶ beautifulsoup4>=4.3.2
- ▶ python-dateutil>=2.0
- ▶ charade>=1.0.3

You will also need NLTK-Trainer, which is available at the following link:
`https://github.com/japerk/nltk-trainer`

Beyond Python, there are a couple recipes that use MongoDB and Redis, both NoSQL databases. These can be downloaded at `http://www.mongodb.org/` and `http://redis.io/`, respectively.

Who this book is for

If you are an intermediate to advanced Python programmer who wants to quickly get to grips with using NLTK for natural language processing, this is the book for you. It will help if you are somewhat familiar with basic text processing techniques, such as regular expressions. Programmers with NLTK experience may learn something new, and students of linguistics will find it invaluable.

Conventions

In this book, you will find a number of styles of text that distinguish between different kinds of information. Here are some examples of these styles, and an explanation of their meaning.

Code words in text, database table names, folder names, filenames, file extensions, pathnames, dummy URLs, user input, and Twitter handles are shown as follows: "The `sent_tokenize` function uses an instance of `PunktSentenceTokenizer` from the `nltk.tokenize.punkt` module."

A block of code is set as follows:

```
>>> from nltk.tokenize import sent_tokenize
>>> sent_tokenize(para)
['Hello World.', "It's good to see you.", 'Thanks for buying this
book.']
```

When we wish to draw your attention to a particular part of a code block, the relevant lines or items are set in bold:

```
>>> doc.make_links_absolute('http://hello')
>>> abslinks = list(doc.iterlinks())
>>> (el, attr, link, pos) = abslinks[0]
>>> link
'http://hello/world'
```

Any command-line input or output is written as follows:

```
$ python train_chunker.py treebank_chunk
```

New terms and **important words** are shown in bold. Words that you see on the screen, in menus or dialog boxes for example, appear in the text like this: "Luckily, this will produce an exception with the message **'DictVectorizer' object has no attribute 'vocabulary_'**".

> Warnings or important notes appear in a box like this.

> Tips and tricks appear like this.

Reader feedback

Feedback from our readers is always welcome. Let us know what you think about this book—what you liked or may have disliked. Reader feedback is important for us to develop titles that you really get the most out of.

To send us general feedback, simply send an e-mail to feedback@packtpub.com, and mention the book title via the subject of your message.

If there is a topic that you have expertise in and you are interested in either writing or contributing to a book, see our author guide on www.packtpub.com/authors.

Customer support

Now that you are the proud owner of a Packt book, we have a number of things to help you to get the most from your purchase.

Downloading the example code

You can download the example code files for all Packt books you have purchased from your account at http://www.packtpub.com. If you purchased this book elsewhere, you can visit http://www.packtpub.com/support and register to have the files e-mailed directly to you.

Code for this book is also available at https://github.com/japerk/nltk3-cookbook. This is where you can find named modules mentioned in recipes, such as replacers.py.

Errata

Although we have taken every care to ensure the accuracy of our content, mistakes do happen. If you find a mistake in one of our books—maybe a mistake in the text or the code—we would be grateful if you would report this to us. By doing so, you can save other readers from frustration and help us improve subsequent versions of this book. If you find any errata, please report them by visiting http://www.packtpub.com/submit-errata, selecting your book, clicking on the **errata submission form** link, and entering the details of your errata. Once your errata are verified, your submission will be accepted and the errata will be uploaded on our website, or added to any list of existing errata, under the Errata section of that title. Any existing errata can be viewed by selecting your title from http://www.packtpub.com/support.

Piracy

Piracy of copyright material on the Internet is an ongoing problem across all media. At Packt, we take the protection of our copyright and licenses very seriously. If you come across any illegal copies of our works, in any form, on the Internet, please provide us with the location address or website name immediately so that we can pursue a remedy.

Please contact us at copyright@packtpub.com with a link to the suspected pirated material.

We appreciate your help in protecting our authors, and our ability to bring you valuable content.

Questions

You can contact us at questions@packtpub.com if you are having a problem with any aspect of the book, and we will do our best to address it.

1

Tokenizing Text and WordNet Basics

In this chapter, we will cover the following recipes:

- ▶ Tokenizing text into sentences
- ▶ Tokenizing sentences into words
- ▶ Tokenizing sentences using regular expressions
- ▶ Training a sentence tokenizer
- ▶ Filtering stopwords in a tokenized sentence
- ▶ Looking up Synsets for a word in WordNet
- ▶ Looking up lemmas and synonyms in WordNet
- ▶ Calculating WordNet Synset similarity
- ▶ Discovering word collocations

Introduction

Natural Language ToolKit (NLTK) is a comprehensive Python library for natural language processing and text analytics. Originally designed for teaching, it has been adopted in the industry for research and development due to its usefulness and breadth of coverage. NLTK is often used for rapid prototyping of text processing programs and can even be used in production applications. Demos of select NLTK functionality and production-ready APIs are available at `http://text-processing.com`.

This chapter will cover the basics of tokenizing text and using WordNet. **Tokenization** is a method of breaking up a piece of text into many pieces, such as sentences and words, and is an essential first step for recipes in the later chapters. **WordNet** is a dictionary designed for programmatic access by natural language processing systems. It has many different use cases, including:

▶ Looking up the definition of a word

▶ Finding synonyms and antonyms

▶ Exploring word relations and similarity

▶ Word sense disambiguation for words that have multiple uses and definitions

NLTK includes a WordNet corpus reader, which we will use to access and explore WordNet. A corpus is just a body of text, and corpus readers are designed to make accessing a corpus much easier than direct file access. We'll be using WordNet again in the later chapters, so it's important to familiarize yourself with the basics first.

Tokenizing text into sentences

Tokenization is the process of splitting a string into a list of pieces or tokens. A token is a piece of a whole, so a word is a token in a sentence, and a sentence is a token in a paragraph. We'll start with sentence tokenization, or splitting a paragraph into a list of sentences.

Getting ready

Installation instructions for NLTK are available at `http://nltk.org/install.html` and the latest version at the time of writing this is Version 3.0b1. This version of NLTK is built for Python 3.0 or higher, but it is backwards compatible with Python 2.6 and higher. In this book, we will be using Python 3.3.2. If you've used earlier versions of NLTK (such as version 2.0), note that some of the APIs have changed in Version 3 and are not backwards compatible.

Once you've installed NLTK, you'll also need to install the data following the instructions at `http://nltk.org/data.html`. I recommend installing everything, as we'll be using a number of corpora and pickled objects. The data is installed in a data directory, which on Mac and Linux/Unix is usually `/usr/share/nltk_data`, or on Windows is `C:\nltk_data`. Make sure that `tokenizers/punkt.zip` is in the data directory and has been unpacked so that there's a file at `tokenizers/punkt/PY3/english.pickle`.

Finally, to run the code examples, you'll need to start a Python console. Instructions on how to do so are available at `http://nltk.org/install.html`. For Mac and Linux/Unix users, you can open a terminal and type `python`.

How to do it...

Once NLTK is installed and you have a Python console running, we can start by creating a paragraph of text:

```
>>> para = "Hello World. It's good to see you. Thanks for buying this
book."
```

Downloading the example code

You can download the example code files for all Packt books you have purchased from your account at http://www.packtpub.com. If you purchased this book elsewhere, you can visit http://www.packtpub.com/support and register to have the files e-mailed directly to you.

Now we want to split the paragraph into sentences. First we need to import the sentence tokenization function, and then we can call it with the paragraph as an argument:

```
>>> from nltk.tokenize import sent_tokenize
>>> sent_tokenize(para)
['Hello World.', "It's good to see you.", 'Thanks for buying this
book.']
```

So now we have a list of sentences that we can use for further processing.

How it works...

The sent_tokenize function uses an instance of PunktSentenceTokenizer from the nltk.tokenize.punkt module. This instance has already been trained and works well for many European languages. So it knows what punctuation and characters mark the end of a sentence and the beginning of a new sentence.

There's more...

The instance used in sent_tokenize() is actually loaded on demand from a pickle file. So if you're going to be tokenizing a lot of sentences, it's more efficient to load the PunktSentenceTokenizer class once, and call its tokenize() method instead:

```
>>> import nltk.data
>>> tokenizer = nltk.data.load('tokenizers/punkt/PY3/english.pickle')
>>> tokenizer.tokenize(para)
['Hello World.', "It's good to see you.", 'Thanks for buying this
book.']
```

Tokenizing sentences in other languages

If you want to tokenize sentences in languages other than English, you can load one of the other pickle files in `tokenizers/punkt/PY3` and use it just like the English sentence tokenizer. Here's an example for Spanish:

```
>>> spanish_tokenizer = nltk.data.load('tokenizers/punkt/PY3/spanish.pickle')
>>> spanish_tokenizer.tokenize('Hola amigo. Estoy bien.')
['Hola amigo.', 'Estoy bien.']
```

You can see a list of all the available language tokenizers in `/usr/share/nltk_data/tokenizers/punkt/PY3` (or `C:\nltk_data\tokenizers\punkt\PY3`).

See also

In the next recipe, we'll learn how to split sentences into individual words. After that, we'll cover how to use regular expressions to tokenize text. We'll cover how to train your own sentence tokenizer in an upcoming recipe, *Training a sentence tokenizer*.

Tokenizing sentences into words

In this recipe, we'll split a sentence into individual words. The simple task of creating a list of words from a string is an essential part of all text processing.

How to do it...

Basic word tokenization is very simple; use the `word_tokenize()` function:

```
>>> from nltk.tokenize import word_tokenize
>>> word_tokenize('Hello World.')
['Hello', 'World', '.']
```

How it works...

The `word_tokenize()` function is a wrapper function that calls `tokenize()` on an instance of the `TreebankWordTokenizer` class. It's equivalent to the following code:

```
>>> from nltk.tokenize import TreebankWordTokenizer
>>> tokenizer = TreebankWordTokenizer()
>>> tokenizer.tokenize('Hello World.')
['Hello', 'World', '.']
```

It works by separating words using spaces and punctuation. And as you can see, it does not discard the punctuation, allowing you to decide what to do with it.

There's more...

Ignoring the obviously named `WhitespaceTokenizer` and `SpaceTokenizer`, there are two other word tokenizers worth looking at: `PunktWordTokenizer` and `WordPunctTokenizer`. These differ from `TreebankWordTokenizer` by how they handle punctuation and contractions, but they all inherit from `TokenizerI`. The inheritance tree looks like what's shown in the following diagram:

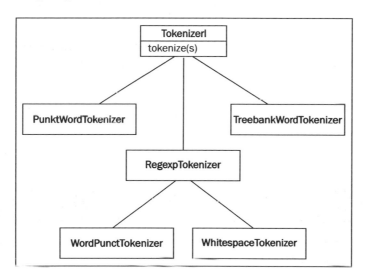

Separating contractions

The `TreebankWordTokenizer` class uses conventions found in the Penn Treebank corpus. This corpus is one of the most used corpora for natural language processing, and was created in the 1980s by annotating articles from the *Wall Street Journal*. We'll be using this later in *Chapter 4, Part-of-speech Tagging*, and *Chapter 5, Extracting Chunks*.

One of the tokenizer's most significant conventions is to separate contractions. For example, consider the following code:

```
>>> word_tokenize("can't")
['ca', "n't"]
```

If you find this convention unacceptable, then read on for alternatives, and see the next recipe for tokenizing with regular expressions.

PunktWordTokenizer

An alternative word tokenizer is `PunktWordTokenizer`. It splits on punctuation, but keeps it with the word instead of creating separate tokens, as shown in the following code:

```
>>> from nltk.tokenize import PunktWordTokenizer
>>> tokenizer = PunktWordTokenizer()
>>> tokenizer.tokenize("Can't is a contraction.")
['Can', "'t", 'is', 'a', 'contraction.']
```

WordPunctTokenizer

Another alternative word tokenizer is `WordPunctTokenizer`. It splits all punctuation into separate tokens:

```
>>> from nltk.tokenize import WordPunctTokenizer
>>> tokenizer = WordPunctTokenizer()
>>> tokenizer.tokenize("Can't is a contraction.")
['Can', "'", 't', 'is', 'a', 'contraction', '.']
```

See also

For more control over word tokenization, you'll want to read the next recipe to learn how to use regular expressions and the `RegexpTokenizer` for tokenization. And for more on the Penn Treebank corpus, visit `http://www.cis.upenn.edu/~treebank/`.

Tokenizing sentences using regular expressions

Regular expressions can be used if you want complete control over how to tokenize text. As regular expressions can get complicated very quickly, I only recommend using them if the word tokenizers covered in the previous recipe are unacceptable.

Getting ready

First you need to decide how you want to tokenize a piece of text as this will determine how you construct your regular expression. The choices are:

- ▸ Match on the tokens
- ▸ Match on the separators or gaps

We'll start with an example of the first, matching alphanumeric tokens plus single quotes so that we don't split up contractions.

How to do it...

We'll create an instance of `RegexpTokenizer`, giving it a regular expression string to use for matching tokens:

```
>>> from nltk.tokenize import RegexpTokenizer
>>> tokenizer = RegexpTokenizer("[\w']+")
>>> tokenizer.tokenize("Can't is a contraction.")
["Can't", 'is', 'a', 'contraction']
```

There's also a simple helper function you can use if you don't want to instantiate the class, as shown in the following code:

```
>>> from nltk.tokenize import regexp_tokenize
>>> regexp_tokenize("Can't is a contraction.", "[\w']+")
["Can't", 'is', 'a', 'contraction']
```

Now we finally have something that can treat contractions as whole words, instead of splitting them into tokens.

How it works...

The `RegexpTokenizer` class works by compiling your pattern, then calling `re.findall()` on your text. You could do all this yourself using the `re` module, but `RegexpTokenizer` implements the `TokenizerI` interface, just like all the word tokenizers from the previous recipe. This means it can be used by other parts of the NLTK package, such as corpus readers, which we'll cover in detail in *Chapter 3, Creating Custom Corpora*. Many corpus readers need a way to tokenize the text they're reading, and can take optional keyword arguments specifying an instance of a `TokenizerI` subclass. This way, you have the ability to provide your own tokenizer instance if the default tokenizer is unsuitable.

There's more...

`RegexpTokenizer` can also work by matching the gaps, as opposed to the tokens. Instead of using `re.findall()`, the `RegexpTokenizer` class will use `re.split()`. This is how the `BlanklineTokenizer` class in `nltk.tokenize` is implemented.

Simple whitespace tokenizer

The following is a simple example of using `RegexpTokenizer` to tokenize on whitespace:

```
>>> tokenizer = RegexpTokenizer('\s+', gaps=True)
>>> tokenizer.tokenize("Can't is a contraction.")
["Can't", 'is', 'a', 'contraction.']
```

Notice that punctuation still remains in the tokens. The `gaps=True` parameter means that the pattern is used to identify gaps to tokenize on. If we used `gaps=False`, then the pattern would be used to identify tokens.

See also

For simpler word tokenization, see the previous recipe.

Training a sentence tokenizer

NLTK's default sentence tokenizer is general purpose, and usually works quite well. But sometimes it is not the best choice for your text. Perhaps your text uses nonstandard punctuation, or is formatted in a unique way. In such cases, training your own sentence tokenizer can result in much more accurate sentence tokenization.

Getting ready

For this example, we'll be using the `webtext` corpus, specifically the `overheard.txt` file, so make sure you've downloaded this corpus. The text in this file is formatted as dialog that looks like this:

```
White guy: So, do you have any plans for this evening?
Asian girl: Yeah, being angry!
White guy: Oh, that sounds good.
```

As you can see, this isn't your standard paragraph of sentences formatting, which makes it a perfect case for training a sentence tokenizer.

How to do it...

NLTK provides a `PunktSentenceTokenizer` class that you can train on raw text to produce a custom sentence tokenizer. You can get raw text either by reading in a file, or from an NLTK corpus using the `raw()` method. Here's an example of training a sentence tokenizer on dialog text, using `overheard.txt` from the `webtext` corpus:

```
>>> from nltk.tokenize import PunktSentenceTokenizer
>>> from nltk.corpus import webtext
>>> text = webtext.raw('overheard.txt')
>>> sent_tokenizer = PunktSentenceTokenizer(text)
```

Let's compare the results to the default sentence tokenizer, as follows:

```
>>> sents1 = sent_tokenizer.tokenize(text)
>>> sents1[0]
'White guy: So, do you have any plans for this evening?'

>>> from nltk.tokenize import sent_tokenize
>>> sents2 = sent_tokenize(text)
>>> sents2[0]
'White guy: So, do you have any plans for this evening?'
>>> sents1[678]
'Girl: But you already have a Big Mac...'
>>> sents2[678]
'Girl: But you already have a Big Mac...\\nHobo: Oh, this is all
theatrical.'
```

While the first sentence is the same, you can see that the tokenizers disagree on how to tokenize sentence 679 (this is the first sentence where the tokenizers diverge). The default tokenizer includes the next line of dialog, while our custom tokenizer correctly thinks that the next line is a separate sentence. This difference is a good demonstration of why it can be useful to train your own sentence tokenizer, especially when your text isn't in the typical paragraph-sentence structure.

How it works...

The PunktSentenceTokenizer class uses an unsupervised learning algorithm to learn what constitutes a sentence break. It is unsupervised because you don't have to give it any labeled training data, just raw text. You can read more about these kinds of algorithms at https://en.wikipedia.org/wiki/Unsupervised_learning. The specific technique used in this case is called sentence boundary detection and it works by counting punctuation and tokens that commonly end a sentence, such as a period or newline, then using the resulting frequencies to decide what the sentence boundaries should actually look like.

This is a simplified description of the algorithm—if you'd like more details, take a look at the source code of the nltk.tokenize.punkt.PunktTrainer class, which can be found online at http://www.nltk.org/_modules/nltk/tokenize/punkt.html#PunktSentenceTokenizer.

There's more...

The `PunktSentenceTokenizer` class learns from any string, which means you can open a text file and read its content. Here is an example of reading `overheard.txt` directly instead of using the `raw()` corpus method. This assumes that the `webtext` corpus is located in the standard directory at `/usr/share/nltk_data/corpora`. We also have to pass a specific encoding to the `open()` function, as follows, because the file is not in ASCII:

```
>>> with open('/usr/share/nltk_data/corpora/webtext/overheard.txt',
encoding='ISO-8859-2') as f:
...     text = f.read()
>>> sent_tokenizer = PunktSentenceTokenizer(text)
>>> sents = sent_tokenizer.tokenize(text)
>>> sents[0]
'White guy: So, do you have any plans for this evening?'
>>> sents[678]
'Girl: But you already have a Big Mac...'
```

Once you have a custom sentence tokenizer, you can use it for your own corpora. Many corpus readers accept a `sent_tokenizer` parameter, which lets you override the default sentence tokenizer object with your own sentence tokenizer. Corpus readers are covered in more detail in *Chapter 3, Creating Custom Corpora*.

See also

Most of the time, the default sentence tokenizer will be sufficient. This is covered in the first recipe, *Tokenizing text into sentences*.

Filtering stopwords in a tokenized sentence

Stopwords are common words that generally do not contribute to the meaning of a sentence, at least for the purposes of information retrieval and natural language processing. These are words such as *the* and *a*. Most search engines will filter out stopwords from search queries and documents in order to save space in their index.

Getting ready

NLTK comes with a `stopwords` corpus that contains word lists for many languages. Be sure to unzip the data file, so NLTK can find these word lists at `nltk_data/corpora/stopwords/`.

How to do it...

We're going to create a set of all English stopwords, then use it to filter stopwords from a sentence with the help of the following code:

```
>>> from nltk.corpus import stopwords
>>> english_stops = set(stopwords.words('english'))
>>> words = ["Can't", 'is', 'a', 'contraction']
>>> [word for word in words if word not in english_stops]
["Can't", 'contraction']
```

How it works...

The `stopwords` corpus is an instance of `nltk.corpus.reader.WordListCorpusReader`. As such, it has a `words()` method that can take a single argument for the file ID, which in this case is `'english'`, referring to a file containing a list of English stopwords. You could also call `stopwords.words()` with no argument to get a list of all stopwords in every language available.

There's more...

You can see the list of all English stopwords using `stopwords.words('english')` or by examining the word list file at `nltk_data/corpora/stopwords/english`. There are also stopword lists for many other languages. You can see the complete list of languages using the `fileids` method as follows:

```
>>> stopwords.fileids()
['danish', 'dutch', 'english', 'finnish', 'french', 'german',
'hungarian', 'italian', 'norwegian', 'portuguese', 'russian',
'spanish', 'swedish', 'turkish']
```

Any of these `fileids` can be used as an argument to the `words()` method to get a list of stopwords for that language. For example:

```
>>> stopwords.words('dutch')
['de', 'en', 'van', 'ik', 'te', 'dat', 'die', 'in', 'een', 'hij',
'het', 'niet', 'zijn', 'is', 'was', 'op', 'aan', 'met', 'als', 'voor',
'had', 'er', 'maar', 'om', 'hem', 'dan', 'zou', 'of', 'wat', 'mijn',
'men', 'dit', 'zo', 'door', 'over', 'ze', 'zich', 'bij', 'ook', 'tot',
'je', 'mij', 'uit', 'der', 'daar', 'haar', 'naar', 'heb', 'hoe',
'heeft', 'hebben', 'deze', 'u', 'want', 'nog', 'zal', 'me', 'zij',
'nu', 'ge', 'geen', 'omdat', 'iets', 'worden', 'toch', 'al', 'waren',
'veel', 'meer', 'doen', 'toen', 'moet', 'ben', 'zonder', 'kan',
'hun', 'dus', 'alles', 'onder', 'ja', 'eens', 'hier', 'wie', 'werd',
'altijd', 'doch', 'wordt', 'wezen', 'kunnen', 'ons', 'zelf', 'tegen',
'na', 'reeds', 'wil', 'kon', 'niets', 'uw', 'iemand', 'geweest',
'andere']
```

See also

If you'd like to create your own `stopwords` corpus, see the *Creating a wordlist corpus* recipe in *Chapter 3, Creating Custom Corpora*, to learn how to use `WordListCorpusReader`. We'll also be using stopwords in the *Discovering word collocations* recipe later in this chapter.

Looking up Synsets for a word in WordNet

WordNet is a lexical database for the English language. In other words, it's a dictionary designed specifically for natural language processing.

NLTK comes with a simple interface to look up words in WordNet. What you get is a list of **Synset** instances, which are groupings of synonymous words that express the same concept. Many words have only one Synset, but some have several. In this recipe, we'll explore a single Synset, and in the next recipe, we'll look at several in more detail.

Getting ready

Be sure you've unzipped the `wordnet` corpus at `nltk_data/corpora/wordnet`. This will allow `WordNetCorpusReader` to access it.

How to do it...

Now we're going to look up the Synset for `cookbook`, and explore some of the properties and methods of a Synset using the following code:

```
>>> from nltk.corpus import wordnet
>>> syn = wordnet.synsets('cookbook')[0]
>>> syn.name()
'cookbook.n.01'
>>> syn.definition()
'a book of recipes and cooking directions'
```

How it works...

You can look up any word in WordNet using `wordnet.synsets(word)` to get a list of Synsets. The list may be empty if the word is not found. The list may also have quite a few elements, as some words can have many possible meanings, and, therefore, many Synsets.

There's more...

Each Synset in the list has a number of methods you can use to learn more about it. The `name()` method will give you a unique name for the Synset, which you can use to get the Synset directly:

```
>>> wordnet.synset('cookbook.n.01')
Synset('cookbook.n.01')
```

The `definition()` method should be self-explanatory. Some Synsets also have an `examples()` method, which contains a list of phrases that use the word in context:

```
>>> wordnet.synsets('cooking')[0].examples()
['cooking can be a great art', 'people are needed who have experience
in cookery', 'he left the preparation of meals to his wife']
```

Working with hypernyms

Synsets are organized in a structure similar to that of an inheritance tree. More abstract terms are known as **hypernyms** and more specific terms are **hyponyms**. This tree can be traced all the way up to a root hypernym.

Hypernyms provide a way to categorize and group words based on their similarity to each other. The *Calculating WordNet Synset similarity* recipe details the functions used to calculate the similarity based on the distance between two words in the hypernym tree:

```
>>> syn.hypernyms()
[Synset('reference_book.n.01')]
>>> syn.hypernyms()[0].hyponyms()
[Synset('annual.n.02'), Synset('atlas.n.02'), Synset('cookbook.n.01'),
Synset('directory.n.01'), Synset('encyclopedia.n.01'),
Synset('handbook.n.01'), Synset('instruction_book.n.01'),
Synset('source_book.n.01'), Synset('wordbook.n.01')]
>>> syn.root_hypernyms()
[Synset('entity.n.01')]
```

As you can see, `reference_book` is a hypernym of `cookbook`, but `cookbook` is only one of the many hyponyms of `reference_book`. And all these types of books have the same root hypernym, which is `entity`, one of the most abstract terms in the English language. You can trace the entire path from entity down to `cookbook` using the `hypernym_paths()` method, as follows:

```
>>> syn.hypernym_paths()
[[Synset('entity.n.01'), Synset('physical_entity.n.01'),
Synset('object.n.01'), Synset('whole.n.02'), Synset('artifact.n.01'),
Synset('creation.n.02'), Synset('product.n.02'), Synset('work.n.02'),
Synset('publication.n.01'), Synset('book.n.01'), Synset('reference_
book.n.01'), Synset('cookbook.n.01')]]
```

The `hypernym_paths()` method returns a list of lists, where each list starts at the root hypernym and ends with the original Synset. Most of the time, you'll only get one nested list of Synsets.

Part of speech (POS)

You can also look up a simplified part-of-speech tag as follows:

```
>>> syn.pos()
'n'
```

There are four common part-of-speech tags (or POS tags) found in WordNet, as shown in the following table:

Part of speech	Tag
Noun	n
Adjective	a
Adverb	r
Verb	v

These POS tags can be used to look up specific Synsets for a word. For example, the word `'great'` can be used as a noun or an adjective. In WordNet, `'great'` has 1 noun Synset and 6 adjective Synsets, as shown in the following code:

```
>>> len(wordnet.synsets('great'))
7
>>> len(wordnet.synsets('great', pos='n'))
1
>>> len(wordnet.synsets('great', pos='a'))
6
```

These POS tags will be referenced more in the *Using WordNet for tagging* recipe in *Chapter 4, Part-of-speech Tagging*.

See also

In the next two recipes, we'll explore lemmas and how to calculate Synset similarity. And in *Chapter 2, Replacing and Correcting Words*, we'll use WordNet for lemmatization, synonym replacement, and then explore the use of antonyms.

Looking up lemmas and synonyms in WordNet

Building on the previous recipe, we can also look up lemmas in WordNet to find synonyms of a word. A **lemma** (in linguistics), is the canonical form or morphological form of a word.

How to do it...

In the following code, we'll find that there are two lemmas for the cookbook Synset using the lemmas() method:

```
>>> from nltk.corpus import wordnet
>>> syn = wordnet.synsets('cookbook')[0]
>>> lemmas = syn.lemmas()
>>> len(lemmas)
2
>>> lemmas[0].name()
'cookbook'
>>> lemmas[1].name()
'cookery_book'
>>> lemmas[0].synset() == lemmas[1].synset()
True
```

How it works...

As you can see, cookery_book and cookbook are two distinct lemmas in the same Synset. In fact, a lemma can only belong to a single Synset. In this way, a Synset represents a group of lemmas that all have the same meaning, while a lemma represents a distinct word form.

There's more...

Since all the lemmas in a Synset have the same meaning, they can be treated as synonyms. So if you wanted to get all synonyms for a Synset, you could do the following:

```
>>> [lemma.name() for lemma in syn.lemmas()]
['cookbook', 'cookery_book']
```

All possible synonyms

As mentioned earlier, many words have multiple Synsets because the word can have different meanings depending on the context. But, let's say you didn't care about the context, and wanted to get all the possible synonyms for a word:

```
>>> synonyms = []
>>> for syn in wordnet.synsets('book'):
...     for lemma in syn.lemmas():
...         synonyms.append(lemma.name())
>>> len(synonyms)
38
```

As you can see, there appears to be 38 possible synonyms for the word 'book'. But in fact, some synonyms are verb forms, and many synonyms are just different usages of 'book'. If, instead, we take the set of synonyms, there are fewer unique words, as shown in the following code:

```
>>> len(set(synonyms))
25
```

Antonyms

Some lemmas also have antonyms. The word good, for example, has 27 Synsets, five of which have lemmas with antonyms, as shown in the following code:

```
>>> gn2 = wordnet.synset('good.n.02')
>>> gn2.definition()
'moral excellence or admirableness'
>>> evil = gn2.lemmas()[0].antonyms()[0]
>>> evil.name
'evil'
>>> evil.synset().definition()
'the quality of being morally wrong in principle or practice'
>>> ga1 = wordnet.synset('good.a.01')
>>> ga1.definition()
'having desirable or positive qualities especially those suitable for
a thing specified'
>>> bad = ga1.lemmas()[0].antonyms()[0]
>>> bad.name()
'bad'
>>> bad.synset().definition()
'having undesirable or negative qualities'
```

The antonyms() method returns a list of lemmas. In the first case, as we can see in the previous code, the second Synset for good as a noun is defined as moral excellence, and its first antonym is evil, defined as morally wrong. In the second case, when good is used as an adjective to describe positive qualities, the first antonym is bad, which describes negative qualities.

See also

In the next recipe, we'll learn how to calculate Synset similarity. Then in Chapter 2, *Replacing and Correcting Words*, we'll revisit lemmas for lemmatization, synonym replacement, and antonym replacement.

Calculating WordNet Synset similarity

Synsets are organized in a *hypernym* tree. This tree can be used for reasoning about the similarity between the Synsets it contains. The closer the two Synsets are in the tree, the more similar they are.

How to do it...

If you were to look at all the hyponyms of `reference_book` (which is the hypernym of `cookbook`), you'd see that one of them is `instruction_book`. This seems intuitively very similar to a `cookbook`, so let's see what WordNet similarity has to say about it with the help of the following code:

```
>>> from nltk.corpus import wordnet
>>> cb = wordnet.synset('cookbook.n.01')
>>> ib = wordnet.synset('instruction_book.n.01')
>>> cb.wup_similarity(ib)
0.9166666666666666
```

So they are over 91% similar!

How it works...

The `wup_similarity` method is short for **Wu-Palmer Similarity**, which is a scoring method based on how similar the word senses are and where the Synsets occur relative to each other in the hypernym tree. One of the core metrics used to calculate similarity is the shortest path distance between the two Synsets and their common hypernym:

```
>>> ref = cb.hypernyms()[0]
>>> cb.shortest_path_distance(ref)
1
>>> ib.shortest_path_distance(ref)
1
>>> cb.shortest_path_distance(ib)
2
```

So `cookbook` and `instruction_book` must be very similar, because they are only one step away from the same `reference_book` hypernym, and, therefore, only two steps away from each other.

There's more...

Let's look at two dissimilar words to see what kind of score we get. We'll compare `dog` with `cookbook`, two seemingly very different words.

```
>>> dog = wordnet.synsets('dog')[0]
>>> dog.wup_similarity(cb)
0.38095238095238093
```

Wow, `dog` and `cookbook` are apparently 38% similar! This is because they share common hypernyms further up the tree:

```
>>> sorted(dog.common_hypernyms(cb))
[Synset('entity.n.01'), Synset('object.n.01'), Synset('physical_
entity.n.01'), Synset('whole.n.02')]
```

Comparing verbs

The previous comparisons were all between nouns, but the same can be done for verbs as well:

```
>>> cook = wordnet.synset('cook.v.01')
>>> bake = wordnet.0('bake.v.02')
>>> cook.wup_similarity(bake)
00.6666666666666666
```

The previous Synsets were obviously handpicked for demonstration, and the reason is that the hypernym tree for verbs has a lot more breadth and a lot less depth. While most nouns can be traced up to the hypernym `object`, thereby providing a basis for similarity, many verbs do not share common hypernyms, making WordNet unable to calculate the similarity. For example, if you were to use the Synset for `bake.v.01` in the previous code, instead of `bake.v.02`, the return value would be `None`. This is because the root hypernyms of both the Synsets are different, with no overlapping paths. For this reason, you also cannot calculate the similarity between words with different parts of speech.

Path and Leacock Chordorow (LCH) similarity

Two other similarity comparisons are the path similarity and the LCH similarity, as shown in the following code:

```
>>> cb.path_similarity(ib)
0.3333333333333333
>>> cb.path_similarity(dog)
0.07142857142857142
>>> cb.lch_similarity(ib)
2.538973871058276
>>> cb.lch_similarity(dog)
0.9985288301111273
```

As you can see, the number ranges are very different for these scoring methods, which is why I prefer the `wup_similarity` method.

See also

The recipe on *Looking up Synsets for a word in WordNet* has more details about hypernyms and the hypernym tree.

Discovering word collocations

Collocations are two or more words that tend to appear frequently together, such as United States. Of course, there are many other words that can come after United, such as United Kingdom and United Airlines. As with many aspects of natural language processing, context is very important. And for collocations, context is everything!

In the case of collocations, the context will be a document in the form of a list of words. Discovering collocations in this list of words means that we'll find common phrases that occur frequently throughout the text. For fun, we'll start with the script for *Monty Python and the Holy Grail*.

Getting ready

The script for *Monty Python and the Holy Grail* is found in the `webtext` corpus, so be sure that it's unzipped at `nltk_data/corpora/webtext/`.

How to do it...

We're going to create a list of all lowercased words in the text, and then produce `BigramCollocationFinder`, which we can use to find bigrams, which are pairs of words. These bigrams are found using association measurement functions in the `nltk.metrics` package, as follows:

```
>>> from nltk.corpus import webtext
>>> from nltk.collocations import BigramCollocationFinder
>>> from nltk.metrics import BigramAssocMeasures
>>> words = [w.lower() for w in webtext.words('grail.txt')]
>>> bcf = BigramCollocationFinder.from_words(words)
>>> bcf.nbest(BigramAssocMeasures.likelihood_ratio, 4)
[("'", 's'), ('arthur', ':'), ('#', '1'), ("'", 't')]
```

Well, that's not very useful! Let's refine it a bit by adding a word filter to remove punctuation and stopwords:

```
>>> from nltk.corpus import stopwords
>>> stopset = set(stopwords.words('english'))
>>> filter_stops = lambda w: len(w) < 3 or w in stopset
>>> bcf.apply_word_filter(filter_stops)
>>> bcf.nbest(BigramAssocMeasures.likelihood_ratio, 4)
[('black', 'knight'), ('clop', 'clop'), ('head', 'knight'), ('mumble',
'mumble')]
```

Much better, we can clearly see four of the most common bigrams in *Monty Python and the Holy Grail*. If you'd like to see more than four, simply increase the number to whatever you want, and the collocation finder will do its best.

How it works...

`BigramCollocationFinder` constructs two frequency distributions: one for each word, and another for bigrams. A frequency distribution, or `FreqDist` in NLTK, is basically an enhanced Python dictionary where the keys are what's being counted, and the values are the counts. Any filtering functions that are applied reduce the size of these two `FreqDists` by eliminating any words that don't pass the filter. By using a filtering function to eliminate all words that are one or two characters, and all English stopwords, we can get a much cleaner result. After filtering, the collocation finder is ready to accept a generic scoring function for finding collocations.

There's more...

In addition to `BigramCollocationFinder`, there's also `TrigramCollocationFinder`, which finds triplets instead of pairs. This time, we'll look for trigrams in Australian singles advertisements with the help of the following code:

```
>>> from nltk.collocations import TrigramCollocationFinder
>>> from nltk.metrics import TrigramAssocMeasures
>>> words = [w.lower() for w in webtext.words('singles.txt')]
>>> tcf = TrigramCollocationFinder.from_words(words)
>>> tcf.apply_word_filter(filter_stops)
>>> tcf.apply_freq_filter(3)
>>> tcf.nbest(TrigramAssocMeasures.likelihood_ratio, 4)
[('long', 'term', 'relationship')]
```

Now, we don't know whether people are looking for a long-term relationship or not, but clearly it's an important topic. In addition to the stopword filter, I also applied a frequency filter, which removed any trigrams that occurred less than three times. This is why only one result was returned when we asked for four because there was only one result that occurred more than two times.

Scoring functions

There are many more scoring functions available besides `likelihood_ratio()`. But other than `raw_freq()`, you may need a bit of a statistics background to understand how they work. Consult the NLTK API documentation for `NgramAssocMeasures` in the `nltk.metrics` package to see all the possible scoring functions.

Scoring ngrams

In addition to the `nbest()` method, there are two other ways to get ngrams (a generic term used for describing bigrams and trigrams) from a collocation finder:

- ▶ `above_score(score_fn, min_score)`: This can be used to get all ngrams with scores that are at least `min_score`. The `min_score` value that you choose will depend heavily on the `score_fn` you use.
- ▶ `score_ngrams(score_fn)`: This will return a list with tuple pairs of (ngram, score). This can be used to inform your choice for `min_score`.

See also

The `nltk.metrics` module will be used again in the *Measuring precision and recall of a classifier* and *Calculating high information words* recipes in *Chapter 7, Text Classification*.

2
Replacing and Correcting Words

In this chapter, we will cover the following recipes:

- ▶ Stemming words
- ▶ Lemmatizing words with WordNet
- ▶ Replacing words matching regular expressions
- ▶ Removing repeating characters
- ▶ Spelling correction with Enchant
- ▶ Replacing synonyms
- ▶ Replacing ncgations with antonyms

Introduction

In this chapter, we will go over various word replacement and correction techniques. The recipes cover the gamut of linguistic compression, spelling correction, and text normalization. All of these methods can be very useful for preprocessing text before search indexing, document classification, and text analysis.

Stemming words

Stemming is a technique to remove affixes from a word, ending up with the stem. For example, the stem of `cooking` is `cook`, and a good stemming algorithm knows that the `ing` suffix can be removed. Stemming is most commonly used by search engines for indexing words. Instead of storing all forms of a word, a search engine can store only the stems, greatly reducing the size of index while increasing retrieval accuracy.

One of the most common stemming algorithms is the **Porter stemming algorithm** by Martin Porter. It is designed to remove and replace well-known suffixes of English words, and its usage in NLTK will be covered in the next section.

 The resulting stem is not always a valid word. For example, the stem of `cookery` is `cookeri`. This is a feature, not a bug.

How to do it...

NLTK comes with an implementation of the Porter stemming algorithm, which is very easy to use. Simply instantiate the `PorterStemmer` class and call the `stem()` method with the word you want to stem:

```
>>> from nltk.stem import PorterStemmer
>>> stemmer = PorterStemmer()
>>> stemmer.stem('cooking')
'cook'
>>> stemmer.stem('cookery')
'cookeri'
```

How it works...

The `PorterStemmer` class knows a number of regular word forms and suffixes and uses this knowledge to transform your input word to a final stem through a series of steps. The resulting stem is often a shorter word, or at least a common form of the word, which has the same root meaning.

There's more...

There are other stemming algorithms out there besides the Porter stemming algorithm, such as the **Lancaster stemming algorithm**, developed at Lancaster University. NLTK includes it as the `LancasterStemmer` class. At the time of writing this book, there is no definitive research demonstrating the superiority of one algorithm over the other. However, Porter stemming algorithm is generally the default choice.

All the stemmers covered next inherit from the `StemmerI` interface, which defines the `stem()` method. The following is an inheritance diagram that explains this:

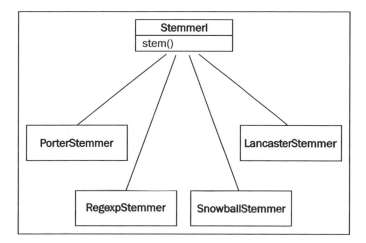

The LancasterStemmer class

The functions of the `LancasterStemmer` class are just like the functions of the `PorterStemmer` class, but can produce slightly different results. It is known to be slightly more aggressive than the `PorterStemmer` functions:

```
>>> from nltk.stem import LancasterStemmer
>>> stemmer = LancasterStemmer()
>>> stemmer.stem('cooking')
'cook'
>>> stemmer.stem('cookery')
'cookery'
```

The RegexpStemmer class

You can also construct your own stemmer using the `RegexpStemmer` class. It takes a single regular expression (either compiled or as a string) and removes any prefix or suffix that matches the expression:

```
>>> from nltk.stem import RegexpStemmer
>>> stemmer = RegexpStemmer('ing')
>>> stemmer.stem('cooking')
'cook'
>>> stemmer.stem('cookery')
'cookery'
>>> stemmer.stem('ingleside')
'leside'
```

A `RegexpStemmer` class should only be used in very specific cases that are not covered by the `PorterStemmer` or the `LancasterStemmer` class because it can only handle very specific patterns and is not a general-purpose algorithm.

The SnowballStemmer class

The `SnowballStemmer` class supports 13 non-English languages. It also provides two English stemmers: the original porter algorithm as well as the new English stemming algorithm. To use the `SnowballStemmer` class, create an instance with the name of the language you are using and then call the `stem()` method. Here is a list of all the supported languages and an example using the Spanish `SnowballStemmer` class:

```
>>> from nltk.stem import SnowballStemmer
>>> SnowballStemmer.languages('danish', 'dutch', 'english', 'finnish',
'french', 'german', 'hungarian', 'italian', 'norwegian', 'porter',
'portuguese', 'romanian', 'russian', 'spanish', 'swedish')
>>> spanish_stemmer = SnowballStemmer('spanish')
>>> spanish_stemmer.stem('hola')
u'hol'
```

See also

In the next recipe, we will cover Lemmatization, which is quite similar to stemming, but subtly different.

Lemmatizing words with WordNet

Lemmatization is very similar to stemming, but is more akin to synonym replacement. A lemma is a root word, as opposed to the root stem. So unlike stemming, you are always left with a valid word that means the same thing. However, the word you end up with can be completely different. A few examples will explain this.

Getting ready

Make sure that you have unzipped the `wordnet` corpus in `nltk_data/corpora/wordnet`. This will allow the `WordNetLemmatizer` class to access WordNet. You should also be familiar with the part-of-speech tags covered in the *Looking up Synsets for a word in WordNet* recipe of *Chapter 1, Tokenizing Text and WordNet Basics*.

How to do it...

We will use the `WordNetLemmatizer` class to find lemmas:

```
>>> from nltk.stem import WordNetLemmatizer
>>> lemmatizer = WordNetLemmatizer()
>>> lemmatizer.lemmatize('cooking')
'cooking'
>>> lemmatizer.lemmatize('cooking', pos='v')
'cook'
>>> lemmatizer.lemmatize('cookbooks')
'cookbook'
```

How it works...

The `WordNetLemmatizer` class is a thin wrapper around the `wordnet` corpus and uses the `morphy()` function of the `WordNetCorpusReader` class to find a lemma. If no lemma is found, or the word itself is a lemma, the word is returned as is. Unlike with stemming, knowing the part of speech of the word is important. As demonstrated previously, `cooking` does not return a different lemma unless you specify that the POS is a verb. This is because the default POS is a noun, and as a noun, `cooking` is its own lemma. On the other hand, `cookbooks` is a noun with its singular form, `cookbook`, as its lemma.

There's more...

Here's an example that illustrates one of the major differences between stemming and lemmatization:

```
>>> from nltk.stem import PorterStemmer
>>> stemmer = PorterStemmer()
>>> stemmer.stem('believes')
'believ'
>>> lemmatizer.lemmatize('believes')
'belief'
```

Instead of just chopping off the `es` like the `PorterStemmer` class, the `WordNetLemmatizer` class finds a valid root word. Where a stemmer only looks at the form of the word, the lemmatizer looks at the meaning of the word. By returning a lemma, you will always get a valid word.

Combining stemming with lemmatization

Stemming and lemmatization can be combined to compress words more than either process can by itself. These cases are somewhat rare, but they do exist:

```
>>> stemmer.stem('buses')
'buse'
>>> lemmatizer.lemmatize('buses')
'bus'
>>> stemmer.stem('bus')
'bu'
```

In this example, stemming saves one character, lemmatization saves two characters, and stemming the lemma saves a total of three characters out of five characters. That is nearly a 60% compression rate! This level of word compression over many thousands of words, while unlikely to always produce such high gains, can still make a huge difference.

See also

In the previous recipe, we covered the basics of stemming and WordNet was introduced in the *Looking up Synsets for a word in WordNet* and *Looking up lemmas and synonyms in WordNet* recipes of *Chapter 1, Tokenizing Text and WordNet Basics*. Looking forward, we will cover the *Using WordNet for tagging* recipe in *Chapter 4, Part-of-speech Tagging*.

Replacing words matching regular expressions

Now, we are going to get into the process of replacing words. If stemming and lemmatization are a kind of linguistic compression, then word replacement can be thought of as error correction or text normalization.

In this recipe, we will replace words based on regular expressions, with a focus on expanding contractions. Remember when we were tokenizing words in *Chapter 1, Tokenizing Text and WordNet Basics*, and it was clear that most tokenizers had trouble with contractions? This recipe aims to fix this by replacing contractions with their expanded forms, for example, by replacing "can't" with "cannot" or "would've" with "would have".

Getting ready

Understanding how this recipe works will require a basic knowledge of regular expressions and the `re` module. The key things to know are matching patterns and the `re.sub()` function.

How to do it...

First, we need to define a number of replacement patterns. This will be a list of tuple pairs, where the first element is the pattern to match with and the second element is the replacement.

Next, we will create a `RegexpReplacer` class that will compile the patterns and provide a `replace()` method to substitute all the found patterns with their replacements.

The following code can be found in the `replacers.py` module in the book's code bundle and is meant to be imported, not typed into the console:

```python
import re

replacement_patterns = [
    (r'won\'t', 'will not'),
    (r'can\'t', 'cannot'),
    (r'i\'m', 'i am'),
    (r'ain\'t', 'is not'),
    (r'(\w+)\'ll', '\g<1> will'),
    (r'(\w+)n\'t', '\g<1> not'),
    (r'(\w+)\'ve', '\g<1> have'),
    (r'(\w+)\'s', '\g<1> is'),
    (r'(\w+)\'re', '\g<1> are'),
    (r'(\w+)\'d', '\g<1> would')
]

class RegexpReplacer(object):
    def __init__(self, patterns=replacement_patterns):
        self.patterns = [(re.compile(regex), repl) for (regex, repl) in
            patterns]

    def replace(self, text):
        s = text
        for (pattern, repl) in self.patterns:
            s = re.sub(pattern, repl, s)
        return s
```

How it works...

Here is a simple usage example:

```
>>> from replacers import RegexpReplacer
>>> replacer = RegexpReplacer()
>>> replacer.replace("can't is a contraction")
'cannot is a contraction'
>>> replacer.replace("I should've done that thing I didn't do")
'I should have done that thing I did not do'
```

The `RegexpReplacer.replace()` function works by replacing every instance of a replacement pattern with its corresponding substitution pattern. In replacement patterns, we have defined tuples such as `r'(\w+)\'ve'` and `'\g<1> have'`. The first element matches a group of ASCII characters followed by `'ve`. By grouping the characters before `'ve` in parenthesis, a match group is found and can be used in the substitution pattern with the `\g<1>` reference. So, we keep everything before `'ve`, then replace `'ve` with the word have. This is how `should've` can become `should have`.

There's more...

This replacement technique can work with any kind of regular expression, not just contractions. So, you can replace any occurrence of & with `and`, or eliminate all occurrences of - by replacing it with an empty string. The `RegexpReplacer` class can take any list of replacement patterns for whatever purpose.

Replacement before tokenization

Let's try using the `RegexpReplacer` class as a preliminary step before tokenization:

```
>>> from nltk.tokenize import word_tokenize
>>> from replacers import RegexpReplacer
>>> replacer = RegexpReplacer()
>>> word_tokenize("can't is a contraction")
['ca', "n't", 'is', 'a', 'contraction']
>>> word_tokenize(replacer.replace("can't is a contraction"))
['can', 'not', 'is', 'a', 'contraction']
```

Much better! By eliminating the contractions in the first place, the tokenizer will produce cleaner results. Cleaning up the text before processing is a common pattern in natural language processing.

For more information on tokenization, see the first three recipes in *Chapter 1, Tokenizing Text and WordNet Basics*. For more replacement techniques, continue reading the rest of this chapter.

Removing repeating characters

In everyday language, people are often not strictly grammatical. They will write things such as I loooooove it in order to emphasize the word love. However, computers don't know that "loooooove" is a variation of "love" unless they are told. This recipe presents a method to remove these annoying repeating characters in order to end up with a *proper* English word.

Getting ready

As in the previous recipe, we will be making use of the re module, and more specifically, backreferences. A **backreference** is a way to refer to a previously matched group in a regular expression. This will allow us to match and remove repeating characters.

How to do it...

We will create a class that has the same form as the RegexpReplacer class from the previous recipe. It will have a replace() method that takes a single word and returns a more correct version of that word, with the dubious repeating characters removed. This code can be found in replacers.py in the book's code bundle and is meant to be imported:

```
import re

class RepeatReplacer(object):
  def __init__(self):
    self.repeat_regexp = re.compile(r'(\w*)(\w)\2(\w*)')
    self.repl = r'\1\2\3'

  def replace(self, word):
    repl_word = self.repeat_regexp.sub(self.repl, word)

    if repl_word != word:
      return self.replace(repl_word)
    else:
      return repl_word
```

And now some example use cases:

```
>>> from replacers import RepeatReplacer
>>> replacer = RepeatReplacer()
>>> replacer.replace('loooove')
'love'
>>> replacer.replace('oooooh')
'oh'
>>> replacer.replace('goose')
'gose'
```

How it works...

The `RepeatReplacer` class starts by compiling a regular expression to match
and define a replacement string with backreferences. The `repeat_regexp` pattern
matches three groups:

▸   0 or more starting characters (`\w*`)

▸   A single character (`\w`) that is followed by another instance of that character (`\2`)

▸   0 or more ending characters (`\w*`)

The replacement string is then used to keep all the matched groups, while discarding the
backreference to the second group. So, the word `loooove` gets split into `(looo)(o)o(ve)`
and then recombined as `loooove`, discarding the last o. This continues until only one o
remains, when `repeat_regexp` no longer matches the string and no more characters
are removed.

There's more...

In the preceding examples, you can see that the `RepeatReplacer` class is a bit too
greedy and ends up changing `goose` into `gose`. To correct this issue, we can augment
the `replace()` function with a WordNet lookup. If WordNet recognizes the word, then
we can stop replacing characters. Here is the WordNet-augmented version:

```
import re
from nltk.corpus import wordnet

class RepeatReplacer(object):
  def __init__(self):
    self.repeat_regexp = re.compile(r'(\w*)(\w)\2(\w*)')
    self.repl = r'\1\2\3'
```

```
def replace(self, word):
  if wordnet.synsets(word):
    return word
  repl_word = self.repeat_regexp.sub(self.repl, word)

  if repl_word != word:
    return self.replace(repl_word)
  else:
    return repl_word
```

Now, `goose` will be found in WordNet, and no character replacement will take place. Also, `oooooh` will become `ooh` instead of `oh` because `ooh` is actually a word in WordNet, defined as an expression of admiration or pleasure.

See also

Read the next recipe to learn how to correct misspellings. For more information on WordNet, refer to the WordNet recipes in *Chapter 1, Tokenizing Text and WordNet Basics*. We will also be using WordNet for antonym replacement later in this chapter.

Spelling correction with Enchant

Replacing repeating characters is actually an extreme form of spelling correction. In this recipe, we will take on the less extreme case of correcting minor spelling issues using **Enchant**—a spelling correction API.

Getting ready

You will need to install Enchant and a dictionary for it to use. Enchant is an offshoot of the AbiWord open source word processor, and more information on it can be found at `http://www.abisource.com/projects/enchant/`.

For dictionaries, **Aspell** is a good open source spellchecker and dictionary that can be found at `http://aspell.net/`.

Finally, you will need the **PyEnchant** library, which can be found at the following link: `http://pythonhosted.org/pyenchant/`

You should be able to install it with the `easy_install` command that comes with Python setuptools, such as by typing `sudo easy_install pyenchant` on Linux or Unix. On a Mac machine, PyEnchant may be difficult to install. If you have difficulties, consult `http://pythonhosted.org/pyenchant/download.html`.

How to do it...

We will create a new class called `SpellingReplacer` in `replacers.py`, and this time, the `replace()` method will check Enchant to see whether the word is valid. If not, we will look up the suggested alternatives and return the best match using `nltk.metrics.edit_distance()`:

```python
import enchant
from nltk.metrics import edit_distance

class SpellingReplacer(object):
    def __init__(self, dict_name='en', max_dist=2):
        self.spell_dict = enchant.Dict(dict_name)
        self.max_dist = max_dist

    def replace(self, word):
        if self.spell_dict.check(word):
            return word
        suggestions = self.spell_dict.suggest(word)

        if suggestions and edit_distance(word, suggestions[0]) <=
            self.max_dist:
            return suggestions[0]
        else:
            return word
```

The preceding class can be used to correct English spellings, as follows:

```python
>>> from replacers import SpellingReplacer
>>> replacer = SpellingReplacer()
>>> replacer.replace('cookbok')
'cookbok'
```

How it works...

The `SpellingReplacer` class starts by creating a reference to an Enchant dictionary. Then, in the `replace()` method, it first checks whether the given word is present in the dictionary. If it is, no spelling correction is necessary and the word is returned. If the word is not found, it looks up a list of suggestions and returns the first suggestion, as long as its edit distance is less than or equal to `max_dist`. The edit distance is the number of character changes necessary to transform the given word into the suggested word. The `max_dist` value then acts as a constraint on the Enchant `suggest` function to ensure that no unlikely replacement words are returned. Here is an example showing all the suggestions for `languege`, a misspelling of `language`:

```
>>> import enchant
>>> d = enchant.Dict('en')
>>> d.suggest('languege')
['language', 'languages', 'languor', "language's"]
```

Except for the correct suggestion, `language`, all the other words have an edit distance of three or greater. You can try this yourself with the following code:

```
>>> from nltk.metrics import edit_distance
>>> edit_distance('language', 'languege')
1
>>> edit_distance('language', 'languo')
3
```

There's more...

You can use language dictionaries other than en, such as en_GB, assuming the dictionary has already been installed. To check which other languages are available, use `enchant.list_languages()`:

```
>>> enchant.list_languages()
['en', 'en_CA', 'en_GB', 'en_US']
```

 If you try to use a dictionary that doesn't exist, you will get `enchant.DictNotFoundError`. You can first check whether the dictionary exists using `enchant.dict_exists()`, which will return `True` if the named dictionary exists, or `False` otherwise.

The en_GB dictionary

Always ensure that you use the correct dictionary for whichever language you are performing spelling correction on. The en_US dictionary can give you different results than en_GB, such as for the word `theater`. The word `theater` is the American English spelling whereas the British English spelling is `theatre`:

```
>>> import enchant
>>> dUS = enchant.Dict('en_US')
>>> dUS.check('theater')
True
>>> dGB = enchant.Dict('en_GB')
>>> dGB.check('theater')
False
```

```
>>> from replacers import SpellingReplacer
>>> us_replacer = SpellingReplacer('en_US')
>>> us_replacer.replace('theater')
'theater'
>>> gb_replacer = SpellingReplacer('en_GB')
>>> gb_replacer.replace('theater')
'theatre'
```

Personal word lists

Enchant also supports personal word lists. These can be combined with an existing dictionary, allowing you to augment the dictionary with your own words. So, let's say you had a file named `mywords.txt` that had `nltk` on one line. You could then create a dictionary augmented with your personal word list as follows:

```
>>> d = enchant.Dict('en_US')
>>> d.check('nltk')
False
>>> d = enchant.DictWithPWL('en_US', 'mywords.txt')
>>> d.check('nltk')
True
```

To use an augmented dictionary with our `SpellingReplacer` class, we can create a subclass in `replacers.py` that takes an existing spelling dictionary:

```
class CustomSpellingReplacer(SpellingReplacer):
  def __init__(self, spell_dict, max_dist=2):
    self.spell_dict = spell_dict
    self.max_dist = max_dist
```

This `CustomSpellingReplacer` class will not replace any words that you put into `mywords.txt`:

```
>>> from replacers import CustomSpellingReplacer
>>> d = enchant.DictWithPWL('en_US', 'mywords.txt')
>>> replacer = CustomSpellingReplacer(d)
>>> replacer.replace('nltk')
'nltk'
```

See also

The previous recipe covered an extreme form of spelling correction by replacing repeating characters. You can also perform spelling correction by simple word replacement as discussed in the next recipe.

Replacing synonyms

It is often useful to reduce the vocabulary of a text by replacing words with common synonyms. By compressing the vocabulary without losing meaning, you can save memory in cases such as *frequency analysis* and *text indexing*. More details about these topics are available at https://en.wikipedia.org/wiki/Frequency_analysis and https://en.wikipedia.org/wiki/Full_text_search. Vocabulary reduction can also increase the occurrence of significant collocations, which was covered in the *Discovering word collocations* recipe of *Chapter 1, Tokenizing Text and WordNet Basics*.

Getting ready

You will need a defined mapping of a word to its synonym. This is a simple controlled vocabulary. We will start by hardcoding the synonyms as a Python dictionary, and then explore other options to store synonym maps.

How to do it...

We'll first create a WordReplacer class in replacers.py that takes a word replacement mapping:

```
class WordReplacer(object):
  def __init__(self, word_map):
    self.word_map = word_map

  def replace(self, word):
    return self.word_map.get(word, word)
```

Then, we can demonstrate its usage for simple word replacement:

```
>>> from replacers import WordReplacer
>>> replacer = WordReplacer({'bday': 'birthday'})
>>> replacer.replace('bday')
'birthday'
>>> replacer.replace('happy')
'happy'
```

How it works...

The WordReplacer class is simply a class wrapper around a Python dictionary. The replace() method looks up the given word in its word_map dictionary and returns the replacement synonym if it exists. Otherwise, the given word is returned as is.

If you were only using the `word_map` dictionary, you wouldn't need the `WordReplacer` class and could instead call `word_map.get()` directly. However, `WordReplacer` can act as a base class for other classes that construct the `word_map` dictionary from various file formats. Read on for more information.

There's more...

Hardcoding synonyms in a Python dictionary is not a good long-term solution. Two better alternatives are to store the synonyms in a CSV file or in a YAML file. Choose whichever format is easiest for those who maintain your synonym vocabulary. Both of the classes outlined in the following section inherit the `replace()` method from `WordReplacer`.

CSV synonym replacement

The `CsvWordReplacer` class extends `WordReplacer` in `replacers.py` in order to construct the `word_map` dictionary from a CSV file:

```python
import csv

class CsvWordReplacer(WordReplacer):
  def __init__(self, fname):
    word_map = {}
    for line in csv.reader(open(fname)):
      word, syn = line
      word_map[word] = syn
    super(CsvWordReplacer, self).__init__(word_map)
```

Your CSV file should consist of two columns, where the first column is the word and the second column is the synonym meant to replace it. If this file is called `synonyms.csv` and the first line is `bday, birthday`, then you can perform the following:

```python
>>> from replacers import CsvWordReplacer
>>> replacer = CsvWordReplacer('synonyms.csv')
>>> replacer.replace('bday')
'birthday'
>>> replacer.replace('happy')
'happy'
```

YAML synonym replacement

If you have PyYAML installed, you can create `YamlWordReplacer` in `replacers.py` as shown in the following:

```
import yaml

class YamlWordReplacer(WordReplacer):
  def __init__(self, fname):
    word_map = yaml.load(open(fname))
    super(YamlWordReplacer, self).__init__(word_map)
```

 Download and installation instructions for PyYAML are located at `http://pyyaml.org/wiki/PyYAML`. You can also type `pip install pyyaml` on the command prompt

Your YAML file should be a simple mapping of `word: synonym`, such as `bday: birthday`. Note that the YAML syntax is very particular, and the space after the colon is required. If the file is named `synonyms.yaml`, then you can perform the following:

```
>>> from replacers import YamlWordReplacer
>>> replacer = YamlWordReplacer('synonyms.yaml')
>>> replacer.replace('bday')
'birthday'
>>> replacer.replace('happy')
'happy'
```

See also

You can use the `WordReplacer` class to perform any kind of word replacement, even spelling correction for more complicated words that can't be automatically corrected, as we did in the previous recipe. In the next recipe, we will cover antonym replacement.

Replacing negations with antonyms

The opposite of synonym replacement is **antonym replacement**. An **antonym** is a word that has the opposite meaning of another word. This time, instead of creating custom word mappings, we can use WordNet to replace words with unambiguous antonyms. Refer to the *Looking up lemmas and synonyms in WordNet* recipe in *Chapter 1, Tokenizing Text and WordNet Basics*, for more details on antonym lookups.

How to do it...

Let's say you have a sentence like `let's not uglify our code`. With antonym replacement, you can replace `not uglify` with `beautify`, resulting in the sentence `let's beautify our code`. To do this, we will create an `AntonymReplacer` class in `replacers.py` as follows:

```python
from nltk.corpus import wordnet

class AntonymReplacer(object):
  def replace(self, word, pos=None):
    antonyms = set()
    for syn in wordnet.synsets(word, pos=pos):
      for lemma in syn.lemmas():
        for antonym in lemma.antonyms():
          antonyms.add(antonym.name())
    if len(antonyms) == 1:
      return antonyms.pop()
    else:
      return None

  def replace_negations(self, sent):
    i, l = 0, len(sent)
    words = []
    while i < l:
      word = sent[i]
      if word == 'not' and i+1 < l:
        ant = self.replace(sent[i+1])
        if ant:
          words.append(ant)
          i += 2
          continue
      words.append(word)
      i += 1
    return words
```

Now, we can tokenize the original sentence into `["let's", 'not', 'uglify', 'our', 'code']` and pass this to the `replace_negations()` function. Here are some examples:

```
>>> from replacers import AntonymReplacer
>>> replacer = AntonymReplacer()
>>> replacer.replace('good')
>>> replacer.replace('uglify')
'beautify'
>>> sent = ["let's", 'not', 'uglify', 'our', 'code']
>>> replacer.replace_negations(sent)
["let's", 'beautify', 'our', 'code']
```

How it works...

The `AntonymReplacer` class has two methods: `replace()` and `replace_negations()`. The `replace()` method takes a single word and an optional part-of-speech tag, then looks up the Synsets for the word in WordNet. Going through all the Synsets and every lemma of each Synset, it creates a set of all antonyms found. If only one antonym is found, then it is an unambiguous replacement. If there is more than one antonym, which can happen quite often, then we don't know for sure which antonym is correct. In the case of multiple antonyms (or no antonyms), `replace()` returns `None` as it cannot make a decision.

In `replace_negations()`, we look through a tokenized sentence for the word `not`. If `not` is found, then we try to find an antonym for the next word using `replace()`. If we find an antonym, then it is appended to the list of words, replacing `not` and the original word. All other words are appended as is, resulting in a tokenized sentence with unambiguous negations replaced by their antonyms.

There's more...

As unambiguous antonyms aren't very common in WordNet, you might want to create a custom antonym mapping in the same way we did for synonyms. This `AntonymWordReplacer` can be constructed by inheriting from both `WordReplacer` and `AntonymReplacer`:

```
class AntonymWordReplacer(WordReplacer, AntonymReplacer):
    pass
```

The order of inheritance is very important, as we want the initialization and replace function of `WordReplacer` combined with the `replace_negations` function from `AntonymReplacer`. The result is a replacer that can perform the following:

```
>>> from replacers import AntonymWordReplacer
>>> replacer = AntonymWordReplacer({'evil': 'good'})
>>> replacer.replace_negations(['good', 'is', 'not', 'evil'])
['good', 'is', 'good']
```

Of course, you can also inherit from `CsvWordReplacer` or `YamlWordReplacer` instead of `WordReplacer` if you want to load the antonym word mappings from a file.

See also

The previous recipe covers the `WordReplacer` from the perspective of synonym replacement. In *Chapter 1, Tokenizing Text and WordNet Basics*, WordNet usage is covered in detail in the *Looking up Synsets for a word in WordNet* and *Looking up lemmas and synonyms in WordNet* recipes.

3
Creating Custom Corpora

In this chapter, we will cover the following recipes:

- ► Setting up a custom corpus
- ► Creating a wordlist corpus
- ► Creating a part-of-speech tagged word corpus
- ► Creating a chunked phrase corpus
- ► Creating a categorized text corpus
- ► Creating a categorized chunk corpus reader
- ► Lazy corpus loading
- ► Creating a custom corpus view
- ► Creating a MongoDB-backed corpus reader
- ► Corpus editing with file locking

Introduction

In this chapter, we'll cover how to use corpus readers and create custom corpora. If you want to train your own model, such as a part-of-speech tagger or text classifier, you will need to create a custom corpus to train on. Model training is covered in the subsequent chapters.

Now you'll learn how to use the existing corpus data that comes with NLTK. This information is essential for future chapters when we'll need to access the corpora as training data. You've already accessed the WordNet corpus in *Chapter 1, Tokenizing Text and WordNet Basics*. This chapter will introduce you to many more corpora.

We'll also cover creating custom corpus readers, which can be used when your corpus is not in a file format that NLTK already recognizes, or if your corpus is not located in files at all, but instead is located in a database such as MongoDB. It is essential to be familiar with tokenization, which was covered in *Chapter 1, Tokenizing Text and WordNet Basics*.

Setting up a custom corpus

A **corpus** is a collection of text documents, and **corpora** is the plural of corpus. This comes from the Latin word for body; in this case, a body of text. So a **custom corpus** is really just a bunch of text files in a directory, often alongside many other directories of text files.

Getting ready

You should already have the NLTK data package installed, following the instructions at `http://www.nltk.org/data`. We'll assume that the data is installed to `C:\nltk_data` on Windows, and `/usr/share/nltk_data` on Linux, Unix, and Mac OS X.

How to do it...

NLTK defines a list of data directories, or paths, in `nltk.data.path`. Our custom corpora must be within one of these paths so it can be found by NLTK. In order to avoid conflict with the official data package, we'll create a custom `nltk_data` directory in our home directory. The following is some Python code to create this directory and verify that it is in the list of known paths specified by `nltk.data.path`:

```
>>> import os, os.path
>>> path = os.path.expanduser('~/nltk_data')
>>> if not os.path.exists(path):
...      os.mkdir(path)
>>> os.path.exists(path)
True
>>> import nltk.data
>>> path in nltk.data.path
True
```

If the last line, `path in nltk.data.path`, is `True`, then you should now have a `nltk_data` directory in your home directory. The path should be `%UserProfile%\nltk_data` on Windows, or `~/nltk_data` on Unix, Linux, and Mac OS X. For simplicity, I'll refer to the directory as `~/nltk_data`.

If the last line does not return `True`, try creating the `nltk_data` directory manually in your home directory, then verify that the absolute path is in `nltk.data.path`. It's essential to ensure that this directory exists and is in `nltk.data.path` before continuing. You can see a list of the directories by running `python -c "import nltk.data; print(nltk.data.path)"`. Once you have your `nltk_data` directory, the convention is that corpora resides in a `corpora` subdirectory. Create this `corpora` directory within the `nltk_data` directory, so that the path is `~/nltk_data/corpora`. Finally, we'll create a subdirectory in `corpora` to hold our custom corpus. Let's call it `cookbook`, giving us the full path, which is `~/nltk_data/corpora/cookbook`. So on Unix, Linux, and Mac OS X, you could run the following to create the directory:

```
mkdir -p ~/nltk_data/corpora/cookbook
```

Now, we can create a simple wordlist file and make sure it loads. In the *Spelling correction with Enchant* recipe in *Chapter 2, Replacing and Correcting Words*, we created a wordlist file called `mywords.txt`. Put this file into `~/nltk_data/corpora/cookbook/`. Now we can use `nltk.data.load()`, as shown in the following code, to load the file:

```
>>> import nltk.data
>>> nltk.data.load('corpora/cookbook/mywords.txt', format='raw')
b'nltk\n'
```

We need to specify `format='raw'` since `nltk.data.load()` doesn't know how to interpret `.txt` files. As we'll see, it does know how to interpret a number of other file formats.

How it works...

The `nltk.data.load()` function recognizes a number of formats, such as `'raw'`, `'pickle'`, and `'yaml'`. If no format is specified, then it tries to guess the format based on the file's extension. In the previous case, we have a `.txt` file, which is not a recognized extension, so we have to specify the `'raw'` format. But, if we used a file that ended in `.yaml`, then we would not need to specify the format.

Filenames passed into `nltk.data.load()` can be *absolute* or *relative* paths. Relative paths must be relative to one of the paths specified in `nltk.data.path`. The file is found using `nltk.data.find(path)`, which searches all known paths combined with the relative path. Absolute paths do not require a search, and are used as is. When using relative paths, be sure to use choose unambiguous names for your files so as not to conflict with any existing NLTK data.

There's more...

For most corpora access, you won't actually need to use `nltk.data.load`, as that will be handled by the `CorpusReader` classes covered in the following recipes. But it's a good function to be familiar with for loading pickle files and `.yaml` files, and it also introduces the idea of putting all of your data files into a path known by NLTK.

Loading a YAML file

If you put the `synonyms.yaml` file from the *Replacing synonyms* recipe in *Chapter 2, Replacing and Correcting Words* into `~/nltk_data/corpora/cookbook` (next to `mywords.txt`), you can use `nltk.data.load()` to load it without specifying a format:

```
>>> import nltk.data
>>> nltk.data.load('corpora/cookbook/synonyms.yaml')
{'bday': 'birthday'}
```

This assumes that PyYAML is installed. If not, you can find download and installation instructions at `http://pyyaml.org/wiki/PyYAML`.

See also

In the next recipes, we'll cover various corpus readers, and then in the *Lazy corpus loading* recipe, we'll use the `LazyCorpusLoader` class, which expects corpus data to be in a `corpora` subdirectory of one of the paths specified by `nltk.data.path`.

Creating a wordlist corpus

The `WordListCorpusReader` class is one of the simplest `CorpusReader` classes. It provides access to a file containing a list of words, one word per line. In fact, you've already used it when we used the stopwords corpus in *Chapter 1, Tokenizing Text and WordNet Basics,* in the *Filtering stopwords in a tokenized sentence* and *Discovering word collocations* recipes.

Getting ready

We need to start by creating a wordlist file. This could be a single column CSV file, or just a normal text file with one word per line. Let's create a file named `wordlist` that looks like this:

```
nltk
corpus
corpora
wordnet
```

How to do it...

Now we can instantiate a `WordListCorpusReader` class that will produce a list of words from our file. It takes two arguments: the directory path containing the files, and a list of filenames. If you open the Python console in the same directory as the files, then `'.'` can be used as the directory path. Otherwise, you must use a directory path such as `nltk_data/corpora/cookbook`:

```
>>> from nltk.corpus.reader import WordListCorpusReader
>>> reader = WordListCorpusReader('.', ['wordlist'])
>>> reader.words()
['nltk', 'corpus', 'corpora', 'wordnet']
>>> reader.fileids()
['wordlist']
```

How it works...

The `WordListCorpusReader` class inherits from `CorpusReader`, which is a common base class for all corpus readers. The `CorpusReader` class does all the work of identifying which files to read, while `WordListCorpusReader` reads the files and tokenizes each line to produce a list of words. The following is an inheritance diagram:

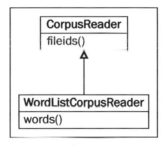

When you call the `words()` function, it calls `nltk.tokenize.line_tokenize()` on the raw file data, which you can access using the `raw()` function as follows:

```
>>> reader.raw()
'nltk\ncorpus\ncorpora\nwordnet\n'
>>> from nltk.tokenize import line_tokenize
>>> line_tokenize(reader.raw())
['nltk', 'corpus', 'corpora', 'wordnet']
```

There's more...

The stopwords corpus is a good example of a multifile WordListCorpusReader. In the *Filtering stopwords in a tokenized sentence* recipe in *Chapter 1, Tokenizing Text and WordNet Basics*, we saw that it had one wordlist file for each language, and you could access the words for that language by calling stopwords.words(fileid). If you want to create your own multifile wordlist corpus, this is a great example to follow.

Names wordlist corpus

Another wordlist corpus that comes with NLTK is the names corpus that is shown in the following code. It contains two files: female.txt and male.txt, each containing a list of a few thousand common first names organized by gender as follows:

```
>>> from nltk.corpus import names
>>> names.fileids()
['female.txt', 'male.txt']
>>> len(names.words('female.txt'))
5001
>>> len(names.words('male.txt'))
2943
```

English words corpus

NLTK also comes with a large list of English words. There's one file with 850 basic words, and another list with over 200,000 known English words, as shown in the following code:

```
>>> from nltk.corpus import words
>>> words.fileids()
['en', 'en-basic']
>>> len(words.words('en-basic'))
850
>>> len(words.words('en'))
234936
```

See also

The *Filtering stopwords in a tokenized sentence* recipe in *Chapter 1, Tokenizing Text and WordNet Basics*, has more details on using the stopwords corpus. In the following recipes, we'll cover more advanced corpus file formats and corpus reader classes.

Creating a part-of-speech tagged word corpus

Part-of-speech tagging is the process of identifying the part-of-speech tag for a word. Most of the time, a tagger must first be trained on a training corpus. How to train and use a tagger is covered in detail in *Chapter 4, Part-of-speech Tagging*, but first we must know how to create and use a training corpus of part-of-speech tagged words.

Getting ready

The simplest format for a tagged corpus is of the form *word/tag*. The following is an excerpt from the brown corpus:

```
The/at-tl expense/nn and/cc time/nn involved/vbn are/ber
    astronomical/jj ./.
```

Each word has a tag denoting its part-of-speech. For example, nn refers to a noun, while a tag that starts with vb is a verb.

 Different corpora can use different tags to mean the same thing. For example, the treebank corpus uses different tags as compared to the brown corpus, even though both are English text. But both sets of tags can be converted into a universal tagset, described at the end of this recipe.

How to do it...

If you were to put the previous excerpt into a file called brown.pos, you could then create a TaggedCorpusReader class using the following code:

```
>>> from nltk.corpus.reader import TaggedCorpusReader
>>> reader = TaggedCorpusReader('.', r'.*\.pos')
>>> reader.words()
['The', 'expense', 'and', 'time', 'involved', 'are', ...]
>>> reader.tagged_words()
[('The', 'AT-TL'), ('expense', 'NN'), ('and', 'CC'), ...]
>>> reader.sents()
[['The', 'expense', 'and', 'time', 'involved', 'are', 'astronomical',
'.']]
>>> reader.tagged_sents()
```

```
[[('The', 'AT-TL'), ('expense', 'NN'), ('and', 'CC'), ('time', 'NN'),
('involved', 'VBN'), ('are', 'BER'), ('astronomical', 'JJ'), ('.',
'.')]]
>>> reader.paras()
[[['The', 'expense', 'and', 'time', 'involved', 'are', 'astronomical',
'.']]]
>>> reader.tagged_paras()
[[[('The', 'AT-TL'), ('expense', 'NN'), ('and', 'CC'), ('time', 'NN'),
('involved', 'VBN'), ('are', 'BER'), ('astronomical', 'JJ'), ('.',
'.')]]]
```

How it works...

This time, instead of naming the file explicitly, we use a regular expression, `r'.*\.pos'`, to match all the files whose names end with `.pos`. We could have done the same thing as we did with the `WordListCorpusReader` class, and pass `['brown.pos']` as the second argument, but this way you can see how to include multiple files in a corpus without naming each one explicitly.

The `TaggedCorpusReader` class provides a number of methods for extracting text from a corpus. First, you can get a list of all words or a list of tagged tokens. A tagged token is simply a tuple of `(word, tag)`. Next, you can get a list of every sentence and also every tagged sentence where the sentence is itself a list of words or tagged tokens. Finally, you can get a list of paragraphs, where each paragraph is a list of sentences and each sentence is a list of words or tagged tokens. The following is an inheritance diagram listing all the major methods:

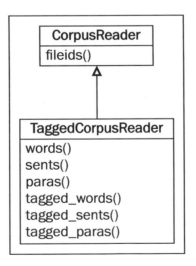

There's more...

All the functions we just demonstrated depend on tokenizers to split the text. The
`TaggedCorpusReader` class tries to have good defaults, but you can customize
them by passing in your own tokenizers at the time of initialization.

Customizing the word tokenizer

The default word tokenizer is an instance of `nltk.tokenize.WhitespaceTokenizer`.
If you want to use a different tokenizer, you can pass that in as `word_tokenizer`, as shown
in the following code:

```
>>> from nltk.tokenize import SpaceTokenizer
>>> reader = TaggedCorpusReader('.', r'.*\.pos', word_
tokenizer=SpaceTokenizer())
>>> reader.words()
['The', 'expense', 'and', 'time', 'involved', 'are', ...]
```

Customizing the sentence tokenizer

The default sentence tokenizer is an instance of `nltk.tokenize.RegexpTokenize`
with `'\n'` to identify the gaps. It assumes that each sentence is on a line all by itself, and
individual sentences do not have line breaks. To customize this, you can pass in your own
tokenizer as `sent_tokenizer`, as shown in the following code:

```
>>> from nltk.tokenize import LineTokenizer
>>> reader = TaggedCorpusReader('.', r'.*\.pos', sent_
tokenizer=LineTokenizer())
>>> reader.sents()
[['The', 'expense', 'and', 'time', 'involved', 'are', 'astronomical',
'.']]
```

Customizing the paragraph block reader

Paragraphs are assumed to be split by blank lines. This is done with the `para_block_reader`
function, which is `nltk.corpus.reader.util.read_blankline_block`. There are a
number of other block reader functions in `nltk.corpus.reader.util`, whose purpose
is to read blocks of text from a stream. Their usage will be covered in more detail later in the
Creating a custom corpus view recipe, where we'll create a custom corpus reader.

Customizing the tag separator

If you don't want to use `'/'` as the word/tag separator, you can pass an alternative string to
`TaggedCorpusReader` for `sep`. The default is `sep='/'`, but if you want to split words and
tags with `'|'`, such as `'word|tag'`, then you should pass in `sep='|'`.

Converting tags to a universal tagset

NLTK 3.0 provides a method for converting known tagsets to a universal tagset. A **tagset** is just a list of part-of-speech tags used by one or more corpora. The **universal tagset** is a simplified and condensed tagset composed of only 12 part-of-speech tags, as shown in the following table:

Universal tag	Description
VERB	All verbs
NOUN	Common and proper nouns
PRON	Pronouns
ADJ	Adjectives
ADV	Adverbs
ADP	Prepositions and postpositions
CONJ	Conjunctions
DET	Determiners
NUM	Cardinal numbers
PRT	Participles
X	Other
.	Punctuation

Mappings from a known tagset to the universal tagset can be found at `nltk_data/taggers/universal_tagset`. For example, `treebank` tag mappings are in `nltk_data/taggers/universal_tagset/en-ptb.map`.

To map corpus tags to the universal tagset, the corpus reader must be initialized with a known tagset name. Then you pass in `tagset='universal'` to a method like `tagged_words()`, as shown in the following code:

```
>>> reader = TaggedCorpusReader('.', r'.*\.pos', tagset='en-brown')
>>> reader.tagged_words(tagset='universal')
[('The', 'DET'), ('expense', 'NOUN'), ('and', 'CONJ'), ...]
```

Most NLTK tagged corpora are initialized with a known tagset, making conversion easy. The following is an example with the `treebank` corpus:

```
>>> from nltk.corpus import treebank
>>> treebank.tagged_words()
[('Pierre', 'NNP'), ('Vinken', 'NNP'), (',', ','), ...]
>>> treebank.tagged_words(tagset='universal')
[('Pierre', 'NOUN'), ('Vinken', 'NOUN'), (',', '.'), ...]
```

If you try to map using an unknown mapping or tagset, every word will be tagged with UNK:

```
>>> treebank.tagged_words(tagset='brown')
[('Pierre', 'UNK'), ('Vinken', 'UNK'), (',', 'UNK'), ...]
```

See also

Chapter 4, *Part-of-speech Tagging*, will cover part-of-speech tags and tagging in much more detail. And for more on tokenizers, see the first three recipes of *Chapter 1, Tokenizing Text and WordNet Basics*.

In the next recipe, we'll create a **chunked phrase** corpus, where each phrase is also part-of-speech tagged.

Creating a chunked phrase corpus

A **chunk** is a short phrase within a sentence. If you remember sentence diagrams from grade school, they were a tree-like representation of phrases within a sentence. This is exactly what chunks are: subtrees within a sentence tree, and they will be covered in much more detail in *Chapter 5, Extracting Chunks*. The following is a sample sentence tree with three **Noun Phrase (NP)** chunks shown as subtrees:

This recipe will cover how to create a corpus with sentences that contain chunks.

Getting ready

The following is an excerpt from the tagged `treebank` corpus. It has part-of-speech tags, as in the previous recipe, but it also has square brackets for denoting chunks. The text within the brackets has been highlighted to make the chunks more apparent. The following sentence is the same sentence as in the previous tree diagram, but in text form:

```
[Earlier/JJR staff-reduction/NN moves/NNS] have/VBP trimmed/VBN about/
IN [300/CD jobs/NNS] ,/, [the/DT spokesman/NN] said/VBD ./.
```

In this format, every chunk is a noun phrase. Words that are not within brackets are part of the sentence tree, but are not part of any noun phrase subtree.

How to do it...

Put the previous excerpt into a file called `treebank.chunk`, and then do the following:

```
>>> from nltk.corpus.reader import ChunkedCorpusReader
>>> reader = ChunkedCorpusReader('.', r'.*\.chunk')
>>> reader.chunked_words()
[Tree('NP', [('Earlier', 'JJR'), ('staff-reduction', 'NN'), ('moves',
'NNS')]), ('have', 'VBP'), ...]
>>> reader.chunked_sents()
[Tree('S', [Tree('NP', [('Earlier', 'JJR'), ('staff-reduction', 'NN'),
('moves', 'NNS')]), ('have', 'VBP'), ('trimmed', 'VBN'), ('about',
'IN'), Tree('NP', [('300', 'CD'), ('jobs', 'NNS')]), (',', ','),
Tree('NP', [('the', 'DT'), ('spokesman', 'NN')]), ('said', 'VBD'),
('.', '.')])]
>>> reader.chunked_paras()
[[Tree('S', [Tree('NP', [('Earlier', 'JJR'), ('staff-reduction',
'NN'), ('moves', 'NNS')]), ('have', 'VBP'), ('trimmed', 'VBN'),
('about', 'IN'), Tree('NP', [('300', 'CD'), ('jobs', 'NNS')]), (',',
','), Tree('NP', [('the', 'DT'), ('spokesman', 'NN')]), ('said',
'VBD'), ('.', '.')])]]]
```

The `ChunkedCorpusReader` class provides the same methods as the `TaggedCorpusReader` for getting tagged tokens, along with three new methods for getting chunks. Each chunk is represented as an instance of `nltk.tree.Tree`. Sentence level trees look like `Tree('S', [...])` while noun phrase trees look like `Tree('NP', [...])`. In `chunked_sents()`, you get a list of sentence trees, with each noun phrase as a subtree of the sentence. In `chunked_words()`, you get a list of noun phrase trees alongside tagged tokens of words that were not in a chunk. The following is an inheritance diagram listing the major methods:

You can draw a tree by calling the `draw()` method. Using the corpus reader defined earlier, you could do `reader.chunked_sents()[0].draw()` to get the same sentence tree diagram shown at the beginning of this recipe.

How it works...

The `ChunkedCorpusReader` class is similar to the `TaggedCorpusReader` class from the previous recipe. It has the same default `sent_tokenizer` and `para_block_reader` functions, but instead of a `word_tokenizer` function, it uses a `str2chunktree()` function. The default is `nltk.chunk.util.tagstr2tree()`, which parses a sentence string containing bracketed chunks into a sentence tree, with each chunk as a noun phrase subtree. Words are split by whitespace, and the default word/tag separator is `'/'`. If you want to customize chunk parsing, then you can pass in your own function for `str2chunktree()`.

There's more...

An alternative format for denoting chunks is called IOB tags. IOB tags are similar to part-of-speech tags, but provide a way to denote the inside, outside, and beginning of a chunk. They also have the benefit of allowing multiple different chunk phrase types, not just noun phrases. The following is an excerpt from the `conll2000` corpus. Each word is on its own line with a part-of-speech tag followed by an IOB tag:

```
Mr. NNP B-NP
Meador NNP I-NP
had VBD B-VP
been VBN I-VP
executive JJ B-NP
vice NN I-NP
president NN I-NP
of IN B-PP
Balcor NNP B-NP
.  .  O
```

`B-NP` denotes the beginning of a noun phrase, while `I-NP` denotes that the word is inside of the current noun phrase. `B-VP` and `I-VP` denote the beginning and inside of a verb phrase. `O` ends the sentence.

To read a corpus using the IOB format, you must use the `ConllChunkCorpusReader` class. Each sentence is separated by a blank line, but there is no separation for paragraphs. This means that the `para_*` methods are not available. If you put the previous IOB example text into a file named `conll.iob`, you can create and use a `ConllChunkCorpusReader` class with the following code. The third argument to `ConllChunkCorpusReader` should be a tuple or list specifying the types of chunks in the file, which in this case is (`'NP'`, `'VP'`, `'PP'`):

```
>>> from nltk.corpus.reader import ConllChunkCorpusReader
>>> conllreader = ConllChunkCorpusReader('.', r'.*\.iob', ('NP', 'VP',
'PP'))
>>> conllreader.chunked_words()
[Tree('NP', [('Mr.', 'NNP'), ('Meador', 'NNP')]), Tree('VP', [('had',
'VBD'), ('been', 'VBN')]), ...]
>>> conllreader.chunked_sents()
[Tree('S', [Tree('NP', [('Mr.', 'NNP'), ('Meador', 'NNP')]),
Tree('VP', [('had', 'VBD'), ('been', 'VBN')]), Tree('NP',
[('executive', 'JJ'), ('vice', 'NN'), ('president', 'NN')]),
Tree('PP', [('of', 'IN')]), Tree('NP', [('Balcor', 'NNP')]), ('.',
'.')])]
>>> conllreader.iob_words()
[('Mr.', 'NNP', 'B-NP'), ('Meador', 'NNP', 'I-NP'), ...]
>>> conllreader.iob_sents()
[[('Mr.', 'NNP', 'B-NP'), ('Meador', 'NNP', 'I-NP'), ('had', 'VBD',
'B-VP'), ('been', 'VBN', 'I-VP'), ('executive', 'JJ', 'B-NP'),
('vice', 'NN', 'I-NP'), ('president', 'NN', 'I-NP'), ('of', 'IN',
'B-PP'), ('Balcor', 'NNP', 'B-NP'), ('.', '.', 'O')]]
```

The previous code also shows the `iob_words()` and `iob_sents()` methods, which return lists of three tuples of (`word`, `pos`, `iob`). The inheritance diagram for `ConllChunkCorpusReader` looks like the following diagram, with most of the methods implemented by its superclass, `ConllCorpusReader`:

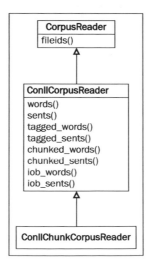

Tree leaves

When it comes to chunk trees, the leaves of a tree are the tagged tokens. So if you want to get a list of all the tagged tokens in a tree, call the `leaves()` method using the following code:

```
>>> reader.chunked_words()[0].leaves()
[('Earlier', 'JJR'), ('staff-reduction', 'NN'), ('moves', 'NNS')]
>>> reader.chunked_sents()[0].leaves()
[('Earlier', 'JJR'), ('staff-reduction', 'NN'), ('moves', 'NNS'),
('have', 'VBP'), ('trimmed', 'VBN'), ('about', 'IN'), ('300', 'CD'),
('jobs', 'NNS'), (',', ','), ('the', 'DT'), ('spokesman', 'NN'),
('said', 'VBD'), ('.', '.')]
>>> reader.chunked_paras()[0][0].leaves()
[('Earlier', 'JJR'), ('staff-reduction', 'NN'), ('moves', 'NNS'),
('have', 'VBP'), ('trimmed', 'VBN'), ('about', 'IN'), ('300', 'CD'),
('jobs', 'NNS'), (',', ','), ('the', 'DT'), ('spokesman', 'NN'),
('said', 'VBD'), ('.', '.')]
```

Treebank chunk corpus

The `nltk.corpus.treebank_chunk` corpus uses `ChunkedCorpusReader` to provide part-of-speech tagged words and noun phrase chunks of *Wall Street Journal* headlines. NLTK comes with a 5 percent sample from the Penn Treebank Project. You can find out more at `http://www.cis.upenn.edu/~treebank/home.html`.

CoNLL2000 corpus

CoNLL stands for the **Conference on Computational Natural Language Learning**. For the year 2000 conference, a shared task was undertaken to produce a corpus of chunks based on the *Wall Street Journal* corpus. In addition to **Noun Phrases** (**NP**), it also contains **Verb Phrases** (**VP**) and **Prepositional Phrases** (**PP**). This chunked corpus is available as `nltk.corpus.conll2000`, which is an instance of `ConllChunkCorpusReader`. You can read more at `http://www.cnts.ua.ac.be/conll2000/chunking/`.

See also

Chapter 5, *Extracting Chunks*, will cover chunk extraction in detail. Also see the previous recipe for details on getting tagged tokens from a corpus reader.

Creating a categorized text corpus

If you have a large corpus of text, you might want to categorize it into separate sections. This can be helpful for organization, or for text classification, which is covered in *Chapter 7, Text Classification*. The brown corpus, for example, has a number of different categories, as shown in the following code:

```
>>> from nltk.corpus import brown
>>> brown.categories()
['adventure', 'belles_lettres', 'editorial', 'fiction', 'government',
'hobbies', 'humor', 'learned', 'lore', 'mystery', 'news', 'religion',
'reviews', 'romance', 'science_fiction']
```

In this recipe, we'll learn how to create our own categorized text corpus.

Getting ready

The easiest way to categorize a corpus is to have one file for each category. The following are two excerpts from the movie_reviews corpus:

▶ movie_pos.txt:

the thin red line is flawed but it provokes .

▶ movie_neg.txt:

a big-budget and glossy production can not make up for a lack of spontaneity that permeates their tv show .

With these two files, we'll have two categories: pos and neg.

How to do it...

We'll use the CategorizedPlaintextCorpusReader class, which inherits from both PlaintextCorpusReader and CategorizedCorpusReader. These two superclasses require three arguments: the root directory, the fileids arguments, and a category specification:

```
>>> from nltk.corpus.reader import CategorizedPlaintextCorpusReader
>>> reader = CategorizedPlaintextCorpusReader('.', r'movie_.*\.txt',
cat_pattern=r'movie_(\w+)\.txt')
>>> reader.categories()
['neg', 'pos']
>>> reader.fileids(categories=['neg'])
['movie_neg.txt']
>>> reader.fileids(categories=['pos'])
['movie_pos.txt']
```

How it works...

The first two arguments to `CategorizedPlaintextCorpusReader` are the root directory and `fileids`, which are passed on to the `PlaintextCorpusReader` class to read in the files. The `cat_pattern` keyword argument is a regular expression for extracting the category names from the `fileids` arguments. In our case, the category is the part of the `fileid` argument after `movie_` and before `.txt`. The category must be surrounded by grouping parenthesis.

The `cat_pattern` keyword is passed to `CategorizedCorpusReader`, which overrides the common corpus reader functions such as `fileids()`, `words()`, `sents()`, and `paras()` to accept a `categories` keyword argument. This way, you could get all the pos sentences by calling `reader.sents(categories=['pos'])`. The `CategorizedCorpusReader` class also provides the `categories()` function, which returns a list of all the known categories in the corpus.

The `CategorizedPlaintextCorpusReader` class is an example of using multiple inheritance to join methods from multiple superclasses, as shown in the following diagram:

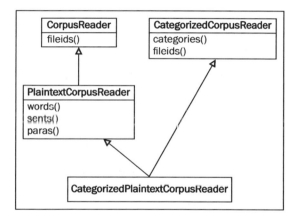

There's more...

Instead of `cat_pattern`, you could pass in a `cat_map`, which is a dictionary mapping a `fileid` argument to a list of category labels, as shown in the following code:

```
>>> reader = CategorizedPlaintextCorpusReader('.', r'movie_.*\.txt',
cat_map={'movie_pos.txt': ['pos'], 'movie_neg.txt': ['neg']})
>>> reader.categories()
['neg', 'pos']
```

Category file

A third way of specifying categories is to use the `cat_file` keyword argument to specify a filename containing a mapping of `fileid` to category. For example, the `brown` corpus has a file called `cats.txt` that looks like the following:

```
ca44 news
cb01 editorial
```

The `reuters` corpus has files in multiple categories, and its `cats.txt` looks like the following:

```
test/14840 rubber coffee lumber palm-oil veg-oil
test/14841 wheat grain
```

Categorized tagged corpus reader

The `brown` corpus reader is actually an instance of `CategorizedTaggedCorpusReader`, which inherits from `CategorizedCorpusReader` and `TaggedCorpusReader`. Just like in `CategorizedPlaintextCorpusReader`, it overrides all the methods of `TaggedCorpusReader` to allow a `categories` argument, so you can call `brown.tagged_sents(categories=['news'])` to get all the tagged sentences from the `news` category. You can use the `CategorizedTaggedCorpusReader` class just like `CategorizedPlaintextCorpusReader` for your own categorized and tagged text corpora.

Categorized corpora

The `movie_reviews` corpus reader is an instance of `CategorizedPlaintextCorpusReader`, as is the `reuters` corpus reader. But where the `movie_reviews` corpus only has two categories (`neg` and `pos`), `reuters` has 90 categories. These corpora are often used for training and evaluating classifiers, which will be covered in *Chapter 7, Text Classification*.

See also

In the next chapter, we'll create a subclass of `CategorizedCorpusReader` and `ChunkedCorpusReader` for reading a categorized chunk corpus. Also, see *Chapter 7, Text Classification* in which we use categorized text for classification.

Creating a categorized chunk corpus reader

NLTK provides a `CategorizedPlaintextCorpusReader` and `CategorizedTaggedCorpusReader` class, but there's no categorized corpus reader for chunked corpora. So in this recipe, we're going to make one.

Getting ready

Refer to the earlier recipe, *Creating a chunked phrase corpus*, for an explanation of `ChunkedCorpusReader`, and refer to the previous recipe for details on `CategorizedPlaintextCorpusReader` and `CategorizedTaggedCorpusReader`, both of which inherit from `CategorizedCorpusReader`.

How to do it...

We'll create a class called `CategorizedChunkedCorpusReader` that inherits from both `CategorizedCorpusReader` and `ChunkedCorpusReader`. It is heavily based on the `CategorizedTaggedCorpusReader` class, and also provides three additional methods for getting categorized chunks. The following code is found in `catchunked.py`:

```python
from nltk.corpus.reader import CategorizedCorpusReader,
    ChunkedCorpusReader

class CategorizedChunkedCorpusReader(CategorizedCorpusReader,
    ChunkedCorpusReader):
    def __init__(self, *args, **kwargs):
        CategorizedCorpusReader.__init__(self, kwargs)
        ChunkedCorpusReader.__init__(self, *args, **kwargs)

    def _resolve(self, fileids, categories):
        if fileids is not None and categories is not None:
            raise ValueError('Specify fileids or categories, not both')
        if categories is not None:
            return self.fileids(categories)
        else:
            return fileids
```

All of the following methods call the corresponding function in `ChunkedCorpusReader` with the value returned from `_resolve()`. We'll start with the plain text methods:

```python
    def raw(self, fileids=None, categories=None):
        return ChunkedCorpusReader.raw(self, self._resolve(fileids,
            categories))

    def words(self, fileids=None, categories=None):
        return ChunkedCorpusReader.words(self, self._resolve(fileids,
            categories))

    def sents(self, fileids=None, categories=None):
        return ChunkedCorpusReader.sents(self, self._resolve(fileids,
            categories))
```

```
def paras(self, fileids=None, categories=None):
  return ChunkedCorpusReader.paras(self, self._resolve(fileids,
    categories))
```

Next is the code for the tagged text methods:

```
def tagged_words(self, fileids=None, categories=None):
  return ChunkedCorpusReader.tagged_words(self,
    self._resolve(fileids, categories))

def tagged_sents(self, fileids=None, categories=None):
  return ChunkedCorpusReader.tagged_sents(self,
    self._resolve(fileids, categories))

def tagged_paras(self, fileids=None, categories=None):
  return ChunkedCorpusReader.tagged_paras(self,
    self._resolve(fileids, categories))
```

And finally, we have code for the chunked methods, which is what we've really been after:

```
def chunked_words(self, fileids=None, categories=None):
  return ChunkedCorpusReader.chunked_words(self,
    self._resolve(fileids, categories))

def chunked_sents(self, fileids=None, categories=None):
  return ChunkedCorpusReader.chunked_sents(self,
    self._resolve(fileids, categories))

def chunked_paras(self, fileids=None, categories=None):
  return ChunkedCorpusReader.chunked_paras(self,
    self._resolve(fileids, categories))
```

All these methods together give us a complete CategorizedChunkedCorpusReader class.

How it works...

The CategorizedChunkedCorpusReader class overrides all the ChunkedCorpusReader methods to take a categories argument for locating fileids. These fileids are found with the internal _resolve() function. This _resolve() function makes use of CategorizedCorpusReader.fileids() to return fileids for a given list of categories. If no categories are given, _resolve() just returns the given fileids, which could be None, in which case all the files are read. The initialization of both CategorizedCorpusReader and ChunkedCorpusReader is what makes all this possible. If you look at the code for CategorizedTaggedCorpusReader, you'll see that it's very similar.

The inheritance diagram looks like this:

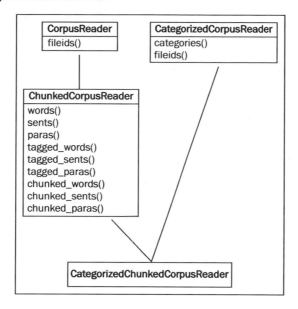

The following is example code for using the `treebank` corpus. All we're doing is making categories out of the `fileids` arguments, but the point is that you could use the same techniques to create your own categorized chunk corpus:

```
>>> import nltk.data
>>> from catchunked import CategorizedChunkedCorpusReader
>>> path = nltk.data.find('corpora/treebank/tagged')
>>> reader = CategorizedChunkedCorpusReader(path, r'wsj_.*\.pos',
cat_pattern=r'wsj_(.*)\.pos')
>>> len(reader.categories()) == len(reader.fileids())
True
>>> len(reader.chunked_sents(categories=['0001']))
16
```

We use `nltk.data.find()` to search the data directories to get a `FileSystemPathPointer` class to the `treebank` corpus. All the `treebank` tagged files start with `wsj_`, followed by a number, and end with `.pos`. The previous code turns that file number into a category.

There's more...

As covered in the *Creating a chunked phrase corpus* recipe, there's an alternative format and reader for a chunk corpus using IOB tags. To have a categorized corpus of IOB chunks, we have to make a new corpus reader.

Categorized CoNLL chunk corpus reader

The following is the code for the subclass of `CategorizedCorpusReader` and `ConllChunkReader` called `CategorizedConllChunkCorpusReader`. It overrides all methods of `ConllCorpusReader` that take a `fileids` argument, so the methods can also take a `categories` argument. The `ConllChunkCorpusReader` is just a small subclass of `ConllCorpusReader` that handles initialization; most of the work is done in `ConllCorpusReader`. This code can also be found in `catchunked.py`.

```
from nltk.corpus.reader import CategorizedCorpusReader,
ConllCorpusReader, ConllChunkCorpusReader

class CategorizedConllChunkCorpusReader(CategorizedCorpusReader,
  ConllChunkCorpusReader):
  def __init__(self, *args, **kwargs):
    CategorizedCorpusReader.__init__(self, kwargs)
    ConllChunkCorpusReader.__init__(self, *args, **kwargs)

  def _resolve(self, fileids, categories):
    if fileids is not None and categories is not None:
      raise ValueError('Specify fileids or categories, not both')
    if categories is not None:
      return self.fileids(categories)
    else:
      return fileids
```

All the following methods call the corresponding method of `ConllCorpusReader` with the value returned from `_resolve()`. We'll start with the plain text methods:

```
def raw(self, fileids=None, categories=None):
  return ConllCorpusReader.raw(self, self._resolve(fileids,
    categories))

def words(self, fileids=None, categories=None):
  return ConllCorpusReader.words(self, self._resolve(fileids,
    categories))

def sents(self, fileids=None, categories=None):
  return ConllCorpusReader.sents(self, self._resolve(fileids,
    categories))
```

The `ConllCorpusReader` class does not recognize paragraphs, so there are no `*_paras()` methods. Next will be the code for the tagged and chunked methods, as follows:

```python
def tagged_words(self, fileids=None, categories=None):
    return ConllCorpusReader.tagged_words(self,
        self._resolve(fileids, categories))
def tagged_sents(self, fileids=None, categories=None):
    return ConllCorpusReader.tagged_sents(self,
        self._resolve(fileids, categories))

def chunked_words(self, fileids=None, categories=None,
    chunk_types=None):
    return ConllCorpusReader.chunked_words(self,
        self._resolve(fileids, categories), chunk_types)

def chunked_sents(self, fileids=None, categories=None,
    chunk_types=None):
    return ConllCorpusReader.chunked_sents(self,
        self._resolve(fileids, categories), chunk_types)
```

For completeness, we must override the following methods of the `ConllCorpusReader` class:

```python
def parsed_sents(self, fileids=None, categories=None,
    pos_in_tree=None):
    return ConllCorpusReader.parsed_sents(
        self, self._resolve(fileids, categories), pos_in_tree)

def srl_spans(self, fileids=None, categories=None):
    return ConllCorpusReader.srl_spans(self,
        self._resolve(fileids, categories))

def srl_instances(self, fileids=None, categories=None,
    pos_in_tree=None, flatten=True):
    return ConllCorpusReader.srl_instances(self,
        self._resolve(fileids, categories), pos_in_tree, flatten)

def iob_words(self, fileids=None, categories=None):
    return ConllCorpusReader.iob_words(self,
        self._resolve(fileids, categories))

def iob_sents(self, fileids=None, categories=None):
    return ConllCorpusReader.iob_sents(self,
        self._resolve(fileids, categories))
```

The inheritance diagram for this class is as follows:

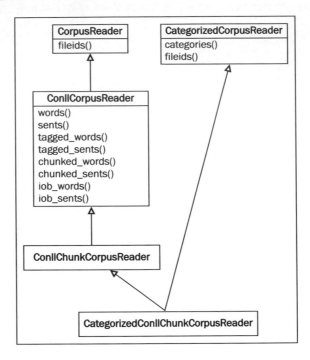

Here is example code using the `conll2000` corpus:

```
>>> import nltk.data
>>> from catchunked import CategorizedConllChunkCorpusReader
>>> path = nltk.data.find('corpora/conll2000')
>>> reader = CategorizedConllChunkCorpusReader(path, r'.*\.txt',
('NP','VP','PP'), cat_pattern=r'(.*)\.txt')
>>> reader.categories()
['test', 'train']
>>> reader.fileids()
['test.txt', 'train.txt']
>>> len(reader.chunked_sents(categories=['test']))
2012
```

Like with `treebank`, we're using the `fileids` for categories. The `ConllChunkCorpusReader` class requires a third argument to specify the chunk types. These chunk types are used to parse the IOB tags. As you learned in the *Creating a chunked phrase corpus* recipe, the `conll2000` corpus recognizes the following three chunk types:

- ▸ NP for noun phrases
- ▸ VP for verb phrases
- ▸ PP for prepositional phrases

See also

In the *Creating a chunked phrase corpus* recipe of this chapter, we covered both the `ChunkedCorpusReader` and `ConllChunkCorpusReader` classes. And in the previous recipe, we covered `CategorizedPlaintextCorpusReader` and `CategorizedTaggedCorpusReader`, which share the same superclass used by `CategorizedChunkedCorpusReader` and `CategorizedConllChunkReader`, that is, `CategorizedCorpusReader`.

Lazy corpus loading

Loading a corpus reader can be an expensive operation due to the number of files, file sizes, and various initialization tasks. And while you'll often want to specify a corpus reader in a common module, you don't always need to access it right away. To speed up module import time when a corpus reader is defined, NLTK provides a `LazyCorpusLoader` class that can transform itself into your actual corpus reader as soon as you need it. This way, you can define a corpus reader in a common module without it slowing down module loading.

How to do it...

The `LazyCorpusLoader` class requires two arguments: the name of the corpus and the corpus reader class, plus any other arguments needed to initialize the corpus reader class.

The `name` argument specifies the root directory name of the corpus, which must be within a `corpora` subdirectory of one of the paths in `nltk.data.path`. See the *Setting up a custom corpus* recipe of this chapter for more details on `nltk.data.path`.

For example, if you have a custom corpora named `cookbook` in your local `nltk_data` directory, its path would be `~/nltk_data/corpora/cookbook`. You'd then pass `'cookbook'` to `LazyCorpusLoader` as the name, and `LazyCorpusLoader` will look in `~/nltk_data/corpora` for a directory named `'cookbook'`.

The second argument to `LazyCorpusLoader` is `reader_cls`, which should be the name of a subclass of `CorpusReader`, such as `WordListCorpusReader`. You will also need to pass in any other arguments required by the `reader_cls` argument for initialization. This will be demonstrated as follows, using the same wordlist file we created in the earlier recipe, *Creating a wordlist corpus*. The third argument to `LazyCorpusLoader` is the list of filenames and `fileids` that will be passed to `WordListCorpusReader` at initialization:

```
>>> from nltk.corpus.util import LazyCorpusLoader
>>> from nltk.corpus.reader import WordListCorpusReader
>>> reader = LazyCorpusLoader('cookbook', WordListCorpusReader,
['wordlist'])
>>> isinstance(reader, LazyCorpusLoader)
True
>>> reader.fileids()
['wordlist']
>>> isinstance(reader, LazyCorpusLoader)
False
>>> isinstance(reader, WordListCorpusReader)
True
```

How it works...

The `LazyCorpusLoader` class stores all the arguments given, but otherwise does nothing until you try to access an attribute or method. This way, initialization is very fast, eliminating the overhead of loading the corpus reader immediately. As soon as you do access an attribute or method, it does the following:

1. Calls `nltk.data.find('corpora/%s' % name)` to find the corpus data root directory.

2. Instantiates the corpus reader class with the root directory and any other arguments.

3. Transforms itself into the corpus reader class.

So in the previous example code, before we call `reader.fileids()`, reader is an instance of `LazyCorpusLoader`, but after the call, reader becomes an instance of `WordListCorpusReader`.

There's more...

All of the corpora included with NLTK and defined in `nltk.corpus` are initially a `LazyCorpusLoader` class. The following is some code from `nltk.corpus` defining the `treebank` corpora:

```
treebank = LazyCorpusLoader('treebank/combined',
  BracketParseCorpusReader, r'wsj_.*\.mrg',tagset='wsj',
  encoding='ascii')
treebank_chunk = LazyCorpusLoader('treebank/tagged',
  ChunkedCorpusReader, r'wsj_.*\.pos',sent_tokenizer
  =RegexpTokenizer(r'(?<=/\.)\s*(?![^\[]*\])', gaps=True),
    para_block_reader=tagged_treebank_para_block_reader,
      encoding='ascii')
treebank_raw = LazyCorpusLoader('treebank/raw',
  PlaintextCorpusReader, r'wsj_.*', encoding='ISO-8859-2')
```

As you can see in the previous code, any number of additional arguments can be passed through by `LazyCorpusLoader` to its `reader_cls` argument.

Creating a custom corpus view

A **corpus view** is a class wrapper around a corpus file that reads in blocks of tokens as needed. Its purpose is to provide a view into a file without reading the whole file at once (since corpus files can often be quite large). If the corpus readers included by NLTK already meet all your needs, then you do not have to know anything about corpus views. But, if you have a custom file format that needs special handling, this recipe will show you how to create and use a custom corpus view. The main corpus view class is `StreamBackedCorpusView`, which opens a single file as a stream, and maintains an internal cache of blocks it has read.

Blocks of tokens are read in with a block reader function. A block can be any piece of text, such as a paragraph or a line, and tokens are parts of a block, such as individual words. In the *Creating a part-of-speech tagged word corpus* recipe, we discussed the default `para_block_reader` function of the `TaggedCorpusReader` class, which reads lines from a file until it finds a blank line, then returns those lines as a single paragraph token. The actual block reader function is `nltk.corpus.reader.util.read_blankline_block`. The `TaggedCorpusReader` class passes this block reader function into a `TaggedCorpusView` class whenever it needs to read blocks from a file. The `TaggedCorpusView` class is a subclass of `StreamBackedCorpusView` that knows to split paragraphs of word/tag into `(word, tag)` tuples.

How to do it...

We'll start with the simple case of a plain text file with a heading that should be ignored by the corpus reader. Let's make a file called `heading_text.txt` that looks like this:

```
A simple heading

Here is the actual text for the corpus.

Paragraphs are split by blanklines.

This is the 3rd paragraph.
```

Normally, we'd use the `PlaintextCorpusReader` class, but by default it will treat `A simple heading` as the first paragraph. To ignore this heading, we need to subclass the `PlaintextCorpusReader` class so we can override its `CorpusView` class variable with our own `StreamBackedCorpusView` subclass. The following is the code found in `corpus.py`:

```python
from nltk.corpus.reader import PlaintextCorpusReader
from nltk.corpus.reader.util import StreamBackedCorpusView

class IgnoreHeadingCorpusView(StreamBackedCorpusView):
  def __init__(self, *args, **kwargs):
    StreamBackedCorpusView.__init__(self, *args, **kwargs)
    # open self._stream
    self._open()
    # skip the heading block
    self.read_block(self._stream)
    # reset the start position to the current position in the stream
    self._filepos = [self._stream.tell()]

class IgnoreHeadingCorpusReader(PlaintextCorpusReader):
  CorpusView = IgnoreHeadingCorpusView
```

To demonstrate that this works as expected, here is code showing that the default `PlaintextCorpusReader` class finds four paragraphs, while our `IgnoreHeadingCorpusReader` class only has three paragraphs:

```python
>>> from nltk.corpus.reader import PlaintextCorpusReader
>>> plain = PlaintextCorpusReader('.', ['heading_text.txt'])
>>> len(plain.paras())
4
>>> from corpus import IgnoreHeadingCorpusReader
>>> reader = IgnoreHeadingCorpusReader('.', ['heading_text.txt'])
>>> len(reader.paras())
3
```

How it works...

The `PlaintextCorpusReader` class by design has a `CorpusView` class variable that can be overridden by subclasses. So we do just that, and make our `IgnoreHeadingCorpusView` class the `CorpusView` class variable.

 Most corpus readers do not have a `CorpusView` class variable because they require very specific corpus views.

The `IgnoreHeadingCorpusView` class is a subclass of `StreamBackedCorpusView` that does the following on initialization:

1. Opens the file using `self._open()`. This function is defined by `StreamBackedCorpusView`, and sets the internal instance variable `self._stream` to the opened file.

2. Reads one block with `read_blankline_block()`, which then reads the heading as a paragraph, and moves the stream's file position forward to the next block.

3. Resets the start file position to the current position of `self._stream`. The `self._filepos` variable is an internal index of where each block is in the file.

The following is a diagram illustrating the relationships between the classes:

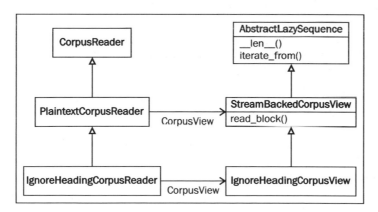

There's more...

Corpus views can get a lot fancier and more complicated, but the core concept is the same: read blocks from a stream to return a list of tokens. There are a number of block readers provided in `nltk.corpus.reader.util`, but you can always create your own. If you do want to define your own block reader function, then you have two choices on how to implement it:

1. Define it as a separate function and pass it into `StreamBackedCorpusView` as `block_reader`. This is a good option if your block reader is fairly simple, reusable, and doesn't require any outside variables or configuration.

2. Subclass `StreamBackedCorpusView` and override the `read_block()` method. This is what many custom corpus views do because the block reading is highly specialized and requires additional functions and configuration, usually provided by the corpus reader when the corpus view is initialized.

Block reader functions

The following is a survey of most of the included block readers in `nltk.corpus.reader.util`. Unless otherwise mentioned, each block reader function takes a single argument: the `stream` argument to read from:

  ▶ `read_whitespace_block()`: This will read 20 lines from the stream, splitting each line into tokens by whitespace.

  ▶ `read_wordpunct_block()`: This reads 20 lines from the stream, splitting each line using `nltk.tokenize.wordpunct_tokenize()`.

  ▶ `read_line_block()`: This reads 20 lines from the stream and returns them as a list, with each line as a token.

  ▶ `read_blankline_block()`: This will read lines from the stream until it finds a blank line. It will then return a single token of all lines found combined into a single string.

  ▶ `read_regexp_block()`: This takes two additional arguments, which must be regular expressions that can be passed to `re.match()`: `start_re` and `end_re`. The `start_re` variable matches the starting line of a block, and `end_re` matches the ending line of the block. The `end_re` variable defaults to `None`, in which case the block will end as soon as a new `start_re` match is found. The return value is a single token of all lines in the block joined into a single string.

Pickle corpus view

If you want to have a corpus of pickled objects, you can use the `PickleCorpusView`, a subclass of `StreamBackedCorpusView`, found in `nltk.corpus.reader.util`. A file consists of blocks of pickled objects, and can be created with the `PickleCorpusView.write()` class method, which takes a sequence of objects and an output file, then pickles each object using `pickle.dump()` and writes it to the file. It overrides the `read_block()` method to return a list of unpickled objects from the stream, using `pickle.load()`.

Concatenated corpus view

Also found in `nltk.corpus.reader.util` is the `ConcatenatedCorpusView` class. This class is useful if you have multiple files that you want a corpus reader to treat as a single file. A `ConcatenatedCorpusView` class is created by giving it a list of `corpus_views`, which are then iterated over as if they were a single view.

See also

The concept of block readers was introduced in the *Creating a part-of-speech tagged word corpus* recipe.

Creating a MongoDB-backed corpus reader

All the corpus readers we've dealt with so far have been file-based. That is in part due to the design of the `CorpusReader` base class, and also the assumption that most corpus data will be in text files. However, sometimes you'll have a bunch of data stored in a database that you want to access and use just like a text file corpus. In this recipe, we'll cover the case where you have documents in MongoDB, and you want to use a particular field of each document as your block of text.

Getting ready

MongoDB is a document-oriented database that has become a popular alternative to relational databases such as MySQL. The installation and setup of MongoDB is outside the scope of this book, but you can find instructions at `http://docs.mongodb.org/manual/`.

You'll also need to install PyMongo, a Python driver for MongoDB. You should be able to do this with either `easy_install` or `pip`, by typing `sudo easy_install pymongo` or `sudo pip install pymongo`.

The following code assumes that your database is on localhost port `27017`, which is the MongoDB default configuration, and that you'll be using the test database with a collection named corpus that contains documents with a text field. Explanations for these arguments are available in the PyMongo documentation at `http://api.mongodb.org/python/current/`.

How to do it...

Since the `CorpusReader` class assumes you have a file-based corpus, we can't directly subclass it. Instead, we're going to emulate both the `StreamBackedCorpusView` and `PlaintextCorpusReader` classes. The `StreamBackedCorpusView` class is a subclass of `nltk.util.AbstractLazySequence`, so we'll subclass `AbstractLazySequence` to create a MongoDB view, and then create a new class that will use the view to provide functionality similar to the `PlaintextCorpusReader` class. The following is the code, which is found in `mongoreader.py`:

```python
import pymongo
from nltk.data import LazyLoader
from nltk.tokenize import TreebankWordTokenizer
from nltk.util import AbstractLazySequence, LazyMap,
  LazyConcatenation

class MongoDBLazySequence(AbstractLazySequence):
  def __init__(self, host='localhost', port=27017, db='test',
    collection='corpus', field='text'):
    self.conn = pymongo.MongoClient(host, port)
    self.collection = self.conn[db][collection]
    self.field = field

  def __len__(self):
    return self.collection.count()

  def iterate_from(self, start):
    f = lambda d: d.get(self.field, '')
    return iter(LazyMap(f, self.collection.find(fields=
      [self.field], skip=start)))

class MongoDBCorpusReader(object):
  def __init__(self, word_tokenizer=TreebankWordTokenizer(),
    sent_tokenizer=LazyLoader('tokenizers/punkt/PY3
      /english.pickle'),**kwargs):
    self._seq = MongoDBLazySequence(**kwargs)
    self._word_tokenize = word_tokenizer.tokenize
    self._sent_tokenize = sent_tokenizer.tokenize

  def text(self):
    return self._seq
```

```
def words(self):
    return LazyConcatenation(LazyMap(self._word_tokenize,
        self.text()))

def sents(self):
    return LazyConcatenation(LazyMap(self._sent_tokenize,
        self.text()))
```

How it works...

The `AbstractLazySequence` class is an abstract class that provides read-only, on-demand iteration. Subclasses must implement the `__len__()` and `iterate_from(start)` methods, while it provides the rest of the list and iterator emulation methods. By creating the `MongoDBLazySequence` subclass as our view, we can iterate over documents in the MongoDB collection on demand, without keeping all the documents in memory. The `LazyMap` class is a lazy version of Python's built-in `map()` function, and is used in `iterate_from()` to transform the document into the specific field that we're interested in. It's also a subclass of `AbstractLazySequence`.

The `MongoDBCorpusReader` class creates an internal instance of `MongoDBLazySequence` for iteration, then defines the word and sentence tokenization methods. The `text()` method simply returns the instance of `MongoDBLazySequence`, which results in a lazily evaluated list of each text field. The `words()` method uses `LazyMap` and `LazyConcatenation` to return a lazily evaluated list of all words, while the `sents()` method does the same for sentences. The `sent_tokenizer` is loaded on demand with `LazyLoader`, which is a wrapper around `nltk.data.load()`, analogous to `LazyCorpusLoader`. The `LazyConcatentation` class is a subclass of `AbstractLazySequence` too, and produces a flat list from a given list of lists (each list may also be lazy). In our case, we're concatenating the results of `LazyMap` to ensure we don't return nested lists.

There's more...

All of the parameters are configurable. For example, if you had a db named website, with a collection named `comments`, whose documents had a field called `comment`, you could create a `MongoDBCorpusReader` class as follows:

```
>>> reader = MongoDBCorpusReader(db='website',
    collection='comments', field='comment')
```

You can also pass in custom instances for `word_tokenizer` and `sent_tokenizer`, as long as the objects implement the `nltk.tokenize.TokenizerI` interface by providing a `tokenize(text)` method.

See also

Corpus views were covered in the previous recipe, and tokenization was covered in *Chapter 1, Tokenizing Text and WordNet Basics*.

Corpus editing with file locking

Corpus readers and views are all read-only, but there will be times when you want to add to or edit the corpus files. However, modifying a corpus file while other processes are using it, such as through a corpus reader, can lead to dangerous undefined behavior. This is where file locking comes in handy.

Getting ready

You must install the `lockfile` library using `sudo easy_install lockfile` or `sudo pip install lockfile`. This library provides cross-platform file locking, and so will work on Windows, Unix/Linux, Mac OS X, and more. You can find detailed documentation on lockfile at `http://packages.python.org/lockfile/`.

How to do it...

Here are two file editing functions: `append_line()` and `remove_line()`. Both try to acquire an exclusive lock on the file before updating it. An exclusive lock means that these functions will wait until no other process is reading from or writing to the file. Once the lock is acquired, any other process that tries to access the file will have to wait until the lock is released. This way, modifying the file will be safe and not cause any undefined behavior in other processes. These functions can be found in `corpus.py`, as follows:

```
import lockfile, tempfile, shutil

def append_line(fname, line): with lockfile.FileLock(fname):
  fp = open(fname, 'a+')
  fp.write(line)
  fp.write('\n')
  fp.close()

def remove_line(fname, line):
```

```
with lockfile.FileLock(fname):
  tmp = tempfile.TemporaryFile()
  fp = open(fname, 'rw+')
  # write all lines from orig file, except if matches given line
  for l in fp:
    if l.strip() != line:
      tmp.write(l)

  # reset file pointers so entire files are copied
  fp.seek(0)
  tmp.seek(0)
  # copy tmp into fp, then truncate to remove trailing line(s)
  shutil.copyfileobj(tmp, fp)
  fp.truncate()
  fp.close()
  tmp.close()
```

The lock acquiring and releasing happens transparently when you do with `lockfile.FileLock(fname)`.

> Instead of using `with lockfile.FileLock(fname)`, you can also get a lock by calling `lock = lockfile.FileLock(fname)`, then call `lock.acquire()` to acquire the lock, and `lock.release()` to release the lock.

How it works...

You can use these functions as follows:

```
>>> from corpus import append_line, remove_line
>>> append_line('test.txt', 'foo')
>>> remove_line('test.txt', 'foo')
```

In `append_line()`, a lock is acquired, the file is opened in *append mode*, the text is written along with an end-of-line character, and then the file is closed, releasing the lock.

> A lock acquired by `lockfile` only protects the file from other processes that also use `lockfile`. In other words, just because your Python process has a lock with `lockfile` doesn't mean a non-Python process can't modify the file. For this reason, it's best to only use `lockfile` with files that will not be edited by an non-Python processes, or Python processes that do not use `lockfile`.

The `remove_line()` function is a bit more complicated. Because we're removing a line, and not a specific section of the file, we need to iterate over the file to find each instance of the line to remove. The easiest way to do this while writing the changes back to the file, is to use a temporary file to hold the changes, then copy that file back into the original file using `shutil.copyfileobj()`.

The `remove_line()` function does not work on Mac OS X, but does work on Linux. For `remove_line()` to work, it must be able to open a file in both read and write modes, and Mac OS X does not allow this.

These functions are best suited for a wordlist corpus, or some other corpus type with presumably unique lines, that may be edited by multiple people at about the same time, such as through a web interface. Using these functions with a more document-oriented corpus such as `brown`, `treebank`, or `conll2000`, is probably a bad idea.

4
Part-of-speech Tagging

In this chapter, we will cover the following recipes:

- ▶ Default tagging
- ▶ Training a unigram part-of-speech tagger
- ▶ Combining taggers with backoff tagging
- ▶ Training and combining ngram taggers
- ▶ Creating a model of likely word tags
- ▶ Tagging with regular expressions
- ▶ Affix tagging
- ▶ Training a Brill tagger
- ▶ Training the TnT tagger
- ▶ Using WordNet for tagging
- ▶ Tagging proper names
- ▶ Classifier-based tagging
- ▶ Training a tagger with NLTK-Trainer

Introduction

Part-of-speech tagging is the process of converting a sentence, in the form of a list of words, into a list of tuples, where each tuple is of the form (**word, tag**). The **tag** is a part-of-speech tag, and signifies whether the word is a noun, adjective, verb, and so on.

Part-of-speech tagging is a necessary step before chunking, which is covered in *Chapter 5, Extracting Chunks*. Without the part-of-speech tags, a chunker cannot know how to extract phrases from a sentence. But with part-of-speech tags, you can tell a chunker how to identify phrases based on tag patterns.

You can also use part-of-speech tags for grammar analysis and word sense disambiguation. For example, the word *duck* could refer to a bird, or it could be a verb indicating a downward motion. Computers cannot know the difference without additional information, such as part-of-speech tags. For more on word sense disambiguation, refer to the URL `https://en.wikipedia.org/wiki/Word_sense_disambiguation`.

Most of the taggers we'll cover are trainable. They use a list of tagged sentences as their training data, such as what you get from the `tagged_sents()` method of a `TaggedCorpusReader` class (see the *Creating a part-of-speech tagged word corpus* recipe in *Chapter 3, Creating Custom Corpora,* for more details). With these training sentences, the tagger generates an internal model that will tell it how to tag a word. Other taggers use external data sources or match word patterns to choose a tag for a word.

All taggers in NLTK are in the `nltk.tag` package and inherit from the `TaggerI` base class. `TaggerI` requires all subclasses to implement a `tag()` method, which takes a list of words as input and returns a list of tagged words as output. `TaggerI` also provides an `evaluate()` method for evaluating the accuracy of the tagger (covered at the end of the *Default tagging* recipe). Many taggers can also be combined into a backoff chain, so that if one tagger cannot tag a word, the next tagger is used, and so on.

Default tagging

Default tagging provides a baseline for part-of-speech tagging. It simply assigns the same part-of-speech tag to every token. We do this using the `DefaultTagger` class. This tagger is useful as a last-resort tagger, and provides a baseline to measure accuracy improvements.

Getting ready

We're going to use the `treebank` corpus for most of this chapter because it's a common standard and is quick to load and test. But everything we do should apply equally well to `brown`, `conll2000`, and any other part-of-speech tagged corpus.

How to do it...

The `DefaultTagger` class takes a single argument, the tag you want to apply. We'll give it NN, which is the tag for a singular noun. `DefaultTagger` is most useful when you choose the most common part-of-speech tag. Since nouns tend to be the most common types of words, a noun tag is recommended.

```
>>> from nltk.tag import DefaultTagger
>>> tagger = DefaultTagger('NN')
>>> tagger.tag(['Hello', 'World'])
[('Hello', 'NN'), ('World', 'NN')]
```

Every tagger has a tag() method that takes a list of tokens, where each token is a single word. This list of tokens is usually a list of words produced by a word tokenizer (see *Chapter 1, Tokenizing Text and WordNet Basics*, for more on tokenization). As you can see, tag() returns a list of tagged tokens, where a tagged token is a tuple of (word, tag).

How it works...

DefaultTagger is a subclass of SequentialBackoffTagger. Every subclass of SequentialBackoffTagger must implement the choose_tag() method, which takes three arguments:

- ▶ The list of tokens
- ▶ The index of the current token whose tag we want to choose
- ▶ The history, which is a list of the previous tags

SequentialBackoffTagger implements the tag() method, which calls the choose_tag() method of the subclass for each index in the tokens list while accumulating a history of the previously tagged tokens. This history is the reason for the *Sequential* in SequentialBackoffTagger. We'll get to the backoff portion of the name in the *Combining taggers with backoff tagging* recipe. Here's a diagram showing the inheritance tree:

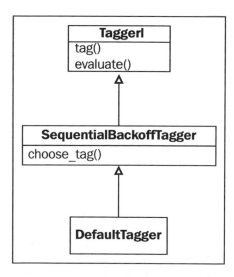

The choose_tag() method of DefaultTagger is very simple: it returns the tag we gave it at the time of initialization. It does not care about the current token or the history.

There's more...

There are a lot of different tags you could give to the `DefaultTagger` class. You can find a complete list of possible tags for the `treebank` corpus at `http://www.ling.upenn.edu/courses/Fall_2003/ling001/penn_treebank_pos.html`. These tags are also documented in *Appendix, Penn Treebank Part-of-speech Tags*.

Evaluating accuracy

To know how accurate a tagger is, you can use the `evaluate()` method, which takes a list of tagged tokens as a gold standard to evaluate the tagger. Using our default tagger created earlier, we can evaluate it against a subset of the `treebank` corpus tagged sentences.

```
>>> from nltk.corpus import treebank
>>> test_sents = treebank.tagged_sents()[3000:]
>>> tagger.evaluate(test_sents)
0.14331966328512843
```

So, by just choosing NN for every tag, we can achieve 14 % accuracy testing on one-fourth of the `treebank` corpus. Of course, accuracy will be different if you choose a different default tag. We'll be reusing these same `test_sents` for evaluating more taggers in the upcoming recipes.

Tagging sentences

`TaggerI` also implements a `tag_sents()` method that can be used to tag a list of sentences, instead of a single sentence. Here's an example of tagging two simple sentences:

```
>>> tagger.tag_sents([['Hello', 'world', '.'], ['How', 'are', 'you',
'?']])
[[('Hello', 'NN'), ('world', 'NN'), ('.', 'NN')], [('How', 'NN'),
('are', 'NN'), ('you', 'NN'), ('?', 'NN')]]
```

The result is a list of two tagged sentences, and of course, every tag is NN because we're using the `DefaultTagger` class. The `tag_sents()` method can be quiet useful if you have many sentences you wish to tag all at once.

Untagging a tagged sentence

Tagged sentences can be untagged using `nltk.tag.untag()`. Calling this function with a tagged sentence will return a list of words without the tags.

```
>>> from nltk.tag import untag
>>> untag([('Hello', 'NN'), ('World', 'NN')])
['Hello', 'World']
```

See also

For more on tokenization, see *Chapter 1, Tokenizing Text and WordNet Basics*. And to learn more about tagged sentences, see the *Creating a part-of-speech tagged word corpus* recipe in *Chapter 3, Creating Custom Corpora*. For a complete list of part-of-speech tags found in the treebank corpus, see *Appendix, Penn Treebank Part-of-speech Tags*.

Training a unigram part-of-speech tagger

A **unigram** generally refers to a single token. Therefore, a unigram tagger only uses a single word as its context for determining the part-of-speech tag.

UnigramTagger inherits from NgramTagger, which is a subclass of ContextTagger, which inherits from SequentialBackoffTagger. In other words, UnigramTagger is a context-based tagger whose context is a single word, or unigram.

How to do it...

UnigramTagger can be trained by giving it a list of tagged sentences at initialization.

```
>>> from nltk.tag import UnigramTagger
>>> from nltk.corpus import treebank
>>> train_sents = treebank.tagged_sents()[:3000]
>>> tagger = UnigramTagger(train_sents)
>>> treebank.sents()[0]
['Pierre', 'Vinken', ',', '61', 'years', 'old', ',', 'will', 'join',
'the', 'board', 'as', 'a', 'nonexecutive', 'director', 'Nov.', '29',
'.']
>>> tagger.tag(treebank.sents()[0])
[('Pierre', 'NNP'), ('Vinken', 'NNP'), (',', ','), ('61', 'CD'),
('years', 'NNS'), ('old', 'JJ'), (',', ','), ('will', 'MD'), ('join',
'VB'), ('the', 'DT'), ('board', 'NN'), ('as', 'IN'), ('a', 'DT'),
('nonexecutive', 'JJ'), ('director', 'NN'), ('Nov.', 'NNP'), ('29',
'CD'), ('.', '.')]
```

We use the first 3000 tagged sentences of the treebank corpus as the training set to initialize the UnigramTagger class. Then, we see the first sentence as a list of words, and can see how it is transformed by the tag() function into a list of tagged tokens.

How it works...

UnigramTagger builds a context model from the list of tagged sentences. Because UnigramTagger inherits from ContextTagger, instead of providing a choose_tag() method, it must implement a context() method, which takes the same three arguments as choose_tag(). The result of context() is, in this case, the word token. The context token is used to create the model, and also to look up the best tag once the model is created. Here's an inheritance diagram showing each class, starting at SequentialBackoffTagger:

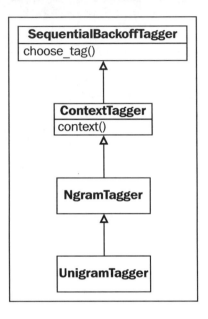

Let's see how accurate the UnigramTagger class is on the test sentences (see the previous recipe for how test_sents is created).

```
>>> tagger.evaluate(test_sents)
0.8588819339520829
```

It has almost 86 % accuracy for a tagger that only uses single word lookup to determine the part-of-speech tag. All accuracy gains from here on will be much smaller.

Actual accuracy values may change each time you run the code. This is because the default iteration order in Python 3 is random. To get consistent accuracy values, run Python with the PYTHONHASHSEED environment variable set to 0 or any positive integer. For example:

$ **PYTHONHASHSEED=0 python chapter4.py**

All accuracy values in this book were calculated with PYTHONHASHSEED=0.

There's more...

The model building is actually implemented in `ContextTagger`. Given the list of tagged sentences, it calculates the frequency that a tag has occurred for each context. The tag with the highest frequency for a context is stored in the model.

Overriding the context model

All taggers that inherit from `ContextTagger` can take a pre-built model instead of training their own. This model is simply a Python `dict` mapping a context key to a tag. The context keys will depend on what the `ContextTagger` subclass returns from its `context()` method. For `UnigramTagger`, context keys are individual words. But for other `NgramTagger` subclasses, the context keys will be tuples.

Here's an example where we pass a very simple model to the `UnigramTagger` class instead of a training set.

```
>>> tagger = UnigramTagger(model={'Pierre': 'NN'})
>>> tagger.tag(treebank.sents()[0])
[('Pierre', 'NN'), ('Vinken', None), (',', None), ('61', None),
('years', None), ('old', None), (',', None), ('will', None), ('join',
None), ('the', None), ('board', None), ('as', None), ('a', None),
('nonexecutive', None), ('director', None), ('Nov.', None), ('29',
None), ('.', None)]
```

Since the model only contained the context key `Pierre`, only the first word got a tag. Every other word got `None` as the tag since the context word was not in the model. So, unless you know exactly what you are doing, let the tagger train its own model instead of passing in your own.

One good case for passing a self-created model to the `UnigramTagger` class is for when you have a dictionary of words and tags, and you know that every word should always map to its tag. Then, you can put this `UnigramTagger` as your first backoff tagger (covered in the next recipe) to look up tags for unambiguous words.

Minimum frequency cutoff

The `ContextTagger` class uses frequency of occurrence to decide which tag is most likely for a given context. By default, it will do this even if the context word and tag occurs only once. If you'd like to set a minimum frequency threshold, then you can pass a `cutoff` value to the `UnigramTagger` class.

```
>>> tagger = UnigramTagger(train_sents, cutoff=3)
>>> tagger.evaluate(test_sents)
0.7757392618173969
```

In this case, using `cutoff=3` has decreased accuracy, but there may be times when a cutoff is a good idea.

See also

In the next recipe, we'll cover **backoff tagging** to combine taggers, and in the *Creating a model of likely word tags* recipe, we'll learn how to statistically determine tags for very common words.

Combining taggers with backoff tagging

Backoff tagging is one of the core features of SequentialBackoffTagger. It allows you to chain taggers together so that if one tagger doesn't know how to tag a word, it can pass the word on to the next backoff tagger. If that one can't do it, it can pass the word on to the next backoff tagger, and so on until there are no backoff taggers left to check.

How to do it...

Every subclass of SequentialBackoffTagger can take a backoff keyword argument whose value is another instance of a SequentialBackoffTagger. So, we'll use the DefaultTagger class from the *Default tagging* recipe in this chapter as the backoff to the UnigramTagger class covered in the previous recipe, *Training a unigram part-of-speech tagger*. Refer to both the recipes for details on train_sents and test_sents.

```
>>> tagger1 = DefaultTagger('NN')
>>> tagger2 = UnigramTagger(train_sents, backoff=tagger1)
>>> tagger2.evaluate(test_sents)
0.8758471832505935
```

By using a default tag of NN whenever the UnigramTagger is unable to tag a word, we've increased the accuracy by almost 2%!

How it works...

When a SequentialBackoffTagger class is initialized, it creates an internal list of backoff taggers with itself as the first element. If a backoff tagger is given, then the backoff tagger's internal list of taggers is appended. Here's some code to illustrate this:

```
>>> tagger1._taggers == [tagger1]
True
>>> tagger2._taggers == [tagger2, tagger1]
True
```

The _taggers list is the internal list of backoff taggers that the SequentialBackoffTagger class uses when the tag() method is called. It goes through its list of taggers, calling choose_tag() on each one. As soon as a tag is found, it stops and returns that tag. This means that if the primary tagger can tag the word, then that's the tag that will be returned. But if it returns None, then the next tagger is tried, and so on until a tag is found, or else None is returned. Of course, None will never be returned if your final backoff tagger is a DefaultTagger.

There's more...

While most of the taggers included in NLTK are subclasses of SequentialBackoffTagger, not all of them are. There's a few taggers that we'll cover in the later recipes that cannot be used as part of a backoff tagging chain, such as the BrillTagger class. However, these taggers generally take another tagger to use as a baseline, and a SequentialBackoffTagger class is often a good choice for that baseline.

Saving and loading a trained tagger with pickle

Since training a tagger can take a while, and you generally only need to do the training once, pickling a trained tagger is a useful way to save it for later usage. If your trained tagger is called tagger, then here's how to dump and load it with pickle:

```
>>> import pickle
>>> f = open('tagger.pickle', 'wb')
>>> pickle.dump(tagger, f)
>>> f.close()
>>> f = open('tagger.pickle', 'rb')
>>> tagger = pickle.load(f)
```

If your tagger picklc file is located in an NLTK data directory, you could also use nltk.data.load('tagger.pickle') to load the tagger.

See also

In the next recipe, we'll combine more taggers with backoff tagging. Also, see the previous two recipes for details on the DefaultTagger and UnigramTagger classes.

Training and combining ngram taggers

In addition to `UnigramTagger`, there are two more `NgramTagger` subclasses: `BigramTagger` and `TrigramTagger`. The `BigramTagger` subclass uses the previous tag as part of its context, while the `TrigramTagger` subclass uses the previous two tags. An **ngram** is a subsequence of *n* items, so the `BigramTagger` subclass looks at two items (the previous tagged word and the current word), and the `TrigramTagger` subclass looks at three items.

These two taggers are good at handling words whose part-of-speech tag is context-dependent. Many words have a different part of speech depending on how they are used. For example, we've been talking about taggers that tag words. In this case, *tag* is used as a verb. But the result of tagging is a part-of-speech tag, so *tag* can also be a noun. The idea with the `NgramTagger` subclasses is that by looking at the previous words and part-of-speech tags, we can better guess the part-of-speech tag for the current word. Internally, each tagger maintains a context dictionary (implemented in the `ContextTagger` parent class) that is used to guess that tag based on the context. In the case of `NgramTagger` subclasses, the context is some number of previous tagged words.

Getting ready

Refer to the first two recipes of this chapter for details on constructing `train_sents` and `test_sents`.

How to do it...

By themselves, `BigramTagger` and `TrigramTagger` perform quite poorly. This is partly because they cannot learn context from the first word(s) in a sentence. Since a `UnigramTagger` class doesn't care about the previous context, it is able to have higher baseline accuracy by simply guessing the most common tag for each word.

```
>>> from nltk.tag import BigramTagger, TrigramTagger
>>> bitagger = BigramTagger(train_sents)
>>> bitagger.evaluate(test_sents)
0.11310166199007123
>>> tritagger = TrigramTagger(train_sents)
>>> tritagger.evaluate(test_sents)
0.0688107058061731
```

Where `BigramTagger` and `TrigramTagger` can make a contribution is when we combine them with backoff tagging. This time, instead of creating each tagger individually, we'll create a function that will take `train_sents`, a list of `SequentialBackoffTagger` classes, and an optional final backoff tagger, then train each tagger with the previous tagger as a backoff. Here's the code from `tag_util.py`:

```
def backoff_tagger(train_sents, tagger_classes, backoff=None):
    for cls in tagger_classes:
        backoff = cls(train_sents, backoff=backoff)

    return backoff
```

And to use it, we can do the following:

```
>>> from tag_util import backoff_tagger
>>> backoff = DefaultTagger('NN')
>>> tagger = backoff_tagger(train_sents, [UnigramTagger, BigramTagger,
TrigramTagger], backoff=backoff)
>>> tagger.evaluate(test_sents)
0.8806820634578028
```

So, we've gained almost 1% accuracy by including the `BigramTagger` and `TrigramTagger` subclasses in the backoff chain. For corpora other than `treebank`, the accuracy gain may be more or less significant, depending on the nature of the text.

How it works...

The `backoff_tagger` function creates an instance of each tagger class in the list, giving it `train_sents` and the previous tagger as a backoff. The order of the list of tagger classes is quite important: the first class in the list (`UnigramTagger`) will be trained first and given the initial backoff tagger (the `DefaultTagger`). This tagger will then become the backoff tagger for the next tagger class in the list. The final tagger returned will be an instance of the last tagger class in the list (`TrigramTagger`). Here's some code to clarify this chain:

```
>>> tagger._taggers[-1] == backoff
True
>>> isinstance(tagger._taggers[0], TrigramTagger)
True
>>> isinstance(tagger._taggers[1], BigramTagger)
True
```

So, we get a `TrigramTagger`, whose first backoff is a `BigramTagger`. Then, the next backoff will be a `UnigramTagger`, whose backoff is the `DefaultTagger`.

There's more...

The `backoff_tagger` function doesn't just work with `NgramTagger` classes, it can also be used for constructing a chain containing any subclasses of `SequentialBackoffTagger`.

`BigramTagger` and `TrigramTagger`, because they are subclasses of `NgramTagger` and `ContextTagger`, can also take a model and cutoff argument, just like the `UnigramTagger`. But unlike for `UnigramTagger`, the context keys of the model must be two tuples, where the first element is a section of the history and the second element is the current token. For the `BigramTagger`, an appropriate context key looks like `((prevtag,), word)`, and for `TrigramTagger`, it looks like `((prevtag1, prevtag2), word)`.

Quadgram tagger

The `NgramTagger` class can be used by itself to create a tagger that uses more than three ngrams for its context key.

```
>>> from nltk.tag import NgramTagger
>>> quadtagger = NgramTagger(4, train_sents)
>>> quadtagger.evaluate(test_sents)
0.058234405352903085
```

It's even worse than the `TrigramTagger`! Here's an alternative implementation of a `QuadgramTagger` class that we can include in a list to `backoff_tagger`. This code can be found in `taggers.py`.

```
from nltk.tag import NgramTagger

class QuadgramTagger(NgramTagger):
  def __init__(self, *args, **kwargs):
    NgramTagger.__init__(self, 4, *args, **kwargs)
```

This is essentially how `BigramTagger` and `TrigramTagger` are implemented: simple subclasses of `NgramTagger` that pass in the number of ngrams to look at in the `history` argument of the `context()` method.

Now, let's see how it does as part of a backoff chain.

```
>>> from taggers import QuadgramTagger
>>> quadtagger = backoff_tagger(train_sents, [UnigramTagger,
BigramTagger, TrigramTagger, QuadgramTagger], backoff=backoff)
>>> quadtagger.evaluate(test_sents)
0.8806388948845241
```

It's actually slightly worse than before, when we stopped with the `TrigramTagger`. So, the lesson is that too much context can have a negative effect on accuracy.

See also

The previous two recipes cover the `UnigramTagger` and backoff tagging.

Creating a model of likely word tags

As previously mentioned in the *Training a unigram part-of-speech tagger* recipe, using a custom model with a `UnigramTagger` class should only be done if you know exactly what you're doing. In this recipe, we're going to create a model for the most common words, most of which always have the same tag no matter what.

How to do it...

To find the most common words, we can use `nltk.probability.FreqDist` to count word frequencies in the `treebank` corpus. Then, we can create a `ConditionalFreqDist` class for tagged words, where we count the frequency of every tag for every word. Using these counts, we can construct a model of the 200 most frequent words as keys, with the most frequent tag for each word as a value. Here's the model creation function defined in `tag_util.py`.

```python
from nltk.probability import FreqDist, ConditionalFreqDist

def word_tag_model(words, tagged_words, limit=200):
    fd = FreqDist(words)
    cfd = ConditionalFreqDist(tagged_words)
    most_freq = (word for word, count in fd.most_common(limit))
    return dict((word, cfd[word].max()) for word in most_freq)
```

And to use it with a `UnigramTagger` class, we can do the following:

```python
>>> from tag_util import word_tag_model
>>> from nltk.corpus import treebank
>>> model = word_tag_model(treebank.words(), treebank.tagged_words())
>>> tagger = UnigramTagger(model=model)
>>> tagger.evaluate(test_sents)
0.559680552557738
```

An accuracy of almost 56% is ok, but nowhere near as good as the trained `UnigramTagger`. Let's try adding it to our backoff chain.

```python
>>> default_tagger = DefaultTagger('NN')
>>> likely_tagger = UnigramTagger(model=model, backoff=default_tagger)
>>> tagger = backoff_tagger(train_sents, [UnigramTagger, BigramTagger, TrigramTagger], backoff=likely_tagger)
>>> tagger.evaluate(test_sents)
0.8806820634578028
```

The final accuracy is exactly the same as without the `likely_tagger`. This is because the frequency calculations we did to create the model are almost exactly the same as what happens when we train a `UnigramTagger` class.

How it works...

The `word_tag_model()` function takes a list of all words, a list of all tagged words, and the maximum number of words we want to use for our model. We give the list of words to a `FreqDist` class, which counts the frequency of each word. Then, we get the top 200 words from the `FreqDist` class by calling `fd.most_common()`, which obviously returns a list of the most common words and counts. The `FreqDist` class is actually a subclass of `collections.Counter`, which provides the `most_common()` method.

Next, we give the list of tagged words to `ConditionalFreqDist`, which creates a `FreqDist` class of tags for each word, with the word as the condition. Finally, we return a `dict` of the top 200 words mapped to their most likely tag.

> In the previous edition of this book, we used the `keys()` method of the `FreqDist` class because in NLTK2, the keys were returned in sorted order, from the most frequent to the least. But in NLTK3, `FreqDist` inherits from `collections.Counter`, and the `keys()` method does not use any predictable ordering.

There's more...

It may seem useless to include this tagger as it does not change the accuracy. But the point of this recipe is to demonstrate how to construct a useful model for a `UnigramTagger` class. Custom model construction is a way to create a manual override of trained taggers that are otherwise black boxes. And by putting the `likely_tagger` at the front of the chain, we can actually improve accuracy a little bit:

```
>>> tagger = backoff_tagger(train_sents, [UnigramTagger, BigramTagger,
TrigramTagger], backoff=default_tagger)
>>> likely_tagger = UnigramTagger(model=model, backoff=tagger)
>>> likely_tagger.evaluate(test_sents)
0.8824088063889488
```

Putting custom model taggers at the front of the backoff chain gives you complete control over how specific words are tagged, while letting the trained taggers handle everything else.

See also

The *Training a unigram part-of-speech tagger* recipe has details on the `UnigramTagger` class and a simple custom model example. See the earlier *recipes Combining taggers with backoff tagging* and *Training and combining ngram taggers* for details on backoff tagging.

Tagging with regular expressions

You can use regular expression matching to tag words. For example, you can match numbers with \d to assign the tag **CD** (which refers to a Cardinal number). Or you could match on known word patterns, such as the suffix "ing". There's a lot of flexibility here, but be careful of over-specifying since language is naturally inexact, and there are always exceptions to the rule.

Getting ready

For this recipe to make sense, you should be familiar with the regular expression syntax and Python's `re` module.

How to do it...

The `RegexpTagger` class expects a list of two tuples, where the first element in the tuple is a regular expression and the second element is the tag. The patterns shown in the following code can be found in `tag_util.py`:

```
patterns = [
  (r'^\d+$', 'CD'),
  (r'.*ing$', 'VBG'), # gerunds, i.e. wondering
  (r'.*ment$', 'NN'), # i.e. wonderment
  (r'.*ful$', 'JJ') # i.e. wonderful
]
```

Once you've constructed this list of patterns, you can pass it into `RegexpTagger`.

```
>>> from tag_util import patterns
>>> from nltk.tag import RegexpTagger
>>> tagger = RegexpTagger(patterns)
>>> tagger.evaluate(test_sents)
0.037470321605870924
```

So, it's not too great with just a few patterns, but since `RegexpTagger` is a subclass of `SequentialBackoffTagger`, it can be a useful part of a backoff chain. For example, it could be positioned just before a `DefaultTagger` class, to tag words that the ngram tagger(s) missed.

How it works...

The `RegexpTagger` class saves the patterns given at initialization, then on each call to `choose_tag()`, it iterates over the patterns and returns the tag for the first expression that matches the current word using `re.match()`. This means that if you have two expressions that could match, the tag of the first one will always be returned, and the second expression won't even be tried.

There's more...

The `RegexpTagger` class can replace the `DefaultTagger` class if you give it a pattern such as `(r'.*', 'NN')`. This pattern should, of course, be last in the list of patterns, otherwise no other patterns will match.

See also

In the next recipe, we'll cover the `AffixTagger` class, which learns how to tag based on prefixes and suffixes of words. See the *Default tagging* recipe for details on the `DefaultTagger` class.

Affix tagging

The `AffixTagger` class is another `ContextTagger` subclass, but this time the context is either the prefix or the suffix of a word. This means the `AffixTagger` class is able to learn tags based on fixed-length substrings of the beginning or ending of a word.

How to do it...

The default arguments for an `AffixTagger` class specify three-character suffixes, and that words must be at least five characters long. If a word is less than five characters, then `None` is returned as the tag.

```
>>> from nltk.tag import AffixTagger
>>> tagger = AffixTagger(train_sents)
>>> tagger.evaluate(test_sents)
0.27558817181092166
```

So, it does ok by itself with the default arguments. Let's try it by specifying three-character prefixes.

```
>>> prefix_tagger = AffixTagger(train_sents, affix_length=3)
>>> prefix_tagger.evaluate(test_sents)
0.23587308439456076
```

To learn on two-character suffixes, the code will look like this:

```
>>> suffix_tagger = AffixTagger(train_sents, affix_length=-2)
>>> suffix_tagger.evaluate(test_sents)
0.31940427368875457
```

How it works...

A positive value for `affix_length` means that the `AffixTagger` class will learn word prefixes, essentially `word[:affix_length]`. If `affix_length` is negative, then suffixes are learned using `word[affix_length:]`.

There's more...

You can combine multiple affix taggers in a backoff chain if you want to learn on multiple character length affixes. Here's an example of four `AffixTagger` classes learning on 2 and 3 character prefixes and suffixes:

```
>>> pre3_tagger = AffixTagger(train_sents, affix_length=3)
>>> pre3_tagger.evaluate(test_sents)
0.23587308439456076
>>> pre2_tagger = AffixTagger(train_sents, affix_length=2,
backoff=pre3_tagger)
>>> pre2_tagger.evaluate(test_sents)
0.29786315562270665
>>> suf2_tagger = AffixTagger(train_sents, affix_length=-2,
backoff=pre2_tagger)
>>> suf2_tagger.evaluate(test_sents)
0.32467083962875026
>>> suf3_tagger = AffixTagger(train_sents, affix_length=-3,
backoff=suf2_tagger)
>>> suf3_tagger.evaluate(test_sents)
0.3590761925318368
```

As you can see, the accuracy goes up each time.

> The ordering in the previous block of code is not the best, nor is it the worst. I'll leave it to you to explore the possibilities and discover the best backoff chain of values for `AffixTagger` and `affix_length`.

Working with min_stem_length

The `AffixTagger` class also takes a `min_stem_length` keyword argument, with a default value of 2. If the word length is less than `min_stem_length` plus the absolute value of `affix_length`, then `None` is returned by the `context()` method. Increasing `min_stem_length` forces the `AffixTagger` class to only learn on longer words, while decreasing `min_stem_length` will allow it to learn on shorter words. Of course, for shorter words, the `affix_length` argument could be equal to or greater than the word length, and `AffixTagger` would essentially be acting like a `UnigramTagger` class.

See also

You can manually specify prefixes and suffixes using regular expressions, as shown in the previous recipe. The *Training a unigram part-of-speech tagger* and *Training and combining ngram taggers* recipes have details on `NgramTagger` subclasses, which are also subclasses of `ContextTagger`.

Training a Brill tagger

The `BrillTagger` class is a transformation-based tagger. It is the first tagger that is not a subclass of `SequentialBackoffTagger`. Instead, the `BrillTagger` class uses a series of rules to correct the results of an initial tagger. These rules are scored based on how many errors they correct minus the number of new errors they produce.

How to do it...

Here's a function from `tag_util.py` that trains a `BrillTagger` class using `BrillTaggerTrainer`. It requires an `initial_tagger` and `train_sents`.

```
from nltk.tag import brill, brill_trainer

def train_brill_tagger(initial_tagger, train_sents, **kwargs):
    templates = [
        brill.Template(brill.Pos([-1])),
        brill.Template(brill.Pos([1])),
        brill.Template(brill.Pos([-2])),
        brill.Template(brill.Pos([2])),
        brill.Template(brill.Pos([-2, -1])),
        brill.Template(brill.Pos([1, 2])),
        brill.Template(brill.Pos([-3, -2, -1])),
        brill.Template(brill.Pos([1, 2, 3])),
        brill.Template(brill.Pos([-1]), brill.Pos([1])),
        brill.Template(brill.Word([-1])),
        brill.Template(brill.Word([1])),
```

```
    brill.Template(brill.Word([-2])),
    brill.Template(brill.Word([2])),
    brill.Template(brill.Word([-2, -1])),
    brill.Template(brill.Word([1, 2])),
    brill.Template(brill.Word([-3, -2, -1])),
    brill.Template(brill.Word([1, 2, 3])),
    brill.Template(brill.Word([-1]), brill.Word([1])),
  ]

    trainer = brill_trainer.BrillTaggerTrainer(initial_tagger,
  templates, deterministic=True)
    return trainer.train(train_sents, **kwargs)
```

To use it, we can create our `initial_tagger` from a backoff chain of `NgramTagger` classes, then pass that into the `train_brill_tagger()` function to get a `BrillTagger` back.

```
>>> default_tagger = DefaultTagger('NN')
>>> initial_tagger = backoff_tagger(train_sents, [UnigramTagger,
BigramTagger, TrigramTagger], backoff=default_tagger)
>>> initial_tagger.evaluate(test_sents)
0.8806820634578028
>>> from tag_util import train_brill_tagger
>>> brill_tagger = train_brill_tagger(initial_tagger, train_sents)
>>> brill_tagger.evaluate(test_sents)
0.8827541549751781
```

So, the `BrillTagger` class has slightly increased accuracy over the `initial_tagger`.

How it works...

The `BrillTaggerTrainer` class takes an `initial_tagger` argument and a list of templates. These templates must implement the `BrillTemplateI` interface, which is found in the `nltk.tbl.template` module. The `brill.Template` class is such an implementation, and is actually imported from `nltk.tbl.template`. The `brill.Pos` and `brill.Word` classes are subclasses of `nltk.tbl.template.Feature`, and they describe what kind of features to use in the template, in this case, one or more part-of-speech tags or words.

The templates specify how to learn transformation rules. For example, `brill.Template(brill.Pos([-1]))` means that a rule can be generated using the previous part-of-speech tag. The `brill.Template(brill.Pos([1]))` statement means that you can look at the next part-of-speech tag to generate a rule. And `brill.Template(brill.Word([-2, -1]))` means you can look at the combination of the previous two words to learn a transformation rule.

The thinking behind a transformation-based tagger is this: given the correct training sentences, the output of the initial tagger, and the templates specifying features, try to generate transformation rules that correct the initial tagger's output to be more in-line with the training sentences. The job of `BrillTaggerTrainer` is to produce these rules, and to do so in a way that increases accuracy. A transformation rule that fixes one problem may cause an error in another condition; thus, every rule must be measured by how many errors it corrects versus how many new errors it introduces.

The workflow looks something like this:

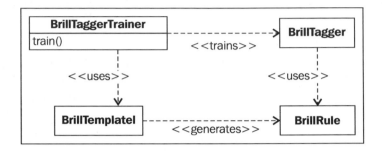

There's more...

You can control the number of rules generated using the `max_rules` keyword argument to the `BrillTaggerTrainer.train()` method. The default value is `200`. You can also control the quality of rules used with the `min_score` keyword argument. The default value is `2`, though `3` can be a good choice as well. The score is a measure of how well a rule corrects errors compared to how many new errors it introduces.

 Increasing `max_rules` or `min_score` will greatly increase training time, without necessarily increasing accuracy. Change these values with care.

Tracing

You can watch the `BrillTaggerTrainer` class do its work by passing `trace=True` into the constructor, for example, `trainer = brill.BrillTaggerTrainer(initial_tagger, templates, deterministic=True, trace=True)`. This will give you the following output:

```
TBL train (fast) (seqs: 3000; tokens: 77511; tpls: 18; min score: 2;
min acc: None)
    Finding initial useful rules...
        Found 9869 useful rules.
    Selecting rules...
```

This means it found `77511` rules with a score of at least `min_score`, and then it selects the best rules, keeping no more than `max_rules`.

The default is `trace=False`, which means the trainer will work silently without printing its status.

See also

The *Training and combining ngram taggers* recipe details the construction of the `initial_tagger` argument used earlier, and the *Default tagging* recipe explains the `default_tagger` argument.

Training the TnT tagger

TnT stands for **Trigrams'n'Tags**. It is a statistical tagger based on second order Markov models. The details of this are out of the scope of this book, but you can read more about the original implementation at `http://www.coli.uni-saarland.de/~thorsten/tnt/`.

How to do it...

The `TnT` tagger has a slightly different API than the previous taggers we've encountered. You must explicitly call the `train()` method after you've created it. Here's a basic example.

```
>>> from nltk.tag import tnt
>>> tnt_tagger = tnt.TnT()
>>> tnt_tagger.train(train_sents)
>>> tnt_tagger.evaluate(test_sents)
0.8756313403842003
```

It's quite a good tagger all by itself, only slightly less accurate than the `BrillTagger` class from the previous recipe. But if you do not call `train()` before `evaluate()`, you'll get an accuracy of 0%.

How it works...

The `TnT` tagger maintains a number of internal `FreqDist` and `ConditionalFreqDist` instances based on the training data. These frequency distributions count unigrams, bigrams, and trigrams. Then, during tagging, the frequencies are used to calculate the probabilities of possible tags for each word. So, instead of constructing a backoff chain of `NgramTagger` subclasses, the `TnT` tagger uses all the ngram models together to choose the best tag. It also tries to guess the tags for the whole sentence at once by choosing the most likely model for the entire sentence, based on the probabilities of each possible tag.

Training is fairly quick, but tagging is significantly slower than the other taggers we've covered. This is due to all the floating point math that must be done to calculate the tag probabilities of each word.

There's more...

The TnT tagger accepts a few optional keyword arguments. You can pass in a tagger for unknown words as unk. If this tagger is already trained, then you must also pass in Trained=True. Otherwise, it will call unk.train(data) with the same data you pass into the train() method. Since none of the previous taggers have a public train() method, I recommend always passing Trained=True if you also pass an unk tagger. Here's an example using a DefaultTagger class, which does not require any training.

```
>>> from nltk.tag import DefaultTagger
>>> unk = DefaultTagger('NN')
>>> tnt_tagger = tnt.TnT(unk=unk, Trained=True)
>>> tnt_tagger.train(train_sents)
>>> tnt_tagger.evaluate(test_sents)
0.892467083962875
```

So, we got an almost 2% increase in accuracy! You must use a tagger that can tag a single word without having seen that word before. This is because the unknown tagger's tag() method is only called with a single word sentence. Other good candidates for an unknown tagger are RegexpTagger and AffixTagger. Passing in a UnigramTagger class that's been trained on the same data is pretty much useless, as it will have seen the exact same words and, therefore, have the same unknown word blind spots.

Controlling the beam search

Another parameter you can modify for TnT is N, which controls the number of possible solutions the tagger maintains while trying to guess the tags for a sentence. N defaults to 1000. Increasing it will greatly increase the amount of memory used during tagging, without necessarily increasing the accuracy. Decreasing N will decrease memory usage, but could also decrease accuracy. Here's what happens when the value is changed to N=100.

```
>>> tnt_tagger = tnt.TnT(N=100)
>>> tnt_tagger.train(train_sents)
>>> tnt_tagger.evaluate(test_sents)
0.8756313403842003
```

So, the accuracy is exactly the same, but we use significantly less memory to achieve it. However, don't assume that accuracy will not change if you decrease N; experiment with your own data to be sure.

Significance of capitalization

You can pass C=True to the TnT constructor if you want capitalization of words to be significant. The default is C=False, which means all words are lowercase. The documentation on C says that treating capitalization as significant probably will not increase accuracy. In my own testing, there was a very slight (< 0.01%) increase in accuracy with C=True, probably because case-sensitivity can help identify proper nouns.

See also

We have covered the DefaultTagger class in the *Default tagging* recipe, backoff tagging in the *Combining taggers with backoff tagging* recipe, NgramTagger subclasses in the *Training a unigram part-of-speech tagger* and *Training and combining ngram taggers* recipes, RegexpTagger in the *Tagging with regular expressions recipe*, and the AffixTagger class in the *Affix tagging recipe*.

Using WordNet for tagging

If you remember from the *Looking up Synsets for a word in WordNet* recipe in *Chapter 1, Tokenizing Text and WordNet Basics*, WordNet Synsets specify a part-of-speech tag. It's a very restricted set of possible tags, and many words have multiple Synsets with different part-of-speech tags, but this information can be useful for tagging unknown words. WordNet is essentially a giant dictionary, and it's likely to contain many words that are not in your training data.

Getting ready

First, we need to decide how to map WordNet part-of-speech tags to the Penn Treebank part-of-speech tags we've been using. The following is a table mapping one to the other. See the *Looking up Synsets for a word in WordNet* recipe in *Chapter 1, Tokenizing Text and WordNet Basics*, for more details. The s, which was not shown before, is just another kind of adjective, at least for tagging purposes.

WordNet tag	Treebank tag
n	NN
a	JJ
s	JJ
r	RB
v	VB

How to do it...

Now we can create a class that will look up words in WordNet, and then choose the most common tag from the Synsets it finds. The `WordNetTagger` class defined in the following code can be found in `taggers.py`:

```python
from nltk.tag import SequentialBackoffTagger
from nltk.corpus import wordnet
from nltk.probability import FreqDist

class WordNetTagger(SequentialBackoffTagger):
  '''
  >>> wt = WordNetTagger()
  >>> wt.tag(['food', 'is', 'great'])
  [('food', 'NN'), ('is', 'VB'), ('great', 'JJ')]
  '''
  def __init__(self, *args, **kwargs):
    SequentialBackoffTagger.__init__(self, *args, **kwargs)

    self.wordnet_tag_map = {
      'n': 'NN',
      's': 'JJ',
      'a': 'JJ',
      'r': 'RB',
      'v': 'VB'
    }

  def choose_tag(self, tokens, index, history):
    word = tokens[index]
    fd = FreqDist()

    for synset in wordnet.synsets(word):
      fd[synset.pos()] += 1

    return self.wordnet_tag_map.get(fd.max())
```

Another way the `FreqDist` API has changed between NLTK2 and NLTK3 is that the `inc()` method has been removed. Instead, you must use `fd[key] += 1`. Since `FreqDist` inherits from `collections.Counter`, it's ok if `fd[key]` doesn't exist the first time you increment.

How it works...

The `WordNetTagger` class simply counts the number of each part-of-speech tag found in the Synsets for a word. The most common tag is then mapped to a `treebank` tag using internal mapping. Here's some sample usage code:

```
>>> from taggers import WordNetTagger
>>> wn_tagger = WordNetTagger()
>>> wn_tagger.evaluate(train_sents)
0.17914876598160262
```

So, it's not too accurate, but that's to be expected. We only have enough information to produce four different kinds of tags, while there are 36 possible tags in `treebank`. There are many words that can have different part-of-speech tags depending on their context. But if we put the `WordNetTagger` class at the end of an `NgramTagger` backoff chain, then we can improve accuracy over the `DefaultTagger` class.

```
>>> from tag_util import backoff_tagger
>>> from nltk.tag import UnigramTagger, BigramTagger, TrigramTagger
>>> tagger = backoff_tagger(train_sents, [UnigramTagger, DigramTagger, TrigramTagger], backoff=wn_tagger)
>>> tagger.evaluate(test_sents)
0.8848262464925534
```

See also

The *Looking up Synsets for a word in WordNet* recipe in *Chapter 1, Tokenizing Text and WordNet Basics*, details how to use the `wordnet` corpus and what kinds of part-of-speech tags it knows about. And in the *Combining taggers with backoff tagging* and *Training and combining ngram taggers* recipes, we went over backoff tagging with ngram taggers.

Tagging proper names

Using the included `names` corpus, we can create a simple tagger for tagging names as proper nouns.

How to do it...

The `NamesTagger` class is a subclass of `SequentialBackoffTagger` as it's probably only useful near the end of a backoff chain. At initialization, we create a set of all names in the `names` corpus, lower-casing each name to make lookup easier. Then, we implement the `choose_tag()` method, which simply checks whether the current word is in the `names_set` list. If it is, we return the `NNP` tag (which is the tag for proper nouns). If it isn't, we return `None`, so the next tagger in the chain can tag the word. The following code can be found in `taggers.py`:

```
from nltk.tag import SequentialBackoffTagger
from nltk.corpus import names

class NamesTagger(SequentialBackoffTagger):
  def __init__(self, *args, **kwargs):
    SequentialBackoffTagger.__init__(self, *args, **kwargs)
    self.name_set = set([n.lower() for n in names.words()])

  def choose_tag(self, tokens, index, history):
    word = tokens[index]

    if word.lower() in self.name_set:
      return 'NNP'
    else:
      return None
```

How it works...

The `NamesTagger` class should be pretty self-explanatory. The usage is also simple.

```
>>> from taggers import NamesTagger
>>> nt = NamesTagger()
>>> nt.tag(['Jacob'])
[('Jacob', 'NNP')]
```

It's probably best to use the `NamesTagger` class right before a `DefaultTagger` class, so it's at the end of a backoff chain. But it could probably go anywhere in the chain since it's unlikely to mis-tag a word.

See also

The *Combining taggers with backoff tagging* recipe goes over the details of using the
SequentialBackoffTagger subclasses.

Classifier-based tagging

The ClassifierBasedPOSTagger class uses classification to do part-of-speech tagging.
Features are extracted from words, and then passed to an internal classifier. The classifier
classifies the features and returns a label, in this case, a part-of-speech tag. Classification
will be covered in detail in *Chapter 7, Text Classification*.

The ClassifierBasedPOSTagger class is a subclass of ClassifierBasedTagger that
implements a feature detector that combines many of the techniques of the previous taggers
into a single feature set. The feature detector finds multiple length suffixes, does some regular
expression matching, and looks at the unigram, bigram, and trigram history to produce a fairly
complete set of features for each word. The feature sets it produces are used to train the
internal classifier, and are used for classifying words into part-of-speech tags.

How to do it...

The basic usage of the ClassifierBasedPOSTagger class is much like any other
SequentialBackoffTaggger. You pass in training sentences, it trains an internal
classifier, and you get a very accurate tagger.

```
>>> from nltk.tag.sequential import ClassifierBasedPOSTagger
>>> tagger = ClassifierBasedPOSTagger(train=train_sents)
>>> tagger.evaluate(test_sents)
0.9309734513274336
```

> Notice a slight modification to initialization: train_sents must be
> passed in as the train keyword argument.

How it works...

The ClassifierBasedPOSTagger class inherits from ClassifierBasedTagger and
only implements a feature_detector() method. All the training and tagging is done in
ClassifierBasedTagger. It defaults to training a NaiveBayesClassifier class with
the given training data. Once this classifier is trained, it is used to classify word features
produced by the feature_detector() method.

The `ClassifierBasedTagger` class is often the most accurate tagger, but it's also one of the slowest taggers. If speed is an issue, you should stick with a `BrillTagger` class based on a backoff chain of `NgramTagger` subclasses and other simple taggers.

The `ClassifierBasedTagger` class also inherits from `FeatursetTaggerI` (which is just an empty class), creating an inheritance tree that looks like this:

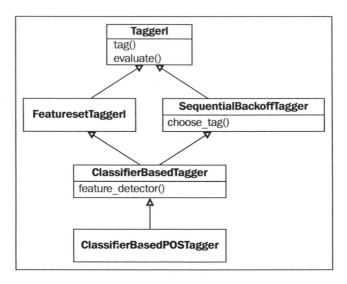

There's more...

You can use a different classifier instead of `NaiveBayesClassifier` by passing in your own `classifier_builder` function. For example, to use a `MaxentClassifier`, you'd do the following:

```
>>> from nltk.classify import MaxentClassifier
>>> me_tagger = ClassifierBasedPOSTagger(train=train_sents,
classifier_builder=MaxentClassifier.train)
>>> me_tagger.evaluate(test_sents)
0.9258363911072739
```

 The `MaxentClassifier` class takes even longer to train than `NaiveBayesClassifier`. If you have SciPy and NumPy installed, training will be faster than normal, but still slower than `NaiveBayesClassifier`.

Detecting features with a custom feature detector

If you want to do your own feature detection, there are two ways to do it:

1. Subclass `ClassifierBasedTagger` and implement a `feature_detector()` method.

2. Pass a function as the `feature_detector` keyword argument into `ClassifierBasedTagger` at initialization.

Either way, you need a feature detection method that can take the same arguments as `choose_tag()`: `tokens`, `index`, `history`. But instead of returning a tag, you return a `dict` of key-value features, where the key is the feature name and the value is the feature value. A very simple example would be a unigram feature detector (found in `tag_util.py`).

```
def unigram_feature_detector(tokens, index, history):
    return {'word': tokens[index]}
```

Then, using the second method, you'd pass this into `ClassifierBasedTagger` as `feature_detector`.

```
>>> from nltk.tag.sequential import ClassifierBasedTagger
>>> from tag_util import unigram_feature_detector
>>> tagger = ClassifierBasedTagger(train-train_sents, feature
detector=unigram_feature_detector)
>>> tagger.evaluate(test_sents)
0.8733865745737104
```

Setting a cutoff probability

Because a classifier will always return the best result it can, passing in a backoff tagger is useless unless you also pass in a `cutoff_prob` argument to specify the probability threshold for classification. Then, if the probability of the chosen tag is less than `cutoff_prob`, the backoff tagger will be used. Here's an example using the `DefaultTagger` class as the backoff, and setting `cutoff_prob` to `0.3`:

```
>>> default = DefaultTagger('NN')
>>> tagger = ClassifierBasedPOSTagger(train=train_sents,
backoff=default, cutoff_prob=0.3)
>>> tagger.evaluate(test_sents)
0.9311029570472696
```

So, we get a slight increase in accuracy if the `ClassifierBasedPOSTagger` class uses the `DefaultTagger` class whenever its tag probability is less than 30%.

Using a pre-trained classifier

If you want to use a classifier that's already been trained, then you can pass that into `ClassifierBasedTagger` or `ClassifierBasedPOSTagger` as the `classifier`. In this case, the `classifier_builder` argument is ignored and no training takes place. However, you must ensure that the classifier has been trained on and can classify feature sets produced by whatever `feature_detector()` method you use.

See also

Chapter 7, Text Classification, will cover classification in depth.

Training a tagger with NLTK-Trainer

As you can tell from all the previous recipes in this chapter, there are many different ways to train taggers, and it's impossible to know which methods and parameters will work best without doing training experiments. But training experiments can be tedious, since they often involve many small code changes (and lots of cut and paste) before you converge on an optimal tagger. In an effort to simplify the process, and make my own work easier, I created a project called `NLTK-Trainer`.

NLTK-Trainer is a collection of scripts that give you the ability to run training experiments without writing a single line of code. The project is available on GitHub at `https://github.com/japerk/nltk-trainer` and has documentation at `http://nltk-trainer.readthedocs.org/`. This recipe will introduce the tagging related scripts, and will show you how to combine many of the previous recipes into a single training command. For download and installation instructions, please go to `http://nltk-trainer.readthedocs.org/`.

How to do it...

The simplest way to run `train_tagger.py` is with the name of an `NLTK` corpus. If we use the `treebank` corpus, the command and output should look something like this:

```
$ python train_tagger.py treebank
loading treebank
3914 tagged sents, training on 3914
training AffixTagger with affix -3 and backoff <DefaultTagger: tag=-
None->
training <class 'nltk.tag.sequential.UnigramTagger'> tagger with backoff
<AffixTagger: size=2536>
training <class 'nltk.tag.sequential.BigramTagger'> tagger with backoff
<UnigramTagger: size=4933>
```

```
training <class 'nltk.tag.sequential.TrigramTagger'> tagger with backoff
<BigramTagger: size=2325>
evaluating TrigramTagger
accuracy: 0.992372
dumping TrigramTagger to /Users/jacob/nltk_data/taggers/treebank_aubt.
pickle
```

That's all it takes to train a tagger on `treebank` and have it dumped to a `pickle` file at `~/nltk_data/taggers/treebank_aubt.pickle`. "Wow, and it's over 99% accurate!" I hear you saying. But look closely at the second line of output: `3914 tagged sents, training on 3914`. This means that the tagger was trained on the entire `treebank` corpus, and then tested against those same training sentences. This is a very misleading way to evaluate any trained model. In the previous recipes, we used the first 3000 sentences for training and the remaining 914 sentences for testing, or about a 75% split. Here's how to do that with `train_tagger.py`, and also skip dumping a `pickle` file:

```
$ python train_tagger.py treebank --fraction 0.75 --no-pickle
loading treebank
3914 tagged sents, training on 2936
training AffixTagger with affix -3 and backoff <DefaultTagger: tag=-
None->
training <class 'nltk.tag.sequential.UnigramTagger'> tagger with backoff
<AffixTagger: size=2287>
training <class 'nltk.tag.sequential.BigramTagger'> tagger with backoff
<UnigramTagger: size=4176>
training <class 'nltk.tag.sequential.TrigramTagger'> tagger with backoff
<BigramTagger: size=1836>
evaluating TrigramTagger
accuracy: 0.906082
```

How it works...

The `train_tagger.py` script roughly performers the following steps:

1. Construct training and testing sentences from corpus arguments.
2. Build tagger training function from tagger arguments.
3. Train a tagger on the training sentences using the training function.
4. Evaluate and/or save the tagger.

The first argument to the script is `corpus`. This could be the name of an NLTK corpus that can be found in the `nltk.corpus` module, such as `treebank` or `brown`. It could also be the path to a custom corpus directory. If it's a path to a custom corpus, then you'll also need to use the `--reader` argument to specify the corpus reader class, such as `nltk.corpus.reader.tagged.TaggedCorpusReader`.

The default training algorithm is `aubt`, which is shorthand for a sequential backoff tagger composed of `AffixTagger` + `UnigramTagger` + `BigramTagger` + `TrigramTagger`. It's probably easiest to understand by replicating many of the previous recipes using `train_tagger.py`. Let's start with a default tagger.

```
$ python train_tagger.py treebank --no-pickle --default NN --sequential
' '

loading treebank

3914 tagged sents, training on 3914

evaluating DefaultTagger

accuracy: 0.130776
```

Using `--default NN` lets us assign a default tag of NN, while `--sequential ''` disables the default `aubt` sequential backoff algorithm. The `--fraction` argument is omitted in this case because there's not actually any training happening.

Now let's try a unigram tagger:

```
$ python train_tagger.py treebank --no-pickle --fraction 0.75
--sequential u

loading treebank

3914 tagged sents, training on 2936

training <class 'nltk.tag.sequential.UnigramTagger'> tagger with backoff
<DefaultTagger: tag=-None->

evaluating UnigramTagger

accuracy: 0.855603
```

Specifying `--sequential u` tells `train_tagger.py` to train with a unigram tagger. As we did earlier, we can boost the accuracy a bit by using a default tagger:

```
$ python train_tagger.py treebank --no-pickle --default NN --fraction
0.75 --sequential u

loading treebank

3914 tagged sents, training on 2936

training <class 'nltk.tag.sequential.UnigramTagger'> tagger with backoff
<DefaultTagger: tag=NN>

evaluating UnigramTagger

accuracy: 0.873462
```

Now, let's try adding a bigram tagger and trigram tagger:

```
$ python train_tagger.py treebank --no-pickle --default NN --fraction
0.75 --sequential ubt

loading treebank

3914 tagged sents, training on 2936

training <class 'nltk.tag.sequential.UnigramTagger'> tagger with backoff
<DefaultTagger: tag=NN>

training <class 'nltk.tag.sequential.BigramTagger'> tagger with backoff
<UnigramTagger: size=8709>

training <class 'nltk.tag.sequential.TrigramTagger'> tagger with backoff
<BigramTagger: size=1836>

evaluating TrigramTagger

accuracy: 0.879012
```

> The PYTHONHASHSEED environment variable has been omitted for
> clarity. This means that when you run train_tagger.py, your
> output and accuracy may vary. To get consistent accuracy values, run
> train_tagger.py like this:
> ```
> $ PYTHONHASHSEED=0 python train_tagger.py treebank …
> ```

The default training algorithm is --sequential aubt, and the default affix is -3. But you can modify this with one or more -a arguments. So, if we want to use an affix of -2 as well as an affix of -3, you can do the following:

```
$ python train_tagger.py treebank --no-pickle --default NN --fraction
0.75 -a -3 -a -2

loading treebank

3914 tagged sents, training on 2936

training AffixTagger with affix -3 and backoff <DefaultTagger: tag=NN>

training AffixTagger with affix -2 and backoff <AffixTagger: size=2143>

training <class 'nltk.tag.sequential.UnigramTagger'> tagger with backoff
<AffixTagger: size=248>

training <class 'nltk.tag.sequential.BigramTagger'> tagger with backoff
<UnigramTagger: size=5204>

training <class 'nltk.tag.sequential.TrigramTagger'> tagger with backoff
<BigramTagger: size=1838>

evaluating TrigramTagger

accuracy: 0.908696
```

The order of multiple -a arguments matters, and if you switch the order, the results and accuracy will change, because the backoff order changes:

```
$ python train_tagger.py treebank --no-pickle --default NN --fraction
0.75 -a -2 -a -3
loading treebank
3914 tagged sents, training on 2936
training AffixTagger with affix -2 and backoff <DefaultTagger: tag=NN>
training AffixTagger with affix -3 and backoff <AffixTagger: size=606>
training <class 'nltk.tag.sequential.UnigramTagger'> tagger with backoff
<AffixTagger: size=1313>
training <class 'nltk.tag.sequential.BigramTagger'> tagger with backoff
<UnigramTagger: size=4169>
training <class 'nltk.tag.sequential.TrigramTagger'> tagger with backoff
<BigramTagger: size=1829>
evaluating TrigramTagger
accuracy: 0.914367
```

You can also train a Brill tagger using the --brill argument. The template bounds the default to (1, 1) but can be customized with the --template_bounds argument.

```
$ python train_tagger.py treebank --no-pickle --default NN --fraction
0.75 --brill
loading treebank
3914 tagged sents, training on 2936
training AffixTagger with affix -3 and backoff <DefaultTagger: tag=NN>
training <class 'nltk.tag.sequential.UnigramTagger'> tagger with backoff
<AffixTagger: size=2143>
training <class 'nltk.tag.sequential.BigramTagger'> tagger with backoff
<UnigramTagger: size=4179>
training <class 'nltk.tag.sequential.TrigramTagger'> tagger with backoff
<BigramTagger: size=1824>
Training Brill tagger on 2936 sentences...
Finding initial useful rules...
    Found 1304 useful rules.
Selecting rules...
evaluating BrillTagger
accuracy: 0.909138
```

Finally, you can train a classifier-based tagger with the `--classifier` argument, which specifies the name of a classifier. Be sure to also pass in `--sequential ''` because, as we learned previously, training a sequential backoff tagger in addition to a classifier-based tagger is useless. The `--default` argument is also useless, because the classifier will always guess something.

```
$ python train_tagger.py treebank --no-pickle --fraction 0.75
--sequential '' --classifier NaiveBayes
loading treebank
3914 tagged sents, training on 2936
training ['NaiveBayes'] ClassifierBasedPOSTagger
Constructing training corpus for classifier.
Training classifier (75814 instances)
training NaiveBayes classifier
evaluating ClassifierBasedPOSTagger
accuracy: 0.928646
```

There are a few other classifier algorithms available besides `NaiveBayes`, and even more if you have NumPy and SciPy installed.

 While classifier-based taggers tend to be more accurate, they are also slower to train, and much slower at tagging. If speed is important to you, I recommend sticking with sequential taggers.

There's more...

The `train_tagger.py` script supports many other arguments not shown here, all of which you can see by running the script with `--help`. A few additional arguments are presented next, followed by an introduction to two other tagging-related scripts available in `NLTK-Trainer`.

Saving a pickled tagger

Without the `--no-pickle` argument, `train_tagger.py` will save a pickled tagger at `~/nltk_data/taggers/NAME.pickle`, where `NAME` is a combination of the corpus name and training algorithm. You can specify a custom filename for your tagger using the `--filename` argument like this:

```
$ python train_tagger.py treebank --filename path/to/tagger.pickle
```

Training on a custom corpus

If you have a custom corpus that you want to use for training a tagger, you can do that by passing in the path to the corpus and the classname of a corpus reader in the --reader argument. The corpus path can either be absolute or relative to a nltk_data directory. The corpus reader class must provide a tagged_sents() method. Here's an example using a relative path to the treebank tagged corpus:

```
$ python train_tagger.py corpora/treebank/tagged --reader nltk.corpus.
reader.ChunkedCorpusReader --no-pickle --fraction 0.75

loading corpora/treebank/tagged

51002 tagged sents, training on 38252

training AffixTagger with affix -3 and backoff <DefaultTagger: tag=-
None->

training <class 'nltk.tag.sequential.UnigramTagger'> tagger with backoff
<AffixTagger: size=2092>

training <class 'nltk.tag.sequential.BigramTagger'> tagger with backoff
<UnigramTagger: size=4121>

training <class 'nltk.tag.sequential.TrigramTagger'> tagger with backoff
<BigramTagger: size=1627>

evaluating TrigramTagger

accuracy: 0.883175
```

Training with universal tags

You can train a tagger with the universal tagset using the --tagset argument as follows:

```
$ python train_tagger.py treebank --no-pickle --fraction 0.75 --tagset
universal

loading treebank

using universal tagset

3914 tagged sents, training on 2936

training AffixTagger with affix -3 and backoff <DefaultTagger: tag=-
None->

training <class 'nltk.tag.sequential.UnigramTagger'> tagger with backoff
<AffixTagger: size=2287>

training <class 'nltk.tag.sequential.BigramTagger'> tagger with backoff
<UnigramTagger: size=2889>

training <class 'nltk.tag.sequential.TrigramTagger'> tagger with backoff
<BigramTagger: size=1014>

evaluating TrigramTagger

accuracy: 0.934800
```

Because the universal tagset has fewer tags, these taggers tend to be more accurate; this will only work on a corpus that has universal tagset mappings. The universal tagset was covered in the *Creating a part-of-speech tagged word corpus* recipe in *Chapter 3, Creating Custom Corpora*.

Analyzing a tagger against a tagged corpus

Every previous example in this chapter has been about training and evaluating a tagger on a single corpus. But how do you know how well that tagger will perform on a different corpus? The `analyze_tagger_coverage.py` script gives you a simple way to test the performance of a tagger against another tagged corpus. Here's how to test NLTK's built-in tagger against the `treebank` corpus:

```
$ python analyze_tagger_coverage.py treebank --metrics
```

The output has been omitted for brevity, but I encourage you to run it yourself to see the results. It's especially useful for evaluating a tagger's performance on a corpus that it was not trained on, such as `conll2000` or `brown`.

If you only provide a corpus argument, this script will use NLTK's built-in tagger. To evaluate your own tagger, you can use the `--tagger` argument, which takes a path to a pickled tagger. The path can be absolute or relative to a `nltk_data` directory. For example:

```
$ python analyze_tagger_coverage.py treebank --metrics --tagger path/to/
tagger.pickle
```

You can also use a custom corpus just like we did earlier with `train_tagger.py`, but if your corpus is not tagged, then you must omit the `--metrics` argument. In that case, you will only get tag counts, with no notion of accuracy, because there are no tags to compare to.

Analyzing a tagged corpus

Finally, there is a script called `analyze_tagged_corpus.py`, which, as the name implies, will read in a tagged corpus and print out stats about the number of words and tags. You can run it as follows:

```
$ python analyze_tagged_corpus.py treebank
```

The results are available in *Appendix, Penn Treebank Part-of-speech Tags*. As with the other commands, you can pass in a custom corpus path and reader to analyze your own tagged corpus.

See also

The previous recipes in this chapter cover the details of the classes and methods that power the functionality of `train_tagger.py`. The *Training a chunker with NLTK-Trainer* recipe at the end of *Chapter 5, Extracting Chunks*, will introduce NLTK-Trainer's chunking-related scripts, and classification-related scripts will be covered in the *Training a classifier with NLTK-Trainer* recipe at the end of *Chapter 7, Text Classification*.

Extracti

Extracting Chunks

As in Chapter 4, Par
training and testi
a simpler and r
the conll20
Chapter 3

In this chapter, we will cover the following recipes:

- ▸ Chunking and chinking with regular expressions
- ▸ Merging and splitting chunks with regular expressions
- ▸ Expanding and removing chunks with regular expressions
- ▸ Partial parsing with regular expressions
- ▸ Training a tagger-based chunker
- ▸ Classification-based chunking
- ▸ Extracting named entities
- ▸ Extracting proper noun chunks
- ▸ Extracting location chunks
- ▸ Training a named entity chunker
- ▸ Training a chunker with NLTK-Trainer

Introduction

Chunk extraction, or **partial parsing**, is the process of extracting short phrases from a part-of-speech tagged sentence. This is different from full parsing in that we're interested in standalone **chunks**, or **phrases**, instead of full parse trees (for more on parse trees, see https://en.wikipedia.org/wiki/Parse_tree). The idea is that meaningful phrases can be extracted from a sentence by looking for particular patterns of part-of-speech tags.

-of-speech Tagging, we'll be using the **Penn Treebank** corpus for basic chunk extraction. We'll also be using the **CoNLL2000** corpus as it has more flexible format that supports multiple chunk types (for more details on 00 corpus and IOB tags, see the *Creating a chunked phrase corpus* recipe in *Creating Custom Corpora*).

Chunking and chinking with regular expressions

Using modified regular expressions, we can define **chunk patterns**. These are patterns of part-of-speech tags that define what kinds of words make up a chunk. We can also define patterns for what kinds of words should not be in a chunk. These unchunked words are known as **chinks**.

A `ChunkRule` class specifies what to *include* in a chunk, while a `ChinkRule` class specifies what to *exclude* from a chunk. In other words, chunking creates chunks, while chinking breaks up those chunks.

Getting ready

We first need to know how to define chunk patterns. These are modified regular expressions designed to match sequences of part-of-speech tags. An individual tag is specified by surrounding angle brackets, such as <NN> to match a noun tag. Multiple tags can then be combined, as in <DT><NN> to match a determiner followed by a noun. Regular expression syntax can be used within the angle brackets to match individual tag patterns, so you can do <NN.*> to match all nouns including NN and NNS. You can also use regular expression syntax outside of the angle brackets to match patterns of tags. <DT>?<NN.*>+ will match an optional determiner followed by one or more nouns. The chunk patterns are internally converted to regular expressions using the `tag_pattern2re_pattern()` function.

```
>>> from nltk.chunk.regexp import tag_pattern2re_pattern
>>> tag_pattern2re_pattern('<DT>?<NN.*>+')
'(<(DT)>)?(<(NN[^\\{\\}<>]*)>)+'
```

You don't have to use this function to do chunking, but it might be useful or interesting to see how your chunk patterns convert to regular expressions. This function is used by the `RegexpParser` class (explained in the next section) to convert chunk patterns into regular expressions to match chunking rules.

How to do it...

The pattern for specifying a chunk is to use surrounding curly braces, such as `{<DT><NN>}`. To specify a chink, you flip the braces, such as `}<VB>{`. These rules can be combined into a **grammar** for a particular phrase type. Here's a grammar for noun phrases that combines both a chunk and a chink pattern, along with the result of parsing the sentence the book has many chapters:

```
>>> from nltk.chunk import RegexpParser
>>> chunker = RegexpParser(r'''
... NP:
...    {<DT><NN.*><.*>*<NN.*>}
...    }<VB.*>{
... ''')
>>> chunker.parse([('the', 'DT'), ('book', 'NN'), ('has', 'VBZ'),
('many', 'JJ'), ('chapters', 'NNS')])

Tree('S', [Tree('NP', [('the', 'DT'), ('book', 'NN')]), ('has',
'VBZ'), Tree('NP', [('many', 'JJ'), ('chapters', 'NNS')])])
```

The grammar tells the `RegexpParser` class that there are two rules for parsing NP chunks. The first chunk pattern says that a chunk starts with a determiner followed by any kind of noun. Then, any number of other words are allowed until a final noun is found. The second pattern says that verbs should be chinked, thus separating any large chunks that contain a verb. The result is a tree with two noun-phrase chunks: the book and many chapters.

> Tagged sentences are always parsed into a `Tree` (found in the `nltk.tree` module). The top label of the `Tree` is S, which stands for sentence. Any chunks found will be subtrees whose labels will refer to the chunk type. In this case, the chunk type is NP for noun-phrase chunks. Trees can be drawn calling the `draw()` method using `t.draw()`.

How it works...

Here's what happens, step-by-step:

1. The sentence is converted into a flat `Tree`:

2. The `Tree` is used to create a `ChunkString`.

3. The `RegexpParser` parses the grammar to create a `NP RegexpChunkParser` with the given rules.

4. A `ChunkRule` is created and applied to the `ChunkString`, which matches the entire sentence into a chunk:

5. A `ChinkRule` is created and applied to the same `ChunkString`, which splits the big chunk into two smaller chunks with a verb between them:

6. The `ChunkString` is converted back to a `Tree`, now with two `NP` chunk subtrees:

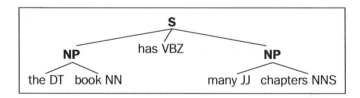

You can do this yourself using the classes in `nltk.chunk.regexp`. The `ChunkRule` and `ChinkRule` classes are both subclasses of `RegexpChunkRule`, and require two arguments: the pattern and a description of the rule. `ChunkString` is an object that starts with a flat tree, which is then modified by each rule when it is passed into the rule's `apply()` method. A `ChunkString` is converted back to a `Tree` with the `to_chunkstruct()` method. Here's some code to demonstrate this:

```
>>> from nltk.chunk.regexp import ChunkString, ChunkRule, ChinkRule
>>> from nltk.tree import Tree
>>> t = Tree('S', [('the', 'DT'), ('book', 'NN'), ('has', 'VBZ'),
```

```
'many', 'JJ'), ('chapters', 'NNS')])
>>> cs = ChunkString(t)
>>> cs
<ChunkString: '<DT><NN><VBZ><JJ><NNS>'>
>>> ur = ChunkRule('<DT><NN.*><.*>*<NN.*>', 'chunk determiners and
nouns')
>>> ur.apply(cs)
>>> cs
<ChunkString: '{<DT><NN><VBZ><JJ><NNS>}'>
>>> ir = ChinkRule('<VB.*>', 'chink verbs')
>>> ir.apply(cs)
>>> cs
<ChunkString: '{<DT><NN>}<VBZ>{<JJ><NNS>}'>
>>> cs.to_chunkstruct()
Tree('S', [Tree('CHUNK', [('the', 'DT'), ('book', 'NN')]), ('has',
'VBZ'), Tree('CHUNK', [('many', 'JJ'), ('chapters', 'NNS')])])
```

The tree diagrams shown earlier can be drawn at each step by calling
`cs.to_chunkstruct().draw()`.

There's more...

You'll notice that the subtrees from the `ChunkString` class are tagged as CHUNK and not NP.
That's because the rules mentioned earlier are phrase agnostic; they create chunks without
needing to know what kind of chunks they are.

Internally, the `RegexpParser` class creates a `RegexpChunkParser` for each chunk phrase
type. So, if you're only chunking NP phrases, there will only be one `RegexpChunkParser`. The
`RegexpChunkParser` class gets all the rules for the specific chunk type, and handles applying
the rules in order and converting the CHUNK trees to the specific chunk type, such as NP.

Here's some code to illustrate the usage of `RegexpChunkParser`. We pass both the rules
mentioned earlier into the `RegexpChunkParser` class, and then parse the same sentence
tree we created before. The resulting tree is just like what we got from applying both rules in
order, except that CHUNK has been replaced with NP in both the subtrees. This is because
`RegexpChunkParser` defaults to `chunk_label='NP'`.

```
>>> from nltk.chunk import RegexpChunkParser
>>> chunker = RegexpChunkParser([ur, ir])
>>> chunker.parse(t)
Tree('S', [Tree('NP', [('the', 'DT'), ('book', 'NN')]), ('has',
'VBZ'), Tree('NP', [('many', 'JJ'), ('chapters', 'NNS')])])
```

Parsing different chunk types

If you wanted to parse a different chunk type, then you could pass that in as `chunk_label` to `RegexpChunkParser`. Here's the same code that we saw in the previous section, but instead of NP subtrees, we'll call them CP for custom phrase:

```
>>> from nltk.chunk import RegexpChunkParser
>>> chunker = RegexpChunkParser([ur, ir], chunk_label='CP')
>>> chunker.parse(t)
Tree('S', [Tree('CP', [('the', 'DT'), ('book', 'NN')]), ('has',
'VBZ'), Tree('CP', [('many', 'JJ'), ('chapters', 'NNS')])])
```

The `RegexpParser` class does this internally when you specify multiple phrase types. This will be covered in the *Partial parsing with regular expressions* recipe.

Parsing alternative patterns

The same parsing results can be obtained using two chunk patterns in the grammar and discarding the chink pattern:

```
>>> chunker = RegexpParser(r'''
... NP:
... {<DT><NN.*>}
... {<JJ><NN.*>}
... ''')
>>> chunker.parse(t)
Tree('S', [Tree('NP', [('the', 'DT'), ('book', 'NN')]), ('has',
'VBZ'), Tree('NP', [('many', 'JJ'), ('chapters', 'NNS')])])
```

In fact, you could reduce the two chunk patterns into a single pattern.

```
>>> chunker = RegexpParser(r'''
... NP:
... {(<DT>|<JJ>)<NN.*>}
... ''')
>>> chunker.parse(t)
Tree('S', [Tree('NP', [('the', 'DT'), ('book', 'NN')]), ('has',
'VBZ'), Tree('NP', [('many', 'JJ'), ('chapters', 'NNS')])])
```

How you create and combine patterns is really up to you. Pattern creation is a process of trial and error, and entirely depends on what your data looks like and which patterns are easiest to express.

Chunk rule with context

You can also create chunk rules with a surrounding tag context. For example, if your pattern is <DT>{<NN>}, that will be parsed into a ChunkRuleWithContext class. So, context in this case is referring to the parts of the rule that are not chinks or chunks, such as <DT>. For example, in the phrase the dog, the would be context to the noun dog. Any time there's a tag on either side of the curly braces, you'll get a ChunkRuleWithContext class instead of a ChunkRule class. This can allow you to be more specific about when to parse particular kinds of chunks.

Here's an example of using ChunkRuleWithContext directly. It takes four arguments: the left context, the pattern to chunk, the right context, and a description:

```
>>> from nltk.chunk.regexp import ChunkRuleWithContext
>>> ctx = ChunkRuleWithContext('<DT>', '<NN.*>', '<.*>', 'chunk nouns
only after determiners')
>>> cs = ChunkString(t)
>>> cs
<ChunkString: '<DT><NN><VBZ><JJ><NNS>'>
>>> ctx.apply(cs)
>>> cs
<ChunkString: '<DT>{<NN>}<VBZ><JJ><NNS>'>
>>> cs.to_chunkstruct()
Tree('S', [('the', 'DT'), Tree('CHUNK', [('book', 'NN')]), ('has',
'VBZ'), ('many', 'JJ'), ('chapters', 'NNS')])
```

This example only chunks nouns that follow a determiner, therefore ignoring the noun that follows an adjective. Here's how it would look using the RegexpParser class:

```
>>> chunker = RegexpParser(r'''
... NP:
... <DT>{<NN.*>}
... ''')
>>> chunker.parse(t)
Tree('S', [('the', 'DT'), Tree('NP', [('book', 'NN')]), ('has',
'VBZ'), ('many', 'JJ'), ('chapters', 'NNS')])
```

See also

In the next recipe, we'll cover merging and splitting chunks.

Merging and splitting chunks with regular expressions

In this recipe, we'll cover two more rules for chunking. A `MergeRule` class can merge two chunks together based on the end of the first chunk and the beginning of the second chunk. A `SplitRule` class will split a chunk into two chunks based on the specified split pattern.

How to do it...

A `SplitRule` class is specified with two opposing curly braces surrounded by a pattern on either side. To split a chunk after a noun, you would do `<NN.*>}{<.*>`. A `MergeRule` class is specified by flipping the curly braces, and will join chunks where the end of the first chunk matches the left pattern and the beginning of the next chunk matches the right pattern. To merge two chunks where the first ends with a noun and the second begins with a noun, you'd use `<NN.*>{}<NN.*>`.

> Note that the order of rules is very important, and reordering can affect the results. The `RegexpParser` class applies the rules one at a time from top to bottom, so each rule will be applied to the `ChunkString` resulting from the previous rule.

An example of splitting and merging, starting with the sentence tree, is shown next:

The whole sentence is chunked, as shown in the following diagram:

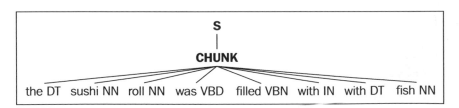

The chunk is split into multiple chunks after every noun, as shown in the following tree:

Each chunk with a determiner is split into separate chunks, creating four chunks where there were three:

Chunks ending with a noun are merged with the next chunk if it begins with a noun, reducing the four chunks back down to three, as shown in the following diagram:

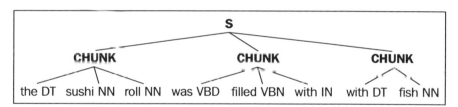

Using the `RegexpParser` class, the code looks like this:

```
>>> chunker = RegexpParser(r'''
... NP:
... {<DT><.*>*<NN.*>}
... <NN.*>}{<.*>
... <.*>}{<DT>
... <NN.*>{}<NN.*>
... ''')
>>> sent = [('the', 'DT'), ('sushi', 'NN'), ('roll', 'NN'), ('was',
'VBD'), ('filled', 'VBN'), ('with', 'IN'), ('the', 'DT'), ('fish',
'NN')]
>>> chunker.parse(sent)
Tree('S', [Tree('NP', [('the', 'DT'), ('sushi', 'NN'), ('roll',
'NN')]), Tree('NP', [('was', 'VBD'), ('filled', 'VBN'), ('with',
'IN')]), Tree('NP', [('the', 'DT'), ('fish', 'NN')])])
```

And the final tree of NP chunks is shown in the following diagram:

How it works...

The MergeRule and SplitRule classes take two arguments: the left pattern and the right pattern. The RegexpParser class takes care of splitting the original patterns on the curly braces to get the left and right sides, but you can also create these manually. Here's a step-by-step walkthrough of how the original sentence is modified by applying each rule:

```
>>> from nltk.chunk.regexp import MergeRule, SplitRule
>>> cs = ChunkString(Tree('S', sent))
>>> cs
<ChunkString: '<DT><NN><NN><VBD><VBN><IN><DT><NN>'>
>>> ur = ChunkRule('<DT><.*>*<NN.*>', 'chunk determiner to noun')
>>> ur.apply(cs)
>>> cs
<ChunkString: '{<DT><NN><NN><VBD><VBN><IN><DT><NN>}'>
>>> sr1 = SplitRule('<NN.*>', '<.*>', 'split after noun')
>>> sr1.apply(cs)
>>> cs
<ChunkString: '{<DT><NN>}{<NN>}{<VBD><VBN><IN><DT><NN>}'>
>>> sr2 = SplitRule('<.*>', '<DT>', 'split before determiner')
>>> sr2.apply(cs)
>>> cs
<ChunkString: '{<DT><NN>}{<NN>}{<VBD><VBN><IN>}{<DT><NN>}'>
>>> mr = MergeRule('<NN.*>', '<NN.*>', 'merge nouns')
>>> mr.apply(cs)
>>> cs
<ChunkString: '{<DT><NN><NN>}{<VBD><VBN><IN>}{<DT><NN>}'>
>>> cs.to_chunkstruct()
Tree('S', [Tree('CHUNK', [('the', 'DT'), ('sushi', 'NN'), ('roll',
'NN')]), Tree('CHUNK', [('was', 'VBD'), ('filled', 'VBN'), ('with',
'IN')]), Tree('CHUNK', [('the', 'DT'), ('fish', 'NN')])])
```

There's more...

The parsing of the rules and splitting of left and right patterns is done in the static `parse()` method of the `RegexpChunkRule` superclass. This is called by the `RegexpParser` class to get the list of rules to pass into the `RegexpChunkParser` class. Here are some examples of parsing the patterns we used earlier:

```
>>> from nltk.chunk.regexp import RegexpChunkRule
>>> RegexpChunkRule.fromstring('{<DT><.*>*<NN.*>}')
<ChunkRule: '<DT><.*>*<NN.*>'>
>>> RegexpChunkRule.fromstring('<.*>}{<DT>')
<SplitRule: '<.*>', '<DT>'>
>>> RegexpChunkRule.fromstring('<NN.*>{}<NN.*>')
<MergeRule: '<NN.*>', '<NN.*>'>
```

Specifying rule descriptions

Descriptions for each rule can be specified with a comment string after the rule (a comment string must start with #). If no comment string is found, the rule's description will be empty. Here's an example:

```
>>> RegexpChunkRule.fromstring('{<DT><.*>*<NN.*>} # chunk
everything').descr()
'chunk everything'
>>> RegexpChunkRule.fromstring('{<DT><.*>*<NN.*>}').descr()
''
```

Comment string descriptions can also be used within grammar strings that are passed to `RegexpParser`.

See also

The previous recipe goes over how to use `ChunkRule`, and how rules are passed into `RegexpChunkParser`.

Expanding and removing chunks with regular expressions

There are three `RegexpChunkRule` subclasses that are not supported by `RegexpChunkRule.fromstring()` or `RegexpParser`, and therefore must be created manually if you want to use them. These rules are as follows:

- `ExpandLeftRule`: Add unchunked (chink) words to the left of a chunk
- `ExpandRightRule`: Add unchunked (chink) words to the right of a chunk
- `UnChunkRule`: Unchunk any matching chunk

How to do it...

`ExpandLeftRule` and `ExpandRightRule` both take two patterns along with a description as arguments. For `ExpandLeftRule`, the first pattern is the chink we want to add to the beginning of the chunk, while the right pattern will match the beginning of the chunk we want to expand. With `ExpandRightRule`, the left pattern should match the end of the chunk we want to expand, and the right pattern matches the chink we want to add to the end of the chunk. The idea is similar to the `MergeRule` class, but in this case, we're merging chink words instead of other chunks.

`UnChunkRule` is the opposite of `ChunkRule`. Any chunk that exactly matches the `UnChunkRule` pattern will be unchunked and become a chink. Here's some code demonstrating the usage with the `RegexpChunkParser` class:

```
>>> from nltk.chunk.regexp import ChunkRule, ExpandLeftRule,
ExpandRightRule, UnChunkRule
>>> from nltk.chunk import RegexpChunkParser
>>> ur = ChunkRule('<NN>', 'single noun')
>>> el = ExpandLeftRule('<DT>', '<NN>', 'get left determiner')
>>> er = ExpandRightRule('<NN>', '<NNS>', 'get right plural noun')
>>> un = UnChunkRule('<DT><NN.*>*', 'unchunk everything')
>>> chunker = RegexpChunkParser([ur, el, er, un])
>>> sent = [('the', 'DT'), ('sushi', 'NN'), ('rolls', 'NNS')]
>>> chunker.parse(sent)
Tree('S', [('the', 'DT'), ('sushi', 'NN'), ('rolls', 'NNS')])
```

You'll notice that the end result is a flat sentence, which is exactly what we started with. That's because the final `UnChunkRule` undid the chunk created by the previous rules. Read on to see what happened step by step.

How it works...

The rules mentioned earlier were applied in the following order, starting with the sentence tree as follows:

1. Make single nouns into a chunk:

2. Expand left determiners into chunks that begin with a noun:

3. Expand right plural nouns into chunks that end with a noun, chunking the whole sentence as follows:

4. Unchunk every chunk that is a *determiner + noun + plural noun*, resulting in the original sentence tree:

Here's the code showing each step:

```
>>> from nltk.chunk.regexp import ChunkString
>>> from nltk.tree import Tree
>>> cs = ChunkString(Tree('S', sent))
>>> cs
```

```
<ChunkString: '<DT><NN><NNS>'>
>>> ur.apply(cs)
>>> cs
<ChunkString: '<DT>{<NN>}<NNS>'>
>>> el.apply(cs)
>>> cs
<ChunkString: '{<DT><NN>}<NNS>'>
>>> er.apply(cs)
>>> cs
<ChunkString: '{<DT><NN><NNS>}'>
>>> un.apply(cs)
>>> cs
<ChunkString: '<DT><NN><NNS>'>
```

There's more...

In practice, you can probably get away with only using the previous four rules: `ChunkRule`, `ChinkRule`, `MergeRule`, and `SplitRule`. But if you do need very fine-grained control over chunk parsing and removing chunks, now you know how to do it with the expansion and unchunk rules.

See also

The previous two recipes covered the more common chunk rules that are supported by `RegexpChunkRule.fromstring()` and `RegexpParser`.

Partial parsing with regular expressions

So far, we've only been parsing noun phrases. But `RegexpParser` supports grammars with multiple phrase types, such as verb phrases and prepositional phrases. We can put the rules we've learned to use and define a grammar that can be evaluated against the `conll2000` corpus, which has NP, VP, and PP phrases.

How to do it...

Now, we will define a grammar to parse three phrase types. For noun phrases, we have a `ChunkRule` class that looks for an optional determiner followed by one or more nouns. We then have a `MergeRule` class for adding an adjective to the front of a noun chunk. For prepositional phrases, we simply chunk any IN word, such as in or on. For verb phrases, we chunk an optional modal word (such as should) followed by a verb.

Each grammar rule is followed by a # comment. This comment is passed into each rule as the description. Comments are optional, but they can be helpful notes for understanding what the rule does, and will be included in trace output.

```
>>> chunker = RegexpParser(r'''
... NP:
... {<DT>?<NN.*>+}   # chunk optional determiner with nouns
... <JJ>{}<NN.*>   # merge adjective with noun chunk
... PP:
... {<IN>}         # chunk preposition
... VP:
... {<MD>?<VB.*>}   # chunk optional modal with verb
... ''')
>>> from nltk.corpus import conll2000
>>> score = chunker.evaluate(conll2000.chunked_sents())
>>> score.accuracy()
0.6148573545757688
```

When we call `evaluate()` on the `chunker` argument, we give it a list of chunked sentences and get back a `ChunkScore` object, which can give us the accuracy of the `chunker` along with a number of other metrics.

How it works...

The `RegexpParser` class parses the grammar string into sets of rules, one set of rules for each phrase type. These rules are used to create a `RegexpChunkParser` class. The rules are parsed using `RegexpChunkRule.fromstring()`, which returns one of the five subclasses: `ChunkRule`, `ChinkRule`, `MergeRule`, `SplitRule`, or `ChunkRuleWithContext`.

Now that the grammar has been translated into sets of rules, these rules are used to parse a tagged sentence into a `Tree` structure. The `RegexpParser` class inherits from `ChunkParserI`, which provides a `parse()` method to parse the tagged words. Whenever a part of the tagged tokens matches a chunk rule, a subtree is constructed so that the tagged tokens become the leaves of a `Tree` whose label is the chunk tag. The `ChunkParserI` interface also provides the `evaluate()` method, which compares the given chunked sentences to the output of the `parse()` method to construct and return a `ChunkScore` object.

You can also evaluate this `chunker` argument on the `treebank_chunk` corpus:

```
>>> from nltk.corpus import treebank_chunk
>>> treebank_score = chunker.evaluate(treebank_chunk.chunked_sents())
>>> treebank_score.accuracy()
0.49033970276008493
```

The `treebank_chunk` corpus is a special version of the `treebank` corpus that provides a `chunked_sents()` method. The regular `treebank` corpus cannot provide that method due to its file format.

The ChunkScore metrics

The `ChunkScore` metrics provide a few other metrics besides accuracy. Of the chunks the `chunker` argument was able to guess, **precision** tells you how many were correct and **recall** tells you how well the chunker did at finding correct chunks compared to how many total chunks there were. For more about `precision` and `recall`, see https://en.wikipedia.org/wiki/Precision_and_recall.

```
>>> score.precision()
0.60201948127375
>>> score.recall()
0.606072502505847
```

You can also get lists of chunks that were missed by the `chunker`, chunks that were incorrectly found, correct chunks, and the total guessed chunks. These can be useful to figure out how to improve your chunk grammar:

```
>>> len(score.missed())
47161
>>> len(score.incorrect())
47967
>>> len(score.correct())
119720
>>> len(score.guessed())
120526
```

As you can see by the number of incorrect chunks, and by comparing `guessed()` and `correct()`, our chunker guessed that there were more chunks than actually existed. And it also missed a good number of correct chunks.

Looping and tracing chunk rules

If you want to apply the chunk rules in your grammar more than once, you can pass `loop=2` into `RegexpParser` at initialization. The default is `loop=1`, which will apply each rule once. Since a chunk can change after every rule application, it may sometimes make sense to re-apply the same rules multiple times.

To watch an internal trace of the chunking process, pass `trace=1` into `RegexpParser`. To get even more output, pass in `trace=2`. This will give you a printout of what the `chunker` is doing as it is doing it. Rule comments/descriptions will be included in the trace output, giving you a good idea of which rule is applied when.

See also

If coming up with regular expression chunk patterns seems like too much work, then read the next recipes, where we'll cover how to train a chunker based on a corpus of chunked sentences.

Training a tagger-based chunker

Training a chunker can be a great alternative to manually specifying regular expression chunk patterns. Instead of a pain-staking process of trial and error to get the exact right patterns, we can use existing corpus data to train chunkers much like we did for part-of-speech tagging in the previous chapter.

How to do it...

As with the part-of-speech tagging, we'll use the `treebank` corpus data for training. But this time, we'll use the `treebank_chunk` corpus, which is specifically formatted to produce chunked sentences in the form of trees. These `chunked_sents()` methods will be used by a `TagChunker` class to train a tagger-based chunker. The `TagChunker` class uses a helper function, `conll_tag_chunks()`, to extract a list of (`pos`, `iob`) tuples from a list of `Trees`. These (`pos`, `iob`) tuples are then used to train a tagger in the same way (`word`, `pos`) tuples were used in *Chapter 4*, *Part-of-speech Tagging*, to train part-of-speech taggers. But instead of learning part-of-speech tags for words, we're learning IOB tags for part-of-speech tags. Here's the code from `chunkers.py`:

```
from nltk.chunk import ChunkParserI
from nltk.chunk.util import tree2conlltags, conlltags2tree
from nltk.tag import UnigramTagger, BigramTagger
from tag_util import backoff_tagger
```

```
def conll_tag_chunks(chunk_sents):
    tagged_sents = [tree2conlltags(tree) for tree in chunk_sents]
    return [[(t, c) for (w, t, c) in sent] for sent in tagged_sents]

class TagChunker(ChunkParserI):
    def __init__(self, train_chunks, tagger_classes=[UnigramTagger,
BigramTagger]):
        train_sents = conll_tag_chunks(train_chunks)
        self.tagger = backoff_tagger(train_sents, tagger_classes)

    def parse(self, tagged_sent):
        if not tagged_sent: return None
        (words, tags) = zip(*tagged_sent)
        chunks = self.tagger.tag(tags)
        wtc = zip(words, chunks)
        return conlltags2tree([(w,t,c) for (w,(t,c)) in wtc])
```

Once we have our trained `TagChunker`, we can then evaluate the `ChunkScore` class the same way we did for the `RegexpParser` class in the previous recipes:

```
>>> from chunkers import TagChunker
>>> from nltk.corpus import treebank_chunk
>>> train_chunks = treebank_chunk.chunked_sents()[:3000]
>>> test_chunks = treebank_chunk.chunked_sents()[3000:]
>>> chunker = TagChunker(train_chunks)
>>> score = chunker.evaluate(test_chunks)
>>> score.accuracy()
0.9732039335251428
>>> score.precision()
0.9166534370535006
>>> score.recall()
0.9465573770491803
```

Pretty darn accurate! Training a chunker is clearly a great alternative to manually specified grammars and regular expressions.

How it works...

Recall from the *Creating a chunked phrase corpus* recipe in *Chapter 3*, *Creating Custom Corpora*, that the conll2000 corpus defines chunks using IOB tags, which specify the type of chunk and where it begins and ends. We can train a part-of-speech tagger on these IOB tag patterns and then use that to power a ChunkerI subclass. But first, we need to transform a Tree that you'd get from the chunked_sents() method of a corpus into a format usable by a part-of-speech tagger. This is what conll_tag_chunks() does. It uses tree2conlltags() to convert a sentence Tree into a list of three tuples of the form (word, pos, iob), where pos is the part-of-speech tag and iob is an IOB tag, such as B-NP to mark the beginning of a noun-phrase, or I-NP to mark that the word is inside the noun-phrase. The reverse of this method is conlltags2tree(). Here's some code to demonstrate these nltk.chunk functions:

```
>>> from nltk.chunk.util import tree2conlltags, conlltags2tree
>>> from nltk.tree import Tree
>>> t = Tree('S', [Tree('NP', [('the', 'DT'), ('book', 'NN')])])
>>> tree2conlltags(t)
[('the', 'DT', 'B-NP'), ('book', 'NN', 'I-NP')]
>>> conlltags2tree([('the', 'DT', 'B-NP'), ('book', 'NN', 'I-NP')])
Tree('S', [Tree('NP', [('the', 'DT'), ('book', 'NN')])])
```

The next step is to convert these 3-tuples into 2-tuples that the tagger can recognize. Because the RegexpParser class uses part-of-speech tags for chunk patterns, we'll do that here too and use part-of-speech tags as if they were words to tag. By simply dropping the word from the 3-tuples (word, pos, iob), the conll_tag_chunks() function returns a list of 2-tuples of the form (pos, iob). When we consider the previous example Tree in a list, the results are in a format we can feed to a tagger:

```
>>> conll_tag_chunks([t])
[[('DT', 'B-NP'), ('NN', 'I-NP')]]
```

The final step is a subclass of ChunkParserI called TagChunker. It trains on a list of chunk trees using an internal tagger. This internal tagger is composed of a UnigramTagger and a BigramTagger class in a backoff chain, using the backoff_tagger() method created in the *Training and combining ngram taggers* recipe in *Chapter 4*, *Part-of-speech Tagging*.

Finally, ChunkerI subclasses must implement a parse() method that expects a part-of-speech tagged sentence. We unzip that sentence into a list of words and part-of-speech tags. The tags are then tagged by the tagger to get IOB tags, which are then recombined with the words and part-of-speech tags to create 3-tuples we can pass to conlltags2tree() to return a final Tree.

There's more...

Since we've been talking about the `conll` IOB tags, let's see how the `TagChunker` class does on the `conll2000` corpus:

```
>>> from nltk.corpus import conll2000
>>> conll_train = conll2000.chunked_sents('train.txt')
>>> conll_test = conll2000.chunked_sents('test.txt')
>>> chunker = TagChunker(conll_train)
>>> score = chunker.evaluate(conll_test)
>>> score.accuracy()
0.8950545623403762
>>> score.precision()
0.8114841974355675
>>> score.recall()
0.8644191676944863
```

Not quite as good as on `treebank_chunk`, but `conll2000` is a much larger corpus, so it's not too surprising.

Using different taggers

If you want to use different tagger classes with the `TagChunker` class, you can pass them in as `tagger_classes`. For example, here's the `TagChunker` class using just a `UnigramTagger` class:

```
>>> from nltk.tag import UnigramTagger
>>> uni_chunker = TagChunker(train_chunks, tagger_
classes=[UnigramTagger])
>>> score = uni_chunker.evaluate(test_chunks)
>>> score.accuracy()
0.9674925924335466
```

The `tagger_classes` argument will be passed directly into the `backoff_tagger()` function, which means they must be subclasses of `SequentialBackoffTagger`. In testing, the default of `tagger_classes=[UnigramTagger, BigramTagger]` generally produces the best results, but it can vary depending on the corpus.

See also

The *Training and combing ngram taggers* recipe in *Chapter 4, Part-of-speech Tagging*, covers backoff tagging with a `UnigramTagger` and `BigramTagger` class. The `ChunkScore` metrics returned by the `evaluate()` method of a chunker are explained in the previous recipe.

Classification-based chunking

Unlike most part-of-speech taggers, the `ClassifierBasedTagger` class learns from features. That means we can create a `ClassifierChunker` class that can learn from both the words and part-of-speech tags, instead of only the part-of-speech tags as the `TagChunker` class does.

How to do it...

For the `ClassifierChunker` class, we don't want to discard the words from the training sentences as we did in the previous recipe. Instead, to remain compatible with the 2-tuple `(word, pos)` format required for training a `ClassiferBasedTagger` class, we convert the `(word, pos, iob)` 3-tuples from `tree2conlltags()` into `((word, pos), iob)` 2-tuples using the `chunk_trees2train_chunks()` function. This code can be found in `chunkers.py`:

```
from nltk.chunk import ChunkParserI
from nltk.chunk.util import tree2conlltags, conlltags2tree
from nltk.tag import ClassifierBasedTagger

def chunk_trees2train_chunks(chunk_sents):
    tag_sents = [tree2conlltags(sent) for sent in chunk_sents]
    return [[((w,t),c) for (w,t,c) in sent] for sent in tag_sents]
```

Next, we need a feature detector function to pass into `ClassifierBasedTagger`. Our default feature detector function, `prev_next_pos_iob()`, knows that the list of tokens is really a list of `(word, pos)` tuples, and can use that to return a feature set suitable for a classifier. In fact, any feature detector function used with the `ClassifierChunker` class (defined next) should recognize that tokens are a list of `(word, pos)` tuples, and have the same function signature as `prev_next_pos_iob()`. To give the classifier as much information as we can, this feature set contains the current, previous, and next word and part-of-speech tag, along with the previous IOB tag:

```
def prev_next_pos_iob(tokens, index, history):
    word, pos = tokens[index]

    if index == 0:
        prevword, prevpos, previob = ('<START>',)*3
    else:
        prevword, prevpos = tokens[index-1]
        previob = history[index-1]
```

```
      if index == len(tokens) - 1:
        nextword, nextpos = ('<END>',)*2
      else:
        nextword, nextpos = tokens[index+1]

      feats = {
        'word': word,
        'pos': pos,
        'nextword': nextword,
        'nextpos': nextpos,
        'prevword': prevword,
        'prevpos': prevpos,
        'previob': previob
      }
      return feats
```

Now, we can define the `ClassifierChunker` class, which uses an internal `ClassifierBasedTagger` with features extracted using `prev_next_pos_iob()` and training sentences from `chunk_trees2train_chunks()`. As a subclass of `ChunkerParserI`, it implements the `parse()` method, which converts the `((w, t), c)` tuples produced by the internal tagger into `Trees` using `conlltags2tree()`:

```
class ClassifierChunker(ChunkParserI):
  def __init__(self, train_sents, feature_detector=prev_next_pos_iob,
**kwargs):
    if not feature_detector:
      feature_detector = self.feature_detector

    train_chunks = chunk_trees2train_chunks(train_sents)
    self.tagger = ClassifierBasedTagger(train=train_chunks,
      feature_detector=feature_detector, **kwargs)

  def parse(self, tagged_sent):
    if not tagged_sent: return None
    chunks = self.tagger.tag(tagged_sent)
    return conlltags2tree([(w,t,c) for ((w,t),c) in chunks])
```

Using the same `train_chunks` and `test_chunks` from the `treebank_chunk` corpus in the previous recipe, we can evaluate this code from `chunkers.py`:

```
>>> from chunkers import ClassifierChunker
>>> chunker = ClassifierChunker(train_chunks)
>>> score = chunker.evaluate(test_chunks)
>>> score.accuracy()
0.9721733155838022
```

```
>>> score.precision()
0.9258838793383068
>>> score.recall()
0.9359016393442623
```

Compared to the `TagChunker` class, all the scores have gone up a bit. Let's see how it does on `conll2000`:

```
>>> chunker = ClassifierChunker(conll_train)
>>> score = chunker.evaluate(conll_test)
>>> score.accuracy()
0.9264622074002153
>>> score.precision()
0.8737924310910219
>>> score.recall()
0.9007354620620346
```

This is much improved over the `TagChunker` class.

How it works...

Like the `TagChunker` class in the previous recipe, we are training a part-of-speech tagger for IOB tagging. But in this case, we want to include the word as a feature to power a classifier. By creating nested 2-tuples of the form `((word, pos), iob)`, we can pass the word through the tagger into our feature detector function. The `chunk_trees2train_chunks()` method produces these nested 2-tuples, and `prev_next_pos_iob()` is aware of them and uses each element as a feature. The following features are extracted:

- The current word and part-of-speech tag
- The previous word, part-of-speech tag, and IOB tag
- The next word and part-of-speech tag

The arguments to `prev_next_pos_iob()` look the same as the `feature_detector()` method of the `ClassifierBasedTagger` class: `tokens`, `index`, and `history`. But this time, `tokens` will be a list of `(word, pos)` two tuples, and `history` will be a list of IOB tags. The special feature values `<START>` and `<END>` are used if there are no previous or next tokens.

The `ClassifierChunker` class uses an internal `ClassifierBasedTagger` and `prev_next_pos_iob()` as its default `feature_detector`. The results from the tagger, which are in the same nested 2-tuple form, are then reformated into 3-tuples to return a final `Tree` using `conlltags2tree()`.

There's more...

You can use your own feature detector function by passing it into the `ClassifierChunker` class as `feature_detector`. The `tokens` argument will contain a list of (`word`, `tag`) tuples, and `history` will be a list of the previous IOB tags found.

Using a different classifier builder

The `ClassifierBasedTagger` class defaults to using `NaiveBayesClassifier.train` as its `classifier_builder`. But you can use any classifier you want by overriding the `classifier_builder` keyword argument. Here's an example using `MaxentClassifier.train`:

```
>>> from nltk.classify import MaxentClassifier
>>> builder = lambda toks: MaxentClassifier.train(toks, trace=0,
max_iter=10, min_lldelta=0.01)
>>> me_chunker = ClassifierChunker(train_chunks,
classifier_builder=builder)
>>> score = me_chunker.evaluate(test_chunks)
>>> score.accuracy()
0.9743204362949285
>>> score.precision()
0.9334423548650859
>>> score.recall()
0.9357377049180328
```

Instead of using `MaxentClassifier.train` directly, I wrapped it in a `lambda` argument so that its output is quite similar to (`trace=0`) and it finishes in a reasonable amount of time. As you can see, the scores are slightly different compared to using the `NaiveBayesClassifier` class.

> The `MaxentClassifier` score values mentioned earlier were computed with the environment variable PYTHONHASHSEED=0. If you use a different value, or do not set this environment variable, your score values may differ.

See also

The previous recipe, *Training a tagger-based chunker*, introduced the idea of using a part-of-speech tagger for training a chunker. The *Classifier-based tagging* recipe in *Chapter 4, Part-of-speech Tagging*, describes `ClassifierBasedPOSTagger`, which is a subclass of `ClassifierBasedTagger`. And in *Chapter 7, Text Classification*, we'll cover classification in detail.

Extracting named entities

Named entity recognition is a specific kind of chunk extraction that uses entity tags of, or in addition to, chunk tags. Common entity tags include PERSON, ORGANIZA LOCATION. Part-of-speech tagged sentences are parsed into chunk trees as with no chunking, but the labels of the trees can be entity tags instead of chunk phrase tags.

How to do it...

NLTK comes with a pre-trained named entity chunker. This chunker has been trained on data from the ACE program, **National Institute of Standards and Technology (NIST)** sponsored program for **Automatic Content Extraction**, which you can read more about at http://www.itl.nist.gov/iad/894.01/tests/ace/. Unfortunately, this data is not included in the NLTK corpora, but the trained chunker is. This chunker can be used through the ne_chunk() method in the nltk.chunk module. The ne_chunk() method will chunk a single sentence into a Tree. The following is an example using ne_chunk() on the first tagged sentence of the treebank_chunk corpus:

```
>>> from nltk.chunk import ne_chunk
>>> ne_chunk(treebank_chunk.tagged_sents()[0])
Tree('S', [Tree('PERSON', [('Pierre', 'NNP')]), Tree('ORGANIZATION',
[('Vinken', 'NNP')]), (',', ','), ('61', 'CD'), ('years', 'NNS'),
('old', 'JJ'), (',', ','), ('will', 'MD'), ('join', 'VB'), ('the',
'DT'), ('board', 'NN'), ('as', 'IN'), ('a', 'DT'), ('nonexecutive',
'JJ'), ('director', 'NN'), ('Nov.', 'NNP'), ('29', 'CD'), ('.', '.')])
```

You can see that two entity tags are found: PERSON and ORGANIZATION. Each of these subtrees contains a list of the words that are recognized as a PERSON or ORGANIZATION. To extract these named entities, we can write a simple helper method that will get the leaves of all the subtrees we are interested in:

```
def sub_leaves(tree, label):
  return [t.leaves() for t in tree.subtrees(lambda s: label() ==
label)]
```

Then, we can call this method to get all the PERSON or ORGANIZATION leaves from a tree:

```
>>> tree = ne_chunk(treebank_chunk.tagged_sents()[0])
>>> from chunkers import sub_leaves
>>> sub_leaves(tree, 'PERSON')
[[('Pierre', 'NNP')]]
>>> sub_leaves(tree, 'ORGANIZATION')
[[('Vinken', 'NNP')]]
```

You will notice that the chunker has mistakenly separated Vinken into its own ORGANIZATION Tree instead of including it with the PERSON Tree containing Pierre. Such is the case with statistical natural language processing—you can't always expect perfection.

How it works...

The pre-trained named entity chunker is much like any other chunker, and in fact uses a `MaxentClassifier` powered `ClassifierBasedTagger` to determine IOB tags. But instead of `B-NP` and `I-NP` IOB tags, it uses `B-PERSON`, `I-PERSON`, `B-ORGANIZATION`, `I-ORGANIZATION`, and more. It also uses the `O` tag to mark words that are not part of a named entity (and thus are *outside* the named entity subtrees).

There's more...

To process multiple sentences at a time, you can use `chunk_ne_sents()`. Here's an example where we process the first 10 sentences from `treebank_chunk.tagged_sents()` and get `ORGANIZATION` `sub_leaves()`:

```
>>> from nltk.chunk import chunk_ne_sents
>>> trees = chunk_ne_sents(treebank_chunk.tagged_sents()[:10])
>>> [sub_leaves(t, 'ORGANIZATION') for t in trees]
[[[('Vinken', 'NNP')]], [[('Elsevier', 'NNP')]], [[('Consolidated',
'NNP'), ('Gold', 'NNP'), ('Fields', 'NNP')]], [], [], [[('Inc.',
'NNP')]], [[('Micronite', 'NN')]], [[('New', 'NNP'), ('England', 'NNP'),
('Journal', 'NNP')]], [[('Lorillard', 'NNP')]], [], []]
```

You can see that there are a couple of multiword `ORGANIZATION` chunks, such as `New England Journal`. There were also a few sentences that had no `ORGANIZATION` chunks, as indicated by the empty lists `[]`.

Binary named entity extraction

If you don't care about the particular kind of named entity to extract, you can pass `binary=True` into `ne_chunk()` or `chunk_ne_sents()`. Now, all named entities will be tagged with `NE`:

```
>>> ne_chunk(treebank_chunk.tagged_sents()[0], binary=True)
Tree('S', [Tree('NE', [('Pierre', 'NNP'), ('Vinken', 'NNP')]), (',',
','), ('61', 'CD'), ('years', 'NNS'), ('old', 'JJ'), (',', ','),
('will', 'MD'), ('join', 'VB'), ('the', 'DT'), ('board', 'NN'),
('as', 'IN'), ('a', 'DT'), ('nonexecutive', 'JJ'), ('director', 'NN'),
('Nov.', 'NNP'), ('29', 'CD'), ('.', '.')])
```

So, `binary` in this case means that an arbitrary chunk either is or is not a named entity. If we get the `sub_leaves()`, we can see that `Pierre Vinken` is correctly combined into a single named entity:

```
>>> subleaves(ne_chunk(treebank_chunk.tagged_sents()[0], binary=True),
'NE')
[[('Pierre', 'NNP'), ('Vinken', 'NNP')]]
```

See also

In the next recipe, we'll create our own simple named entity chunker.

Extracting proper noun chunks

A simple way to do named entity extraction is to chunk all proper nouns (tagged with NNP). We can tag these chunks as NAME, since the definition of a proper noun is the name of a person, place, or thing.

How to do it...

Using the RegexpParser class, we can create a very simple grammar that combines all proper nouns into a NAME chunk. Then, we can test this on the first tagged sentence of treebank_chunk to compare the results with the previous recipe:

```
>>> chunker = RegexpParser(r'''
... NAME:
...     {<NNP>+}
... ''')
>>> sub_leaves(chunker.parse(treebank_chunk.tagged_sents()[0]),
'NAME')
[[('Pierre', 'NNP'), ('Vinken', 'NNP')], [('Nov.', 'NNP')]]
```

Although we get Nov. as a NAME chunk, this isn't a wrong result, as Nov. is the name of a month.

How it works...

The NAME chunker is a simple usage of the RegexpParser class, covered in the *Chunking and chinking with regular expressions, Merging and splitting chunks with regular expressions,* and *Partial parsing with regular expressions* recipes. All sequences of NNP tagged words are combined into NAME chunks.

There's more...

If we wanted to be sure to only chunk the names of people, then we can build a PersonChunker class that uses the names corpus for chunking. This class can be found in chunkers.py:

```
from nltk.chunk import ChunkParserI
from nltk.chunk.util import conlltags2tree
from nltk.corpus import names
```

```
class PersonChunker(ChunkParserI):
  def __init__(self):
    self.name_set = set(names.words())

  def parse(self, tagged_sent):
    iobs = []
    in_person = False

    for word, tag in tagged_sent:
      if word in self.name_set and in_person:
        iobs.append((word, tag, 'I-PERSON'))
      elif word in self.name_set:
        iobs.append((word, tag, 'B-PERSON'))
        in_person = True
      else:
        iobs.append((word, tag, 'O'))
        in_person = False


    return conlltags2tree(iobs)
```

The `PersonChunker` class iterates over the tagged sentence, checking whether each word is in its `names_set` (constructed from the `names` corpus). If the current word is in the `names_set`, then it uses either the `B-PERSON` or `I-PERSON` IOB tags, depending on whether the previous word was also in the `names_set`. Any word that's not in the `names_set` argument gets the `O` IOB tag. When complete, the list of IOB tags is converted to a `Tree` using `conlltags2tree()`. Using it on the same tagged sentence as before, we get the following result:

```
>>> from chunkers import PersonChunker
>>> chunker = PersonChunker()
>>> sub_leaves(chunker.parse(treebank_chunk.tagged_sents()[0]),
'PERSON')
[[('Pierre', 'NNP')]]
```

We no longer get `Nov.`, but we've also lost `Vinken`, as it is not found in the `names` corpus. This recipe highlights some of the difficulties of chunk extraction and natural language processing in general:

- ▶ If you use general patterns, you'll get general results
- ▶ If you're looking for specific results, you must use specific data
- ▶ If your specific data is incomplete, your results will be incomplete too

See also

The previous recipe defines the `sub_leaves()` function used to show the found chunks. In the next recipe, we'll cover how to find LOCATION chunks based on the `gazetteers` corpus.

Extracting location chunks

To identify LOCATION chunks, we can make a different kind of `ChunkParserI` subclass that uses the `gazetteers` corpus to identify location words. The `gazetteers` corpus is a `WordListCorpusReader` class that contains the following location words:

- ▶ Country names
- ▶ U.S. states and abbreviations
- ▶ Major U.S. cities
- ▶ Canadian provinces
- ▶ Mexican states

How to do it...

The `LocationChunker` class, found in `chunkers.py`, iterates over a tagged sentence looking for words that are found in the `gazetteers` corpus. When it finds one or more location words, it creates a LOCATION chunk using IOB tags. The helper method `iob_locations()` is where the IOB LOCATION tags are produced, and the `parse()` method converts these IOB tags into a `Tree`:

```
from nltk.chunk import ChunkParserI
from nltk.chunk.util import conlltags2tree
from nltk.corpus import gazetteers

class LocationChunker(ChunkParserI):
  def __init__(self):
    self.locations = set(gazetteers.words())
    self.lookahead = 0

    for loc in self.locations:
      nwords = loc.count(' ')

      if nwords > self.lookahead:
        self.lookahead = nwords
```

```
def iob_locations(self, tagged_sent):
  i = 0
  l = len(tagged_sent)
  inside = False

  while i < l:
    word, tag = tagged_sent[i]
    j = i + 1
    k = j + self.lookahead
    nextwords, nexttags = [], []
    loc = False

    while j < k:
      if ' '.join([word] + nextwords) in self.locations:
        if inside:
          yield word, tag, 'I-LOCATION'
        else:
          yield word, tag, 'B-LOCATION'

        for nword, ntag in zip(nextwords, nexttags):
          yield nword, ntag, 'I-LOCATION'

        loc, inside = True, True
        i = j
        break

      if j < l:
        nextword, nexttag = tagged_sent[j]
        nextwords.append(nextword)
        nexttags.append(nexttag)
        j += 1
      else:
        break

    if not loc:
      inside = False
      i += 1
      yield word, tag, 'O'

def parse(self, tagged_sent):
  iobs = self.iob_locations(tagged_sent)
  return conlltags2tree(iobs)
```

We can use the `LocationChunker` class to parse the following sentence into two locations—San Francisco CA is cold compared to San Jose CA:

```
>>> from chunkers import LocationChunker
>>> t = loc.parse([('San', 'NNP'), ('Francisco', 'NNP'), ('CA',
'NNP'), ('is', 'BE'), ('cold', 'JJ'), ('compared', 'VBD'), ('to',
'TO'), ('San', 'NNP'), ('Jose', 'NNP'), ('CA', 'NNP')])
>>> sub_leaves(t, 'LOCATION')
[[('San', 'NNP'), ('Francisco', 'NNP'), ('CA', 'NNP')], [('San',
'NNP'), ('Jose', 'NNP'), ('CA', 'NNP')]]
```

And the result is that we get two LOCATION chunks, just as expected.

How it works...

The `LocationChunker` class starts by constructing a set of all locations in the gazetteers corpus. Then, it finds the maximum number of words in a single location string so it knows how many words it must look ahead when parsing a tagged sentence.

The `parse()` method calls a helper method, `iob_locations()`, which generates 3-tuples of the form (`word, pos, iob`), where iob is either O if the word is not a location, or B-LOCATION or I-LOCATION for LOCATION chunks. The `iob_locations()` method finds location chunks by looking at the current word and the next words to check if the combined word is in the locations set. Multiple location words that are next to each other are then put into the same LOCATION chunk, such as in the previous example with San Francisco and CA.

Like in the previous recipe, it's simpler and more convenient to construct a list of (`word, pos, iob`) tuples to pass into `conlltags2tree()` to return a `Tree`. The alternative is to construct a `Tree` manually, but that requires keeping track of children, subtrees, and where you currently are in the `Tree`.

There's more...

One of the nice aspects of this `LocationChunker` class is that it doesn't care about the part-of-speech tags. As long as the location words are found in the location's set, any part-of-speech tag will do.

See also

In the next recipe, we'll cover how to train a named entity chunker using the `ieer` corpus.

Training a named entity chunker

You can train your own named entity chunker using the `ieer` corpus, which stands for **Information Extraction: Entity Recognition**. It takes a bit of extra work, though, because the `ieer` corpus has chunk trees but no part-of-speech tags for words.

How to do it...

Using the `ieertree2conlltags()` and `ieer_chunked_sents()` functions in `chunkers.py`, we can create named entity chunk trees from the `ieer` corpus to train the `ClassifierChunker` class created in the *Classification-based chunking* recipe:

```python
import nltk.tag
from nltk.chunk.util import conlltags2tree
from nltk.corpus import ieer

def ieertree2conlltags(tree, tag=nltk.tag.pos_tag):
  words, ents = zip(*tree.pos())
  iobs = []
  prev = None

  for ent in ents:
    if ent == tree.label():
      iobs.append('O')
      prev = None
    elif prev == ent:
      iobs.append('I-%s' % ent)
    else:
      iobs.append('B-%s' % ent)
      prev = ent

  words, tags = zip(*tag(words))
  return zip(words, tags, iobs)

def ieer_chunked_sents(tag=nltk.tag.pos_tag):
  for doc in ieer.parsed_docs():
    tagged = ieertree2conlltags(doc.text, tag)
    yield conlltags2tree(tagged)
```

We'll use 80 out of 94 sentences for training, and the rest for testing. Then, we can see how it does on the first sentence of the `treebank_chunk` corpus:

```
>>> from chunkers import ieer_chunked_sents, ClassifierChunker
>>> from nltk.corpus import treebank_chunk
>>> ieer_chunks = list(ieer_chunked_sents())
>>> len(ieer_chunks)
94
>>> chunker = ClassifierChunker(ieer_chunks[:80])
>>> chunker.parse(treebank_chunk.tagged_sents()[0])
Tree('S', [Tree('LOCATION', [('Pierre', 'NNP'), ('Vinken', 'NNP')]),
(',', ','), Tree('DURATION', [('61', 'CD'), ('years', 'NNS')]),
Tree('MEASURE', [('old', 'JJ')]), (',', ','), ('will', 'MD'), ('join',
'VB'), ('the', 'DT'), ('board', 'NN'), ('as', 'IN'), ('a', 'DT'),
('nonexecutive', 'JJ'), ('director', 'NN'), Tree('DATE', [('Nov.',
'NNP'), ('29', 'CD')]), ('.', '.')])
```

So, it found a correct DURATION and DATE, but tagged `Pierre Vinken` as a LOCATION. Let's see how it scores against the rest of the `ieer` chunk trees:

```
>>> score = chunker.evaluate(ieer_chunks[80:])
>>> score.accuracy()
0.8829018388070625
>>> score.precision()
0.4088717454194793
>>> score.recall()
0.5053635280095352
```

Accuracy is pretty good, but precision and recall are very low. That means lots of false negatives and false positives.

How it works...

The truth is, we're not working with ideal training data. The `ieer` trees generated by `ieer_chunked_sents()` are not entirely accurate. First, there are no explicit sentence breaks, so each document is a single tree. Second, the words are not explicitly tagged, so we have to guess using `nltk.tag.pos_tag()`.

The `ieer` corpus provides a `parsed_docs()` method that returns a list of documents with a `text` attribute. This `text` attribute is a document `Tree` that is converted to a list of 3-tuples of the form (`word, pos, iob`). To get these final 3-tuples, we must first flatten the `Tree` using `tree.pos()`, which returns a list of 2-tuples of the form (`word, entity`), where `entity` is either the entity tag or the top tag of the tree. Any words whose entity is the top tag are outside the named entity chunks and get the IOB tag `O`. All words that have unique entity tags are either the beginning of or inside a named entity chunk. Once we have all the IOB tags, then we can get the part-of-speech tags of all the words and join the words, part-of-speech tags, and IOB tags into 3-tuples using `zip()`.

There's more...

Despite the non-ideal training data, the `ieer` corpus provides a good place to start for training a named entity chunker. The data comes from *New York Times* and *AP Newswire* reports. Each doc from `ieer.parsed_docs()` also contains a headline attribute that is a `Tree`:

```
>>> from nltk.corpus import ieer
>>> ieer.parsed_docs()[0].headline
Tree('DOCUMENT', ['Kenyans', 'protest', 'tax', 'hikes'])
```

See also

The *Extracting named entities* recipe covers the pre-trained named entity chunker that comes included with NLTK.

Training a chunker with NLTK-Trainer

At the end of the previous chapter, *Chapter 4, Part-of-speech Tagging*, we introduced NLTK-Trainer and the `train_tagger.py` script. In this recipe, we will cover the script for training chunkers: `train_chunker.py`.

 You can find NLTK-Trainer at `https://github.com/japerk/nltk-trainer` and the online documentation at `http://nltk-trainer.readthedocs.org/`.

How to do it...

As with `train_tagger.py`, the only required argument to `train_chunker.py` is the name of a corpus. In this case, we need a corpus that provides a `chunked_sents()` method, such as `treebank_chunk`. Here's an example of running `train_chunker.py` on `treebank_chunk`:

```
$ python train_chunker.py treebank_chunk
loading treebank_chunk
4009 chunks, training on 4009
training ub TagChunker
evaluating TagChunker
ChunkParse score:
    IOB Accuracy:    97.0%
    Precision:       90.8%
    Recall:          93.9%
    F-Measure:       92.3%
dumping TagChunker to /Users/jacob/nltk_data/chunkers/treebank_chunk_
ub.pickle
```

Just like with `train_tagger.py`, we can use the `--no-pickle` argument to skip saving a pickled chunker, and the `--fraction` argument to limit the training set and evaluate the chunker against a test set:

```
$ python train_chunker.py treebank_chunk --no-pickle --fraction 0.75
loading treebank_chunk
4009 chunks, training on 3007
training ub TagChunker
evaluating TagChunker
ChunkParse score:
    IOB Accuracy:    97.3%
    Precision:       91.6%
    Recall:          94.6%
    F-Measure:       93.1%
```

The score output you see is what you get when you print a `ChunkScore` object. This `ChunkScore` is the result of calling the chunker's `evaluate()` method, and has been explained in more detail earlier in this chapter in the *Partial parsing with regular expressions* recipe. Surprisingly, the chunker's scores actually increase slightly when using a smaller training set. This may indicate that the chunker training algorithm is susceptible to over-fitting, meaning that too many training examples can cause the chunker to over-value incorrect or noisy data.

The PYTHONHASHSEED environment variable has been omitted for clarity. This means that when you run `train_chunker.py`, your score values may vary. To get consistent score values, run `train_chunker.py` like this:

```
$ PYTHONHASHSEED=0 python train_chunker.py treebank_chunk ...
```

How it works...

The default training algorithm for `train_chunker.py` is to use a tagger-based chunker composed of a `BigramTagger` and `UnigramTagger` class. This is what is meant by the output line `training ub TagChunker`. The details for how to train a tag chunker have been covered earlier in this chapter in the *Training a tagger-based chunker* recipe. You can modify this algorithm using the `--sequential` argument. Here's how to train a `UnigramTagger` based chunker:

```
$ python train_chunker.py treebank_chunk --no-pickle --fraction 0.75
--sequential u
loading treebank_chunk
4009 chunks, training on 3007
training u TagChunker
evaluating TagChunker
```

```
ChunkParse score:
    IOB Accuracy:    96.7%
    Precision:       89.7%
    Recall:          93.1%
    F-Measure:       91.3%
```

And here's how to twith additional BigramTagger and TrigramTagger classes:

```
$ python train_chunker.py treebank_chunk --no-pickle --fraction 0.75
--sequential ubt
loading treebank_chunk
4009 chunks, training on 3007
training ubt TagChunker
evaluating TagChunker
ChunkParse score:
    IOB Accuracy:    97.2%
    Precision:       91.6%
    Recall:          94.4%
    F-Measure:       93.0%
```

You can also train a classifier-based chunker, which was covered in the previous recipe, *Classification-based chunking*.

```
$ python train_chunker.py treebank_chunk --no-pickle --fraction 0.75
--sequential '' --classifier NaiveBayes
loading treebank_chunk
4009 chunks, training on 3007
training ClassifierChunker with ['NaiveBayes'] classifier
Constructing training corpus for classifier.
Training classifier (71088 instances)
training NaiveBayes classifier
evaluating ClassifierChunker
ChunkParse score:
    IOB Accuracy:    97.2%
    Precision:       92.6%
    Recall:          93.6%
    F-Measure:       93.1%
```

There's more...

The `train_chunker.py` script supports many other arguments not shown here, all of which you can see by running the script with `--help`. A few additional arguments are presented next, followed by an introduction to two other chunking-related scripts available in `nltk-trainer`.

Saving a pickled chunker

Without the `--no-pickle` argument, `train_chunker.py` will save a pickled chunker at `~/nltk_data/chunkers/NAME.pickle`, where `NAME` is a combination of the corpus name and training algorithm. You can specify a custom filename for your chunker using the `--filename` argument like this:

```
$ python train_chunker.py treebank_chunker --filename path/to/
tagger.pickle
```

Training a named entity chunker

We can use `train_chunker.py` to replicate the chunker we trained on the `ieer` corpus in the *Training a named entity chunker* recipe. This is possible because the special handling required for training on `ieer` is built-in to NLTK-Trainer.

```
$ python train_chunker.py ieer --no-pickle --fraction 0.85 --sequential
'' --classifier NaiveBayes
loading ieer
converting ieer parsed docs to chunked sentences
94 chunks, training on 80
training ClassifierChunker with ['NaiveBayes'] classifier
Constructing training corpus for classifier.
Training classifier (47000 instances)
training NaiveBayes classifier
evaluating ClassifierChunker
ChunkParse score:
    IOB Accuracy:    88.3%
    Precision:       40.9%
    Recall:          50.5%
    F-Measure:       45.2%
```

Training on a custom corpus

If you have a custom corpus that you want to use for training a chunker, you can do that by passing in the path to the corpus and the classname of a corpus reader in the `--reader` argument. The corpus path can either be absolute or relative to a `nltk_data` directory. The corpus reader class must provide a `chunked_sents()` method. Here's an example using a relative path to the `treebank` chunked corpus:

```
$ python train_chunker.py corpora/treebank/tagged --reader nltk.corpus.
reader.ChunkedCorpusReader --no-pickle --fraction 0.75
loading corpora/treebank/tagged
51002 chunks, training on 38252
training ub TagChunker
evaluating TagChunker
ChunkParse score:
```

```
IOB Accuracy:    98.4%
Precision:       97.7%
Recall:          98.9%
F-Measure:       98.3%
```

Training on parse trees

The `train_chunker.py` script supports two arguments that allow it to train on full parse trees from a corpus reader's `parsed_sents()` method instead of using chunked sentences. A parse tree differs from a chunk tree in that it can be much deeper, with subphrases and even subphrases of those subphrases. But the chunking algorithms we've covered so far cannot learn from deep parse trees, so we need to flatten them somehow. The first argument is `--flatten-deep-tree`, which trains chunks from the leaf labels of a parse tree.

```
$ python train_chunker.py treebank --no-pickle --fraction 0.75 --flatten-
deep-tree
loading treebank
flattening deep trees from treebank
3914 chunks, training on 2936
training ub TagChunker
evaluating TagChunker
ChunkParse score:
     IOB Accuracy:    72.4%
     Precision:       51.6%
     Recall:          52.2%
     F-Measure:       51.9%
```

We use the `treebank` corpus instead of `treebank_chunk`, because it has full parse trees accessible with the `parsed_sents()` method. The other parse tree argument is `--shallow-tree`, which trains chunks from the top-level labels of a parse tree.

```
$ python train_chunker.py treebank --no-pickle --fraction 0.75 --shallow-
tree
loading treebank
creating shallow trees from treebank
3914 chunks, training on 2936
training ub TagChunker
evaluating TagChunker
ChunkParse score:
     IOB Accuracy:    73.1%
     Precision:       60.0%
     Recall:          56.2%
     F-Measure:       58.0%
```

These options are more useful for corpora that don't provide chunked sentences, such as `cess_cat` and `cess_esp`.

Analyzing a chunker against a chunked corpus

So how do you know how well a chunker will perform on a different corpus that you didn't train it on? The `analyze_chunker_coverage.py` script gives you a simple way to test the performance of a chunker against another chunked corpus. Here's how to test NLTK's built-in chunker against the `treebank_chunk` corpus:

```
$ python analyze_chunker_coverage.py treebank_chunk --score
loading tagger taggers/maxent_treebank_pos_tagger/english.pickle
loading chunker chunkers/maxent_ne_chunker/english_ace_multiclass.pickle
evaluating chunker score

ChunkParse     score:
    IOB Accuracy:   45.4%
    Precision:      0.0%
    Recall:         0.0%
    F-Measure:      0.0%

analyzing chunker coverage of treebank_chunk with NEChunkParser
```

IOB	Found
FACILITY	56
GPE	1874
GSP	38
LOCATION	34
ORGANIZATION	1572
PERSON	2108

As you can see, NLTK's default chunker does not do well against the `treebank_chunk` corpus. This is because the default chunker is looking for named entities, not `NP` phrases. This is shown by the coverage analysis of IOB tags that were found. These results do not necessarily mean that the default chunker is bad, just that it was not trained for finding noun phrases, and thus cannot be accurately evaluated against the `treebank_chunk` corpus.

While the `analyze_chunker_coverage.py` script defaults to using NLTK's built-in tagger and chunker, you can evaluate on your own tagger and/or chunker using the `--tagger` and/or `--chunker` arguments, both of which accept a path to a pickled tagger or chunker. Consider the following code:

```
$ python train_chunker.py treebank_chunker --tagger path/to/tagger.pickle
--chunker path/to/chunker.pickle
```

You can also use a custom corpus just like we did earlier with `train_chunker.py`; however, if your corpus is not chunked, then you must omit the `--score` argument, because you have nothing to compare the results to. In that case, you will only get IOB tag counts with no scores, because there are no chunks to compare to.

Analyzing a chunked corpus

Finally, there is a script called `analyze_chunked_corpus.py`, which as the name implies, will read in a chunked corpus and print out stats about the number of words and tags. You can run it like this:

```
$ python analyze_chunked_corpus.py treebank_chunk
```

The results are very similar to `analyze_tagged_corpus.py`, with additional columns for each IOB tag. Each IOB tag column shows the counts for each part-of-speech tag that was present in chunks for that IOB tag. For example, NN words (nouns) may occur 300 times in total, and for 280 of those times, the NN words occurred with a NP IOB tag, meaning that most nouns occur within noun phrases.

As with the other commands, you can pass in a custom corpus path and reader to analyze your own chunked corpus.

See also

- The *Training a tagger-based chunker*, the *Classification-based chunking*, and the *Training a named entity chunker* recipes cover many of the ideas that went into the `train_chunker.py` script
- In *Chapter 4, Part-of-speech Tagging*, we showed how to use NLTK-Trainer for training a tagger in the *Training a tagger with NLTK-Trainer* recipe

6
Transforming Chunks and Trees

In this chapter, we will cover the following recipes:

▸ Filtering insignificant words from a sentence
▸ Correcting verb forms
▸ Swapping verb phrases
▸ Swapping noun cardinals
▸ Swapping infinitive phrases
▸ Singularizing plural nouns
▸ Chaining chunk transformations
▸ Converting a chunk tree to text
▸ Flattening a deep tree
▸ Creating a shallow tree
▸ Converting tree labels

Introduction

Now that you know how to get chunks/phrases from a sentence, what do you do with them? This chapter will show you how to do various transforms on both chunks and trees. The **chunk transforms** are for grammatical correction and rearranging phrases without loss of meaning. The **tree transforms** give you ways to modify and flatten deep parse trees. The functions detailed in these recipes modify data, as opposed to learning from it. This means it's not safe to apply them indiscriminately. A thorough knowledge of the data you want to transform, along with a few experiments, should help you decide which functions to apply and when.

Whenever the term **chunk** is used in this chapter, it could refer to an actual chunk extracted by a chunker, or it could simply refer to a short phrase or sentence in the form of a list of tagged words. What's important in this chapter is what you can do with a chunk, not where it came from.

Filtering insignificant words from a sentence

Many of the most commonly used words are insignificant when it comes to discerning the meaning of a phrase. For example, in the phrase *the movie was terrible*, the most **significant** words are *movie* and *terrible*, while *the* and *was* are almost useless. You could get the same meaning if you took them out, that is, *movie terrible* or *terrible movie*. Either way, the sentiment is the same. In this recipe, we'll learn how to remove the insignificant words and keep the significant ones by looking at their part-of-speech tags.

Getting ready

First, we need to decide which part-of-speech tags are significant and which are not. Looking through the `treebank` corpus for stopwords yields the following table of insignificant words and tags:

Word	Tag
a	DT
all	PDT
an	DT
and	CC
or	CC
that	WDT
the	DT

Other than CC, all the tags end with DT. This means we can filter out insignificant words by looking at the tag's suffix. Refer to *Appendix, Penn Treebank Part-of-speech Tags*, for details on tag meanings.

How to do it...

In `transforms.py` is a function called `filter_insignificant()`. It takes a single chunk, which should be a list of tagged words, and returns a new chunk without any insignificant tagged words. It defaults to filtering out any tags that end with DT or CC:

```
def filter_insignificant(chunk, tag_suffixes=['DT', 'CC']):
    good = []
```

```
for word, tag in chunk:
  ok = True

  for suffix in tag_suffixes:
    if tag.endswith(suffix):
      ok = False
      break

  if ok:
    good.append((word, tag))

return good
```

And now we can use it on the part-of-speech tagged version of *the terrible movie*:

```
>>> from transforms import filter_insignificant
>>> filter_insignificant([('the', 'DT'), ('terrible', 'JJ'),
('movie', 'NN')])
[('terrible', 'JJ'), ('movie', 'NN')]
```

As you can see, the word `the` is eliminated from the chunk.

How it works...

The `filter_insignificant()` function iterates over the tagged words in the chunk. For each tag, it checks whether that tag ends with any of the `tag_suffixes`. If it does, then the tagged word is skipped. But if the tag is ok, then the tagged word is appended to a new good chunk that is returned.

There's more...

The way `filter_insignificant()` is defined, you can pass in your own tag suffixes if DT and CC are not enough, or are incorrect for your case. For example, you might decide that possessive words and pronouns such as *you*, *your*, *their*, and *theirs* are no good, but DT and CC words are ok. The tag suffixes would then be PRP and PRP$:

```
>>> filter_insignificant([('your', 'PRP$'), ('book', 'NN'), ('is',
'VBZ'), ('great', 'JJ')], tag_suffixes=['PRP', 'PRP$'])
[('book', 'NN'), ('is', 'VBZ'), ('great', 'JJ')]
```

Filtering insignificant words can be a good complement to stopword filtering for purposes such as search engine indexing and querying and text classification.

This recipe is analogous to the *Filtering stopwords in a tokenized sentence* recipe in Chapter 1, *Tokenizing Text and WordNet Basics*.

Correcting verb forms

It's fairly common to find incorrect verb forms in real-world language. For example, the correct form of *is our children learning?* is *are our children learning?* The verb *is* should only be used with singular nouns, while *are* is for plural nouns, such as *children*. We can correct these mistakes by creating verb correction mappings that are used depending on whether there's a plural or singular noun in the chunk.

Getting ready

We first need to define the verb correction mappings in `transforms.py`. We'll create two mappings, one for plural to singular and another for singular to plural:

```
plural_verb_forms = {
  ('is', 'VBZ'): ('are', 'VBP'),
  ('was', 'VBD'): ('were', 'VBD')
}

singular_verb_forms = {
  ('are', 'VBP'): ('is', 'VBZ'),
  ('were', 'VBD'): ('was', 'VBD')
}
```

Each mapping has a tagged verb that maps to another tagged verb. These initial mappings cover the basics of mapping **is** to **are**, **was** to **were**, and vice versa.

How to do it...

In `transforms.py` is a function called `correct_verbs()`. Pass it a chunk with incorrect verb forms and you'll get a corrected chunk back. It uses a helper function, `first_chunk_index()`, to search the chunk for the position of the first tagged word where `pred` returns `True`. The `pred` argument should be a callable function that takes a `(word, tag)` tuple and returns `True` or `False`. Here's `first_chunk_index()`:

```
def first_chunk_index(chunk, pred, start=0, step=1):
  l = len(chunk)
  end = l if step > 0 else -1
```

```
for i in range(start, end, step):
    if pred(chunk[i]):
        return i

return None
```

For `first_chunk_index()` to be useful, we need to use a predicate function. In the case of `correct_verbs()`, the predicate function we need should return `True` if the tag in the (`word, tag`) argument starts with a given tag prefix, and `False` otherwise.

```
def tag_startswith(prefix):
    def f(wt):
        return wt[1].startswith(prefix)
    return f
```

The `tag_startswith()` function takes a tag prefix, such as `NN`, and returns a predicate function that will take a (`word, tag`) tuple and return `True` if the tag starts with the given prefix. A function that returns another function is called a **higher order function**. This is not as complicated as it might sound—just as you can use a function to generate and return new variables and values, some programming languages (such as Python) let you generate functions inside of other functions. In this case, we want a function that takes a single argument: (`word, tag`). But we also want this function to have access to a prefix variable. Since we cannot add arguments to the function definition, we instead generate a higher order function that has access to the prefix variable, while preserving the single (`word, tag`) argument.

Now that we have defined `first_chunk_index()` and `tag_startswith()`, we can actually implement `correct_verbs()`. This may seem like overkill for a single function, but we will be using `first_chunk_index()` and `tag_startswith()` in subsequent recipes.

```
def correct_verbs(chunk):
    vbidx = first_chunk_index(chunk, tag_startswith('VB'))
    # if no verb found, do nothing
    if vbidx is None:
        return chunk

    verb, vbtag = chunk[vbidx]
    nnpred = tag_startswith('NN')
    # find nearest noun to the right of verb
    nnidx = first_chunk_index(chunk, nnpred, start=vbidx+1)
    # if no noun found to right, look to the left
    if nnidx is None:
        nnidx = first_chunk_index(chunk, nnpred, start=vbidx-1, step=-1)
    # if no noun found, do nothing
    if nnidx is None:
        return chunk
```

```
    noun, nntag = chunk[nnidx]
    # get correct verb form and insert into chunk
    if nntag.endswith('S'):
      chunk[vbidx] = plural_verb_forms.get((verb, vbtag), (verb, vbtag))
    else:
      chunk[vbidx] = singular_verb_forms.get((verb, vbtag), (verb,
vbtag))

  return chunk
```

When we call the preceding function on a part-of-speech tagged `is our children learning` chunk, we get back the correct form, `are our children learning`.

```
>>> from transforms import correct_verbs
>>> correct_verbs([('is', 'VBZ'), ('our', 'PRP$'), ('children',
'NNS'), ('learning', 'VBG')])
[('are', 'VBP'), ('our', 'PRP$'), ('children', 'NNS'), ('learning',
'VBG')]
```

We can also try this with a *singular noun* and an incorrect *plural verb*:

```
>>> correct_verbs([('our', 'PRP$'), ('child', 'NN'), ('were', 'VBD'),
('learning', 'VBG')])
[('our', 'PRP$'), ('child', 'NN'), ('was', 'VBD'), ('learning',
'VBG')]
```

In this case, `were` becomes `was` because `child` is a singular noun.

How it works...

The `correct_verbs()` function starts by looking for a verb in the chunk. If no verb is found, the chunk is returned with no changes. Once a verb is found, we keep the verb, its tag, and its index in the chunk. Then, we look on either side of the verb to find the nearest noun, starting on the right and looking to the left only if no noun is found on the right. If no noun is found at all, the chunk is returned as is. But if a noun is found, then we look up the correct verb form depending on whether or not the noun is plural.

Recall from *Chapter 4*, *Part-of-speech Tagging*, that plural nouns are tagged with NNS, while singular nouns are tagged with NN. That means we can check the plurality of a noun by looking to see whether its tag ends with S. Once we get the corrected verb form, it is inserted into the chunk to replace the original verb form.

See also

The next four recipes all make use of `first_chunk_index()` to perform chunk transformations.

Swapping verb phrases

Swapping the words around a verb can eliminate the passive voice from particular phrases. For example, the book was great can be transformed into the great book. This kind of normalization can also help with frequency analysis, by counting two apparently different phrases as the same phrase.

How to do it...

In transforms.py is a function called swap_verb_phrase(). It swaps the right-hand side of the chunk with the left-hand side, using the verb as the **pivot point**. It uses the first_chunk_index() function defined in the previous recipe to find the verb to pivot around.

```
def swap_verb_phrase(chunk):
  def vbpred(wt):
    word, tag = wt
    return tag != 'VBG' and tag.startswith('VB') and len(tag) > 2

  vbidx = first_chunk_index(chunk, vbpred)

  if vbidx is None:
    return chunk

  return chunk[vbidx+1:] + chunk[:vbidx]
```

Now we can see how it works on the part-of-speech tagged phrase the book was great:

```
>>> swap_verb_phrase([('the', 'DT'), ('book', 'NN'), ('was', 'VBD'),
('great', 'JJ')])
[('great', 'JJ'), ('the', 'DT'), ('book', 'NN')]
```

And the result is great the book. This phrase clearly isn't grammatically correct, so read on to learn how to fix it.

How it works...

Using first_chunk_index() from the previous recipe with the vbpred() function defined inline, we start by finding the first matching verb that is not a gerund (a word that ends in *ing*) tagged with VBG. Once we've found the verb, we return the chunk with the right side before the left, and remove the verb.

The reason we don't want to pivot around a gerund is that gerunds are commonly used to describe nouns, and pivoting around one would remove that description. Here's an example where you can see how not pivoting around a gerund is a good thing:

```
>>> swap_verb_phrase([('this', 'DT'), ('gripping', 'VBG'), ('book',
'NN'), ('is', 'VBZ'), ('fantastic', 'JJ')])
[('fantastic', 'JJ'), ('this', 'DT'), ('gripping', 'VBG'), ('book',
'NN')]
```

If we had pivoted around the gerund, the result would be `book is fantastic this`, and we'd lose the gerund `gripping`.

There's more...

Filtering insignificant words makes the final result more readable. By filtering either before or after `swap_verb_phrase()`, we get `fantastic gripping book` instead of `fantastic this gripping book`:

```
>>> from transforms import swap_verb_phrase, filter_insignificant
>>> swap_verb_phrase(filter_insignificant([('this', 'DT'),
('gripping', 'VBG'), ('book', 'NN'), ('is', 'VBZ'), ('fantastic',
'JJ')]))
[('fantastic', 'JJ'), ('gripping', 'VBG'), ('book', 'NN')]
>>> filter_insignificant(swap_verb_phrase([('this', 'DT'),
('gripping', 'VBG'), ('book', 'NN'), ('is', 'VBZ'), ('fantastic',
'JJ')]))
[('fantastic', 'JJ'), ('gripping', 'VBG'), ('book', 'NN')]
```

Either way, we get a shorter grammatical chunk with no loss of meaning.

See also

The previous recipe, *Correcting verb forms*, defines `first_chunk_index()`, which is used to find the verb in the chunk.

Swapping noun cardinals

In a chunk, a *cardinal* word, tagged as CD, refers to a number, such as *10*. These cardinals often occur before or after a noun. For normalization purposes, it can be useful to always put the cardinal before the noun.

How to do it...

The swap_noun_cardinal() function is defined in transforms.py. It swaps any cardinal that occurs immediately after a noun with the noun so that the cardinal occurs immediately before the noun. It uses a helper function, tag_equals(), which is similar to tag_startswith(), but in this case, the function it returns does an equality comparison with the given tag:

```
def tag_equals(tag):
  def f(wt):
    return wt[1] == tag
  return f
```

Now we can define swap_noun_cardinal():

```
def swap_noun_cardinal(chunk):
  cdidx = first_chunk_index(chunk, tag_equals('CD'))
  # cdidx must be > 0 and there must be a noun immediately before it
  if not cdidx or not chunk[cdidx-1][1].startswith('NN'):
    return chunk

  noun, nntag = chunk[cdidx-1]
  chunk[cdidx-1] = chunk[cdidx]
  chunk[cdidx] = noun, nntag
  return chunk
```

Let's try it on a date, such as Dec 10, and another common phrase, the top 10.

```
>>> swap_noun_cardinal([('Dec.', 'NNP'), ('10', 'CD')])
[('10', 'CD'), ('Dec.', 'NNP')]
>>> swap_noun_cardinal([('the', 'DT'), ('top', 'NN'), ('10', 'CD')])
[('the', 'DT'), ('10', 'CD'), ('top', 'NN')]
```

The result is that the numbers are now in front of the noun, creating 10 Dec and the 10 top.

How it works...

We start by looking for a CD tag in the chunk. If no CD is found, or if the CD is at the beginning of the chunk, then the chunk is returned as is. There must also be a noun immediately before the CD. If we do find a CD with a noun preceding it, then we swap the noun and cardinal.

See also

The *Correcting verb forms* recipe defines the first_chunk_index() function used to find tagged words in a chunk.

Swapping infinitive phrases

An infinitive phrase has the form *A of B*, such as *book of recipes*. These can often be transformed into a new form while retaining the same meaning, such as *recipes book*.

How to do it...

An infinitive phrase can be found by looking for a word tagged with IN. The `swap_infinitive_phrase()` function, defined in `transforms.py`, will return a chunk that swaps the portion of the phrase after the IN word with the portion before the IN word:

```
def swap_infinitive_phrase(chunk):
  def inpred(wt):
    word, tag = wt
    return tag == 'IN' and word != 'like'

  inidx = first_chunk_index(chunk, inpred)

  if inidx is None:
    return chunk

  nnidx = first_chunk_index(chunk, tag_startswith('NN'), start=inidx,
step=-1) or 0
    return chunk[:nnidx] + chunk[inidx+1:] + chunk[nnidx:inidx]
```

The function can now be used to transform `book of recipes` into `recipes book`:

```
>>> from transforms import swap_infinitive_phrase
>>> swap_infinitive_phrase([('book', 'NN'), ('of', 'IN'), ('recipes',
'NNS')])
[('recipes', 'NNS'), ('book', 'NN')]
```

How it works...

This function is similar to the `swap_verb_phrase()` function described in the *Swapping verb phrases* recipe. The `inpred` function is passed to `first_chunk_index()` to look for a word whose tag is IN. Next, we find the first noun that occurs before the IN word, so we can insert the portion of the chunk after the IN word between the noun and the beginning of the chunk. A more complicated example should demonstrate this:

```
>>> swap_infinitive_phrase([('delicious', 'JJ'), ('book', 'NN'),
('of', 'IN'), ('recipes', 'NNS')])
[('delicious', 'JJ'), ('recipes', 'NNS'), ('book', 'NN')]
```

We don't want the result to be `recipes delicious book`. Instead, we want to insert `recipes` before the noun `book` but after the adjective `delicious`, hence the need to find the `nnidx` occurring before the `inidx`.

There's more...

You'll notice that the `inpred` function checks to make sure the word is not `like`. That's because `like` phrases must be treated differently, as transforming them the same way will result in an ungrammatical phrase. For example, `tastes like chicken` should not be transformed into `chicken tastes`.

```
>>> swap_infinitive_phrase([('tastes', 'VBZ'), ('like', 'IN'),
('chicken', 'NN')])
[('tastes', 'VBZ'), ('like', 'IN'), ('chicken', 'NN')]
```

See also

In the next recipe, we'll learn how to transform `recipes book` into the more normal form `recipe book`.

Singularizing plural nouns

As we saw in the previous recipe, the transformation process can result in phrases such as `recipes book`. This is a NNS followed by a NN, when a more proper version of the phrase would be `recipe book`, which is a NN followed by another NN. We can do another transform to correct these improper plural nouns.

How to do it...

The `transforms.py` script defines a function called `singularize_plural_noun()` which will depluralize a plural noun (tagged with NNS) that is followed by another noun:

```
def singularize_plural_noun(chunk):
    nnsidx = first_chunk_index(chunk, tag_equals('NNS'))

    if nnsidx is not None and nnsidx+1 < len(chunk) and chunk[nnsidx+1]
[1][:2] == 'NN':
        noun, nnstag = chunk[nnsidx]
        chunk[nnsidx] = (noun.rstrip('s'), nnstag.rstrip('S'))

    return chunk
```

And using it on `recipes book`, we get the more correct form, `recipe book`.

```
>>> singularize_plural_noun([('recipes', 'NNS'), ('book', 'NN')])
[('recipe', 'NN'), ('book', 'NN')]
```

How it works...

We start by looking for a plural noun with the tag NNS. If found, and if the next word is a noun (determined by making sure the tag starts with NN), then we depluralize the plural noun by removing s from the right side of both the tag and the word. The tag is assumed to be capitalized, so an uppercase S is removed from the right-hand side of the tag, while a lowercase s is removed from the right-hand side of the word.

See also

The previous recipe shows how a transformation can result in a plural noun followed by a singular noun, though this could also occur naturally in real-world text.

Chaining chunk transformations

The transform functions defined in the previous recipes can be chained together to normalize chunks. The resulting chunks are often shorter with no loss of meaning.

How to do it...

In `transforms.py` is the function `transform_chunk()`. It takes a single chunk and an optional list of transform functions. It calls each transform function on the chunk, one at a time, and returns the final chunk:

```
def transform_chunk(chunk, chain=[filter_insignificant, swap_verb_
phrase, swap_infinitive_phrase, singularize_plural_noun], trace=0):
  for f in chain:
    chunk = f(chunk)

    if trace:
      print f.__name__, ':', chunk

  return chunk
```

Using it on the phrase `the book of recipes is delicious`, we get `delicious recipe book`:

```
>>> from transforms import transform_chunk
>>> transform_chunk([('the', 'DT'), ('book', 'NN'), ('of', 'IN'),
('recipes', 'NNS'), ('is', 'VBZ'), ('delicious', 'JJ')])
[('delicious', 'JJ'), ('recipe', 'NN'), ('book', 'NN')]
```

How it works...

The `transform_chunk()` function defaults to chaining the following functions in the given order:

- `filter_insignificant()`
- `swap_verb_phrase()`
- `swap_infinitive_phrase()`
- `singularize_plural_noun()`

Each function transforms the chunk that results from the previous function, starting with the original chunk.

 The order in which you apply transform functions can be significant. Experiment with your own data to determine which transforms are best, and in which order they should be applied.

There's more...

You can pass `trace=1` into `transform_chunk()` to get an output at each step:

```
>>> from transforms import transform_chunk
>>> transform_chunk([('the', 'DT'), ('book', 'NN'), ('of', 'IN'),
('recipes', 'NNS'), ('is', 'VBZ'), ('delicious', 'JJ')], trace=1)
filter_insignificant : [('book', 'NN'), ('of', 'IN'), ('recipes',
'NNS'), ('is', 'VBZ'), ('delicious', 'JJ')]
swap_verb_phrase : [('delicious', 'JJ'), ('book', 'NN'), ('of', 'IN'),
('recipes', 'NNS')]
swap_infinitive_phrase : [('delicious', 'JJ'), ('recipes', 'NNS'),
('book', 'NN')]
singularize_plural_noun : [('delicious', 'JJ'), ('recipe', 'NN'),
('book', 'NN')]
[('delicious', 'JJ'), ('recipe', 'NN'), ('book', 'NN')]
```

This shows you the result of each transform function, which is then passed in to the next transform until a final chunk is returned.

See also

The transform functions used were defined in the previous recipes of this chapter.

Converting a chunk tree to text

At some point, you may want to convert a `Tree` or subtree back to a sentence or chunk string. This is mostly straightforward, except when it comes to properly outputting punctuation.

How to do it...

We'll use the first tree of the `treebank_chunk` corpus as our example. The obvious first step is to join all the words in the tree with a space:

```
>>> from nltk.corpus import treebank_chunk
>>> tree = treebank_chunk.chunked_sents()[0]
>>> ' '.join([w for w, t in tree.leaves()])
'Pierre Vinken , 61 years old , will join the board as a nonexecutive
director Nov. 29 .'
```

But as you can see, the punctuation isn't quite right. The commas and period are treated as individual words, and so get the surrounding spaces as well. But we can fix this using regular expression substitution. This is implemented in the `chunk_tree_to_sent()` function found in `transforms.py`:

```
import re
punct_re = re.compile(r'\s([,\.;\?])')

def chunk_tree_to_sent(tree, concat=' '):
  s = concat.join([w for w, t in tree.leaves()])
  return re.sub(punct_re, r'\g<1>', s)
```

Using `chunk_tree_to_sent()` results in a cleaner sentence, with no space before each punctuation mark:

```
>>> from transforms import chunk_tree_to_sent
>>> chunk_tree_to_sent(tree)
'Pierre Vinken, 61 years old, will join the board as a nonexecutive
director Nov. 29.'
```

How it works...

To correct the extra spaces in front of the punctuation, we create a regular expression, `punct_re`, that will match a space followed by any of the known punctuation characters. We have to escape both `'.'` and `'?'` with a `'\'` since they are special characters. The punctuation is surrounded by parentheses so we can use the matched group for substitution.

Once we have our regular expression, we define `chunk_tree_to_sent()`, whose first step is to join the words by a concatenation character that defaults to a space. Then, we can call `re.sub()` to replace all the punctuation matches with just the punctuation group. This eliminates the space in front of the punctuation characters, resulting in a more correct string.

There's more...

We can simplify this function a little using `nltk.tag.untag()` to get words from the tree's leaves, instead of using our own list comprehension:

```
import nltk.tag, re
punct_re = re.compile(r'\s([,\.;\?])')

def chunk_tree_to_sent(tree, concat=' '):
    s = concat.join(nltk.tag.untag(tree.leaves()))
    return re.sub(punct_re, r'\g<1>', s)
```

See also

The `nltk.tag.untag()` function is covered at the end of the *Default tagging* recipe in *Chapter 4, Part-of-speech Tagging*.

Flattening a deep tree

Some of the included corpora contain parsed sentences, which are often deep trees of nested phrases. Unfortunately, these trees are too deep to use for training a chunker, since IOB tag parsing is not designed for nested chunks. To make these trees usable for chunker training, we must flatten them.

Getting ready

We're going to use the first parsed sentence of the `treebank` corpus as our example. Here's a diagram showing how deeply nested this tree is:

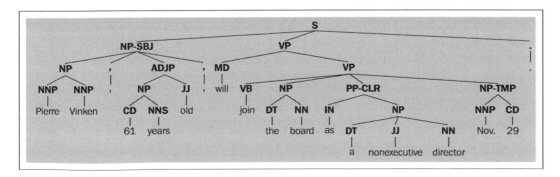

You may notice that the part-of-speech tags are part of the tree structure instead of being included with the word. This will be handled later using the `Tree.pos()` method, which was designed specifically for combining words with preterminal `Tree` labels such as part-of-speech tags.

How to do it...

In `transforms.py` is a function named `flatten_deeptree()`. It takes a single `Tree` and will return a new `Tree` that keeps only the lowest-level trees. It uses a helper function, `flatten_childtrees()`, to do most of the work:

```python
from nltk.tree import Tree

def flatten_childtrees(trees):
  children = []

  for t in trees:
    if t.height() < 3:
      children.extend(t.pos())
    elif t.height() == 3:
      children.append(Tree(t.label(), t.pos()))
    else:
      children.extend(flatten_childtrees([c for c in t]))

  return children

def flatten_deeptree(tree):
    return Tree(tree.label(), flatten_childtrees([c for c in tree]))
```

We can use it on the first parsed sentence of the `treebank` corpus to get a flatter tree:

```python
>>> from nltk.corpus import treebank
>>> from transforms import flatten_deeptree
>>> flatten_deeptree(treebank.parsed_sents()[0])
Tree('S', [Tree('NP', [('Pierre', 'NNP'), ('Vinken', 'NNP')]), (',',
','), Tree('NP', [('61', 'CD'), ('years', 'NNS')]), ('old', 'JJ'),
(',', ','), ('will', 'MD'), ('join', 'VB'), Tree('NP', [('the',
'DT'), ('board', 'NN')]), ('as', 'IN'), Tree('NP', [('a', 'DT'),
('nonexecutive', 'JJ'), ('director', 'NN')]), Tree('NP-TMP', [('Nov.',
'NNP'), ('29', 'CD')]), ('.', '.')])
```

The result is a much flatter `Tree` that only includes `NP` phrases. Words that are not part of an `NP` phrase are separated. This flatter tree is shown in the following diagram:

This `Tree` is quite similar to the first chunk `Tree` from the `treebank_chunk` corpus. The main difference is that the rightmost `NP` `Tree` is separated into two subtrees above, one of them named `NP-TMP`.

The first tree from `treebank_chunk` is shown in the following diagram for comparison. The main difference is the right side of the tree, which has only one `NP` subtree instead of two subtrees:

How it works...

The solution is composed of two functions: `flatten_deeptree()` returns a new `Tree` from the given tree by calling `flatten_childtrees()` on each of the given tree's children.

The `flatten_childtrees()` function is a recursive function that drills down into the `Tree` until it finds child trees whose `height()` is equal to or less than 3. A `Tree` whose `height()` is less than 3 looks like this:

```
>>> from nltk.tree import Tree
>>> Tree('NNP', ['Pierre']).height()
2
```

These short trees are converted into lists of tuples using the `pos()` function.

```
>>> Tree('NNP', ['Pierre']).pos()
[('Pierre', 'NNP')]
```

Trees whose `height()` is equal to 3 are the lowest level trees that we're interested in keeping. These trees look like this:

```
>>> Tree('NP', [Tree('NNP', ['Pierre']), Tree('NNP', ['Vinken'])]).
height()
3
```

And when we call `pos()` on that tree, we get:

```
>>> Tree('NP', [Tree('NNP', ['Pierre']), Tree('NNP', ['Vinken'])]).
pos()
[('Pierre', 'NNP'), ('Vinken', 'NNP')]
```

The recursive nature of `flatten_childtrees()` eliminates all trees whose height is greater than 3.

There's more...

Flattening a deep `Tree` allows us to call `nltk.chunk.util.tree2conlltags()` on the flattened `Tree`, a necessary step to train a chunker. If you try to call this function before flattening the `Tree`, you get a `ValueError` exception:

```
>>> from nltk.chunk.util import tree2conlltags
>>> tree2conlltags(treebank.parsed_sents()[0])
Traceback (most recent call last):
  File "<stdin>", line 1, in <module>
  File "/usr/local/lib/python2.6/dist-packages/nltk/chunk/util.py",
line 417, in tree2conlltags
    raise ValueError, "Tree is too deeply nested to be printed in
CoNLL format"
ValueError: Tree is too deeply nested to be printed in CoNLL format
```

But after flattening, there's no problem:

```
>>> tree2conlltags(flatten_deeptree(treebank.parsed_sents()[0]))
[('Pierre', 'NNP', 'B-NP'), ('Vinken', 'NNP', 'I-NP'), (',', ',',
'O'), ('61', 'CD', 'B-NP'), ('years', 'NNS', 'I-NP'), ('old', 'JJ',
'O'), (',', ',', 'O'), ('will', 'MD', 'O'), ('join', 'VB', 'O'),
('the', 'DT', 'B-NP'), ('board', 'NN', 'I-NP'), ('as', 'IN', 'O'),
('a', 'DT', 'B-NP'), ('nonexecutive', 'JJ', 'I-NP'), ('director',
'NN', 'I-NP'), ('Nov.', 'NNP', 'B-NP-TMP'), ('29', 'CD', 'I-NP-TMP'),
('.', '.', 'O')]
```

Being able to flatten trees opens up the possibility of training a chunker on corpora consisting of deep parse trees.

The cess_esp and cess_cat treebank

The cess_esp and cess_cat corpora are Spanish and Catalan corpora that have parsed sentences but no chunked sentences. In other words, they have deep trees that must be flattened in order to train a chunker. In fact, the trees are so deep that a diagram would be overwhelming, but the flattening can be demonstrated by showing the height() of the tree before and after flattening:

```
>>> from nltk.corpus import cess_esp
>>> cess_esp.parsed_sents()[0].height()
22
>>> flatten_deeptree(cess_esp.parsed_sents()[0]).height()
3
```

See also

The *Training a tagger based chunker* recipe in *Chapter 5, Extracting Chunks*, covers training a chunker using IOB tags.

Creating a shallow tree

In the previous recipe, we flattened a deep Tree by only keeping the lowest level subtrees. In this recipe, we'll keep only the highest level subtrees instead.

How to do it...

We'll be using the first parsed sentence from the `treebank` corpus as our example. Recall from the previous recipe that the sentence `Tree` looks like this:

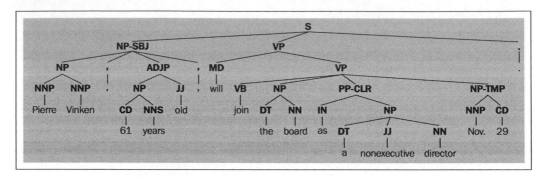

The `shallow_tree()` function defined in `transforms.py` eliminates all the nested subtrees, keeping only the top subtree labels:

```
from nltk.tree import Tree

def shallow_tree(tree):
  children = []

  for t in tree:
    if t.height() < 3:
      children.extend(t.pos())
    else:
      children.append(Tree(t.label(), t.pos()))

  return Tree(tree.label(), children)
```

Using it on the first parsed sentence in `treebank` results in a `Tree` with only two subtrees:

```
>>> from transforms import shallow_tree
>>> shallow_tree(treebank.parsed_sents()[0])
Tree('S', [Tree('NP-SBJ', [('Pierre', 'NNP'), ('Vinken', 'NNP'), (',',
','), ('61', 'CD'), ('years', 'NNS'), ('old', 'JJ'), (',', ',')]),
Tree('VP', [('will', 'MD'), ('join', 'VB'), ('the', 'DT'), ('board',
'NN'), ('as', 'IN'), ('a', 'DT'), ('nonexecutive', 'JJ'), ('director',
'NN'), ('Nov.', 'NNP'), ('29', 'CD')]), ('.', '.')])
```

We can visually and programmatically see the difference in the following diagram:

```
>>> treebank.parsed_sents()[0].height()
7
>>> shallow_tree(treebank.parsed_sents()[0]).height()
3
```

As in the previous recipe, the height of the new tree is 3 so it can be used for training a chunker.

How it works...

The `shallow_tree()` function iterates over each of the top-level subtrees in order to create new child trees. If the `height()` of a subtree is less than 3, then that subtree is replaced by a list of its part-of-speech tagged children. All other subtrees are replaced by a new `Tree` whose children are the part-of-speech tagged leaves. This eliminates all nested subtrees while retaining the top-level subtrees.

This function is an alternative to `flatten_deeptree()` from the previous recipe, for when you want to keep the higher-level tree labels and ignore the lower-level labels.

See also

The previous recipe covers how to flatten a `Tree` and keep the lowest-level subtrees, as opposed to keeping the highest-level subtrees.

Converting tree labels

As you've seen in previous recipes, parse trees often have a variety of `Tree` label types that are not present in chunk trees. If you want to use parse trees to train a chunker, then you'll probably want to reduce this variety by converting some of these tree labels to more common label types.

Getting ready

First, we have to decide which `Tree` labels need to be converted. Let's take a look at that first `Tree` again:

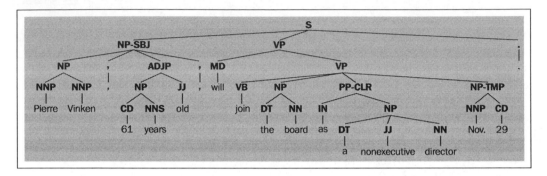

Immediately, you can see that there are two alternative NP subtrees: `NP-SBJ` and `NP-TMP`. Let's convert both of those to `NP`. The mapping will be as follows:

Original Label	New Label
NP-SBJ	NP
NP-TMP	NP

How to do it...

In `transforms.py` is the function `convert_tree_labels()`. It takes two arguments: the `Tree` to convert and a label conversion mapping. It returns a new `Tree` with all matching labels replaced based on the values in the mapping:

```
from nltk.tree import Tree

def convert_tree_labels(tree, mapping):
  children = []

  for t in tree:
    if isinstance(t, Tree):
      children.append(convert_tree_labels(t, mapping))
    else:
      children.append(t)

  label = mapping.get(tree.label(), tree.label())
  return Tree(label, children)
```

Using the mapping table we saw earlier, we can pass it in as a `dict` to `convert_tree_labels()` and convert the first parsed sentence from `treebank`:

```
>>> from transforms import convert_tree_labels
>>> mapping = {'NP-SBJ': 'NP', 'NP-TMP': 'NP'}
>>> convert_tree_labels(treebank.parsed_sents()[0], mapping)
Tree('S', [Tree('NP', [Tree('NP', [Tree('NNP', ['Pierre']),
Tree('NNP', ['Vinken'])]), Tree(',', [',']), Tree('ADJP', [Tree('NP',
[Tree('CD', ['61']), Tree('NNS', ['years'])]), Tree('JJ', ['old'])]),
Tree(',', [','])]), Tree('VP', [Tree('MD', ['will']), Tree('VP',
[Tree('VB', ['join']), Tree('NP', [Tree('DT', ['the']), Tree('NN',
['board'])]), Tree('PP-CLR', [Tree('IN', ['as']), Tree('NP',
[Tree('DT', ['a']), Tree('JJ', ['nonexecutive']), Tree('NN',
['director'])])]), Tree('NP', [Tree('NNP', ['Nov.']), Tree('CD',
['29'])])])]), Tree('.', ['.'])])
```

As you can see in the following diagram, the `NP-*` subtrees have been replaced with `NP` subtrees:

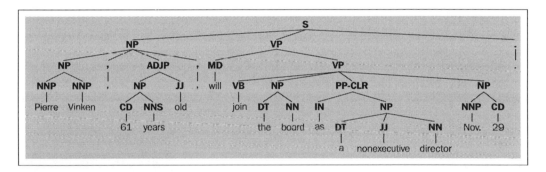

How it works...

The `convert_tree_labels()` function recursively converts every child subtree using the mapping. The `Tree` is then rebuilt with the converted labels and children until the entire `Tree` has been converted.

The result is a brand new `Tree` instance with new subtrees whose labels have been converted.

See also

The previous two recipes cover different methods of flattening a parse `Tree`, both of which can produce subtrees that may require mapping before using them to train a chunker. Chunker training is covered in the *Training a tagger-based chunker* recipe in *Chapter 5, Extracting Chunks*.

7

Text Classification

In this chapter, we will cover the following recipes:

- ▶ Bag of words feature extraction
- ▶ Training a Naive Bayes classifier
- ▶ Training a decision tree classifier
- ▶ Training a maximum entropy classifier
- ▶ Training scikit-learn classifiers
- ▶ Measuring precision and recall of a classifier
- ▶ Calculating high information words
- ▶ Combining classifiers with voting
- ▶ Classifying with multiple binary classifiers
- ▶ Training a classifier with NLTK-Trainer

Introduction

Text classification is a way to categorize documents or pieces of text. By examining the word usage in a piece of text, classifiers can decide what class label to assign to it. A **binary classifier** decides between two labels, such as positive or negative. The text can either be one label or another, but not both, whereas a **multi-label classifier** can assign one or more labels to a piece of text.

Classification works by learning from **labeled feature sets,** or training data, to later classify an **unlabeled feature set**. A labeled feature set is simply a tuple that looks like `(feat, label)`, while an unlabeled feature set is a `feat` by itself. A **feature set** is basically a key-value mapping of feature names to feature values. In the case of text classification, the feature names are usually words, and the values are all `True`. As the documents may have unknown words, and the number of possible words may be very large, words that don't occur in the text are omitted, instead of including them in a feature set with the value `False`.

An **instance** is another term for a feature set. It represents a single occurrence of a combination of features. I will use instance and feature set interchangeably. A **labeled feature set** is an instance with a known class label that we can use for training or evaluation. To summarize, `(feat, label)` is a labeled feature set, or labeled instance. `feat` is a feature set, normally represented as a key-value dictionary. When `feat` does not have an associated label, it is also called an **unlabeled feature set**, or instance.

Bag of words feature extraction

Text feature extraction is the process of transforming what is essentially a list of words into a feature set that is usable by a classifier. The NLTK classifiers expect `dict` style feature sets, so we must therefore transform our text into a `dict`. The **bag of words** model is the simplest method; it constructs a word presence feature set from all the words of an instance. This method doesn't care about the order of the words, or how many times a word occurs, all that matters is whether the word is present in a list of words.

How to do it...

The idea is to convert a list of words into a `dict`, where each word becomes a key with the value `True`. The `bag_of_words()` function in `featx.py` looks like this:

```
def bag_of_words(words):
    return dict([(word, True) for word in words])
```

We can use it with a list of words; in this case, the tokenized sentence the quick brown fox:

```
>>> from featx import bag_of_words
>>> bag_of_words(['the', 'quick', 'brown', 'fox'])
{'quick': True, 'brown': True, 'the': True, 'fox': True}
```

The resulting `dict` is known as a **bag of words** because the words are not in order, and it doesn't matter where in the list of words they occurred, or how many times they occurred. All that matters is that the word is found at least once.

You can use different values than `True`, but it is important to keep in mind that the NLTK classifiers learn from the unique combination of `(key, value)`. That means that `('fox', 1)` is treated as a different feature than `('fox', 2)`.

How it works...

The `bag_of_words()` function is a very simple list comprehension that constructs a `dict` from the given words, where every word gets the value `True`.

Since we have to assign a value to each word in order to create a `dict`, `True` is a logical choice for the value to indicate word presence. If we knew the universe of all possible words, we could assign the value `False` to all the words that are not in the given list of words. But most of the time, we don't know all the possible words beforehand. Plus, the `dict` that would result from assigning `False` to every possible word would be very large (assuming all words in the English language are possible). So instead, to keep feature extraction simple and use less memory, we stick to assigning the value `True` to all words that occur at least once. We don't assign the value `False` to any word since we don't know what the set of possible words are; we only know about the words we are given.

There's more...

In the default bag of words model, all words are treated equally. But that's not always a good idea. As we already know, some words are so common that they are practically meaningless. If you have a set of words that you want to exclude, you can use the `bag_of_words_not_in_set()` function in `featx.py`:

```
def bag_of_words_not_in_set(words, badwords):
    return bag_of_words(set(words) - set(badwords))
```

This function can be used, among other things, to filter stopwords. Here's an example where we filter the word `the` from `the quick brown fox`:

```
>>> from featx import bag_of_words_not_in_set
>>> bag_of_words_not_in_set(['the', 'quick', 'brown', 'fox'], ['the'])
{'quick': True, 'brown': True, 'fox': True}
```

As expected, the resulting `dict` has `quick`, `brown`, and `fox`, but not `the`.

Filtering stopwords

Stopwords are words that are often useless in NLP, in that they don't convey much meaning, such as the word `the`. Here's an example of using the `bag_of_words_not_in_set()` function to filter all English stopwords:

```
from nltk.corpus import stopwords

def bag_of_non_stopwords(words, stopfile='english'):
    badwords = stopwords.words(stopfile)
    return bag_of_words_not_in_set(words, badwords)
```

You can pass a different language filename as the `stopfile` keyword argument if you are using a language other than English. Using this function produces the same result as the previous example:

```
>>> from featx import bag_of_non_stopwords
>>> bag_of_non_stopwords(['the', 'quick', 'brown', 'fox'])
{'quick': True, 'brown': True, 'fox': True}
```

Here, `the` is a stopword, so it is not present in the returned `dict`.

Including significant bigrams

In addition to single words, it often helps to include significant bigrams. As significant bigrams are less common than most individual words, including them in the bag of words model can help the classifier make better decisions. We can use the `BigramCollocationFinder` class covered in the *Discovering word collocations* recipe of *Chapter 1*, *Tokenizing Text and WordNet Basics*, to find significant bigrams. The `bag_of_bigrams_words()` function found in `featx.py` will return a `dict` of all words along with the 200 most significant bigrams:

```
from nltk.collocations import BigramCollocationFinder
from nltk.metrics import BigramAssocMeasures

def bag_of_bigrams_words(words, score_fn=BigramAssocMeasures.chi_sq,
n=200):
    bigram_finder = BigramCollocationFinder.from_words(words)
    bigrams = bigram_finder.nbest(score_fn, n)
    return bag_of_words(words + bigrams)
```

The bigrams will be present in the returned `dict` as `(word1, word2)` and will have the value as `True`. Using the same example words as we did earlier, we get all words plus every bigram:

```
>>> from featx import bag_of_bigrams_words
>>> bag_of_bigrams_words(['the', 'quick', 'brown', 'fox'])
{'brown': True, ('brown', 'fox'): True, ('the', 'quick'):
True, 'fox': True, ('quick', 'brown'): True, 'quick': True, 'the':
True}
```

You can change the maximum number of bigrams found by altering the keyword argument *n*.

The *Discovering word collocations* recipe of *Chapter 1, Tokenizing Text and WordNet Basics*, covers the `BigramCollocationFinder` class in more detail. In the next recipe, we will train a `NaiveBayesClassifier` class using feature sets created with the bag of words model.

Training a Naive Bayes classifier

Now that we can extract features from text, we can train a classifier. The easiest classifier to get started with is the `NaiveBayesClassifier` class. It uses the **Bayes theorem** to predict the probability that a given feature set belongs to a particular label. The formula is:

```
P(label | features) = P(label) * P(features | label) / P(features)
```

The following list describes the various parameters from the previous formula:

- `P(label)`: This is the prior probability of the label occurring, which is the likelihood that a random feature set will have the label. This is based on the number of training instances with the label compared to the total number of training instances. For example, if 60/100 training instances have the label, the prior probability of the label is 60%.

- `P(features | label)`: This is the prior probability of a given feature set being classified as that label. This is based on which features have occurred with each label in the training data.

- `P(features)`: This is the prior probability of a given feature set occurring. This is the likelihood of a random feature set being the same as the given feature set, and is based on the observed feature sets in the training data. For example, if the given feature set occurs twice in 100 training instances, the prior probability is 2%.

- `P(label | features)`: This tells us the probability that the given features should have that label. If this value is high, then we can be reasonably confident that the label is correct for the given features.

Getting ready

We are going to be using the `movie_reviews` corpus for our initial classification examples. This corpus contains two categories of text: `pos` and `neg`. These categories are exclusive, which makes a classifier trained on them a **binary classifier**. Binary classifiers have only two classification labels, and will always choose one or the other.

Each file in the `movie_reviews` corpus is composed of either positive or negative movie reviews. We will be using each file as a single instance for both training and testing the classifier. Because of the nature of the text and its categories, the classification we will be doing is a form of sentiment analysis. If the classifier returns `pos`, then the text expresses a positive sentiment, whereas if we get `neg`, then the text expresses a negative sentiment.

How to do it...

For training, we need to first create a list of labeled feature sets. This list should be of the form `[(featureset, label)]`, where the `featureset` variable is a `dict` and `label` is the known class label for the `featureset`. The `label_feats_from_corpus()` function in `featx.py` takes a corpus, such as `movie_reviews`, and a `feature_detector` function, which defaults to `bag_of_words`. It then constructs and returns a mapping of the form `{label: [featureset]}`. We can use this mapping to create a list of labeled training instances and testing instances. The reason to do it this way is to get a fair sample from each label. It is important to get a fair sample, because parts of the corpus may be (unintentionally) biased towards one label or the other. Getting a fair sample should eliminate this possible bias:

```python
import collections

def label_feats_from_corpus(corp, feature_detector=bag_of_words):
    label_feats = collections.defaultdict(list)
    for label in corp.categories():
        for fileid in corp.fileids(categories=[label]):
            feats = feature_detector(corp.words(fileids=[fileid]))
            label_feats[label].append(feats)
    return label_feats
```

Once we can get a mapping of `label | feature sets`, we want to construct a list of labeled training instances and testing instances. The `split_label_feats()` function in `featx.py` takes a mapping returned from `label_feats_from_corpus()` and splits each list of feature sets into labeled training and testing instances:

```python
def split_label_feats(lfeats, split=0.75):
    train_feats = []
    test_feats = []
    for label, feats in lfeats.items():
        cutoff = int(len(feats) * split)
        train_feats.extend([(feat, label) for feat in feats[:cutoff]])
        test_feats.extend([(feat, label) for feat in feats[cutoff:]])
    return train_feats, test_feats
```

Using these functions with the `movie_reviews` corpus gives us the lists of labeled feature sets we need to train and test a classifier:

```python
>>> from nltk.corpus import movie_reviews
>>> from featx import label_feats_from_corpus, split_label_feats
>>> movie_reviews.categories()
['neg', 'pos']
>>> lfeats = label_feats_from_corpus(movie_reviews)
>>> lfeats.keys()
```

```
dict_keys(['neg', 'pos'])
>>> train_feats, test_feats = split_label_feats(lfeats, split=0.75)
>>> len(train_feats)
1500
>>> len(test_feats)
500
```

So there are 1000 pos files, 1000 neg files, and we end up with 1500 labeled training instances and 500 labeled testing instances, each composed of equal parts of pos and neg. If we were using a different dataset, where the classes were not balanced, our training and testing data would have the same imbalance.

Now we can train a NaiveBayesClassifier class using its train() class method:

```
>>> from nltk.classify import NaiveBayesClassifier
>>> nb_classifier = NaiveBayesClassifier.train(train_feats)
>>> nb_classifier.labels()
['neg', 'pos']
```

Let's test the classifier on a couple of made up reviews. The classify() method takes a single argument, which should be a feature set. We can use the same bag_of_words() feature detector on a list of words to get our feature set:

```
>>> from featx import bag_of_words
>>> negfeat = bag_of_words(['the', 'plot', 'was', 'ludicrous'])
>>> nb_classifier.classify(negfeat)
'neg'
>>> posfeat = bag_of_words(['kate', 'winslet', 'is', 'accessible'])
>>> nb_classifier.classify(posfeat)
'pos'
```

How it works...

The label_feats_from_corpus() function assumes that the corpus is categorized, and that a single file represents a single instance for feature extraction. It iterates over each category label, and extracts features from each file in that category using the feature_detector() function, which defaults to bag_of_words(). It returns a dict whose keys are the category labels, and the values are lists of instances for that category.

If we had label_feats_from_corpus() return a list of labeled feature sets instead of a dict, it would be much harder to get balanced training data. The list would be ordered by label, and if you took a slice of it, you would almost certainly be getting far more of one label than another. By returning a dict, you can take slices from the feature sets of each label, in the same proportion that exists in the data.

Now we need to split the labeled feature sets into training and testing instances using `split_label_feats()`. This function allows us to take a fair sample of labeled feature sets from each label, using the `split` keyword argument to determine the size of the sample. The `split` argument defaults to `0.75`, which means the first 75% of the labeled feature sets for each label will be used for training, and the remaining 25% will be used for testing.

Once we have gotten our training and testing feats split up, we train a classifier using the `NaiveBayesClassifier.train()` method. This class method builds two probability distributions for calculating prior probabilities. These are passed into the `NaiveBayesClassifier` constructor. The `label_probdist` constructor contains the prior probability for each label, or `P(label)`. The `feature_probdist` constructor contains `P(feature name = feature value | label)`. In our case, it will store `P(word=True | label)`. Both are calculated based on the frequency of occurrence of each label and each feature name and value in the training data.

The `NaiveBayesClassifier` class inherits from `ClassifierI`, which requires subclasses to provide a `labels()` method, and at least one of the `classify()` or `prob_classify()` methods. The following diagram shows other methods, which will be covered shortly:

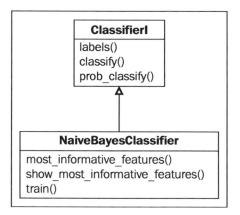

There's more...

We can test the accuracy of the classifier using `nltk.classify.util.accuracy()` and the `test_feats` variable created previously:

```
>>> from nltk.classify.util import accuracy
>>> accuracy(nb_classifier, test_feats)
0.728
```

This tells us that the classifier correctly guessed the label of nearly 73% of the test feature sets.

 The code in this chapter is run with the PYTHONHASHSEED=0 environment variable so that accuracy calculations are consistent. If you run the code with a different value for PYTHONHASHSEED, or without setting this environment variable, your accuracy values may differ.

Classification probability

While the classify() method returns only a single label, you can use the prob_classify() method to get the classification probability of each label. This can be useful if you want to use probability thresholds for classification:

```
>>> probs = nb_classifier.prob_classify(test_feats[0][0])
>>> probs.samples()
dict_keys(['neg', 'pos'])
>>> probs.max()
'pos'
>>> probs.prob('pos')
0.9999999646430913
>>> probs.prob('neg')
3.535688969240647e-08
```

In this case, the classifier says that the first test instance is nearly 100% likely to be pos. Other instances may have more mixed probabilities. For example, if the classifier says an instance is 60% pos and 40% neg, that means the classifier is 60% sure the instance is pos, but there is a 40% chance that it is neg. It can be useful to know this for situations where you only want to use strongly classified instances, with a threshold of 80% or greater.

Most informative features

The NaiveBayesClassifier class has two methods that are quite useful for learning about your data. Both methods take a keyword argument n to control how many results to show. The most_informative_features() method returns a list of the form [(feature name, feature value)] ordered by most informative to least informative. In our case, the feature value will always be True:

```
>>> nb_classifier.most_informative_features(n=5)
[('magnificent', True), ('outstanding', True), ('insulting', True),
('vulnerable', True), ('ludicrous', True)]
```

The `show_most_informative_features()` method will print out the results from `most_informative_features()` and will also include the probability of a feature pair belonging to each label:

```
>>> nb_classifier.show_most_informative_features(n=5)
Most Informative Features

      magnificent = True     pos : neg = 15.0 : 1.0
      outstanding = True     pos : neg = 13.6 : 1.0
        insulting = True     neg : pos = 13.0 : 1.0
       vulnerable = True     pos : neg = 12.3 : 1.0
        ludicrous = True     neg : pos = 11.8 : 1.0
```

The informativeness, or information gain, of each feature pair is based on the prior probability of the feature pair occurring for each label. More informative features are those that occur primarily in one label and not on the other. The less informative features are those that occur frequently with both labels. Another way to state this is that the entropy of the classifier decreases more when using a more informative feature. See `https://en.wikipedia.org/wiki/Information_gain_in_decision_trees` for more on information gain and entropy (while it specifically mentions decision trees, the same concepts are applicable to all classifiers).

Training estimator

During training, the `NaiveBayesClassifier` class constructs probability distributions for each feature using an `estimator` parameter, which defaults to `nltk.probability.ELEProbDist`. The estimator is used to calculate the probability of a `label` parameter given a specific feature. In `ELEProbDist`, **ELE** stands for **Expected Likelihood Estimate**, and the formula for calculating the label probabilities for a given feature is $(c+0.5)/(N+B/2)$. Here, c is the count of times a single feature occurs, N

is the total number of feature outcomes observed, and B is the number of bins or unique features in the feature set. In cases where the feature values are all `True`, $N == B$. In other cases, where the number of times a feature occurs is recorded, then $N >= B$.

You can use any `estimator` parameter you want, and there are quite a few to choose from. The only constraints are that it must inherit from `nltk.probability.ProbDistI` and its constructor must take a `bins` keyword argument. Here's an example using the `LaplaceProdDist` class, which uses the formula $(c+1)/(N+B)$:

```
>>> from nltk.probability import LaplaceProbDist
>>> nb_classifier = NaiveBayesClassifier.train(train_feats,
estimator=LaplaceProbDist)
>>> accuracy(nb_classifier, test_feats)
0.716
```

As you can see, accuracy is slightly lower, so choose your `estimator` parameter carefully.

You cannot use `nltk.probability.MLEProbDist` as the estimator, or any `ProbDistI` subclass that does not take the `bins` keyword argument. Training will fail with `TypeError: __init__() got an unexpected keyword argument 'bins'`.

Manual training

You don't have to use the `train()` class method to construct a `NaiveBayesClassifier`. You can instead create the `label_probdist` and `feature_probdist` variables manually. The `label_probdist` variable should be an instance of `ProbDistI`, and should contain the prior probabilities for each label. The `feature_probdist` variable should be a `dict` whose keys are tuples of the form `(label, feature name)` and whose values are instances of `ProbDistI` that have the probabilities for each feature value. In our case, each `ProbDistI` should have only one value, `True=1`. Here's a very simple example using a manually constructed `DictionaryProbDist` class:

```
>>> from nltk.probability import DictionaryProbDist
>>> label_probdist = DictionaryProbDist({'pos': 0.5, 'neg': 0.5})
>>> true_probdist = DictionaryProbDist({True: 1})
>>> feature_probdist = {('pos', 'yes'): true_probdist, ('neg', 'no'):
true_probdist}
>>> classifier = NaiveBayesClassifier(label_probdist, feature_
probdist)
>>> classifier.classify({'yes': True})
'pos'
>>> classifier.classify({'no': True})
'neg'
```

See also

In the next recipes, we will train two more classifiers, `DecisionTreeClassifier` and `MaxentClassifier`. In the *Measuring precision and recall of a classifier* recipe in this chapter, we will use precision and recall instead of accuracy to evaluate the classifiers. And then in the *Calculating high information words* recipe, we will see how using only the most informative features can improve classifier performance.

The `movie_reviews` corpus is an instance of `CategorizedPlaintextCorpusReader`, which is covered in the *Creating a categorized text corpus* recipe in *Chapter 3, Creating Custom Corpora*.

Training a decision tree classifier

The `DecisionTreeClassifier` class works by creating a tree structure, where each node corresponds to a feature name and the branches correspond to the feature values. Tracing down the branches, you get to the leaves of the tree, which are the classification labels.

How to do it...

Using the same `train_feats` and `test_feats` variables we created from the `movie_reviews` corpus in the previous recipe, we can call the `DecisionTreeClassifier.train()` class method to get a trained classifier. We pass `binary=True` because all of our features are binary: either the word is present or it's not. For other classification use cases where you have multivalued features, you will want to stick to the default `binary=False`.

 In this context, `binary` refers to *feature values*, and is not to be confused with a *binary classifier*. Our word features are binary because the value is either `True` or the word is not present. If our features could take more than two values, we would have to use `binary=False`. A **binary classifier**, on the other hand, is a classifier that only chooses between two labels. In our case, we are training a binary `DecisionTreeClassifier` on binary features. But it's also possible to have a binary classifier with non-binary features, or a non-binary classifier with binary features.

The following is the code for training and evaluating the accuracy of a `DecisionTreeClassifier` class:

```
>>> from nltk.classify import DecisionTreeClassifier
>>> dt_classifier = DecisionTreeClassifier.train(train_feats,
binary=True, entropy_cutoff=0.8, depth_cutoff=5, support_cutoff=30)
>>> accuracy(dt_classifier, test_feats)
0.688
```

The `DecisionTreeClassifier` class can take much longer to train than the `NaiveBayesClassifier` class. For that reason, I have overridden the default parameters so it trains faster. These parameters will be explained later.

How it works...

The `DecisionTreeClassifier` class, like the `NaiveBayesClassifier` class, is also an instance of `ClassifierI`, as shown in the following diagram:

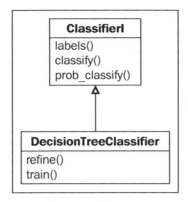

During training, the `DecisionTreeClassifier` class creates a tree where the child nodes are also instances of `DecisionTreeClassifier`. The leaf nodes contain only a single label, while the intermediate child nodes contain decision mappings for each feature. These decisions map each feature value to another `DecisionTreeClassifier`, which itself may contain decisions for another feature, or it may be a final leaf node with a classification label. The `train()` class method builds this tree from the ground up, starting with the leaf nodes. It then refines itself to minimize the number of decisions needed to get to a label by putting the most informative features at the top.

To classify, the `DecisionTreeClassifier` class looks at the given feature set and traces down the tree, using known feature names and values to make decisions. Because we are creating a binary tree, each `DecisionTreeClassifier` instance also has a default decision tree, which it uses when a known feature is not present in the feature set being classified. This is a common occurrence in text-based feature sets, and indicates that a known word was not in the text being classified. This also contributes information towards a classification decision.

There's more...

The parameters passed into `DecisionTreeClassifier.train()` can be tweaked to improve accuracy or decrease training time. Generally, if you want to improve accuracy, you must accept a longer training time and if you want to decrease the training time, the accuracy will most likely decrease as well. But be careful not to optimize for accuracy too much. A really high accuracy may indicate overfitting, which means the classifier will be excellent at classifying the training data, but not so good on data it has never seen. See `https://en.wikipedia.org/wiki/Over_fitting` for more on this concept.

Controlling uncertainty with entropy_cutoff

Entropy is the uncertainty of the outcome. As entropy approaches 1.0, uncertainty increases. Conversely, as entropy approaches 0.0, uncertainty decreases. In other words, when you have similar probabilities, the entropy will be high as each probability has a similar likelihood (or uncertainty of occurrence). But the more the probabilities differ, the lower the entropy will be.

The `entropy_cutoff` value is used during the tree refinement process. The tree refinement process is how the decision tree decides to create new branches. If the entropy of the probability distribution of label choices in the tree is greater than the `entropy_cutoff` value, then the tree is refined further by creating more branches. But if the entropy is lower than the `entropy_cutoff` value, then tree refinement is halted.

Entropy is calculated by giving `nltk.probability.entropy()` a `MLEProbDist` value created from a `FreqDist` of label counts. Here's an example showing the entropy of various `FreqDist` values. The value of `'pos'` is kept at `30`, while the value of `'neg'` is manipulated to show that when `'neg'` is close to `'pos'`, entropy increases, but when it is closer to `1`, entropy decreases:

```
>>> from nltk.probability import FreqDist, MLEProbDist, entropy
>>> fd = FreqDist({'pos': 30, 'neg': 10})
>>> entropy(MLEProbDist(fd))
0.8112781244591328
>>> fd['neg'] = 25
>>> entropy(MLEProbDist(fd))
0.9940302114769565
>>> fd['neg'] = 30
>>> entropy(MLEProbDist(fd))
1.0
>>> fd['neg'] = 1
>>> entropy(MLEProbDist(fd))
0.20559250818508304
```

What this all means is that if the label occurrence is very skewed one way or the other, the tree doesn't need to be refined because entropy/uncertainty is low. But when the entropy is greater than `entropy_cutoff`, then the tree must be refined with further decisions to reduce the uncertainty. Higher values of `entropy_cutoff` will decrease both accuracy and training time.

Controlling tree depth with depth_cutoff

The `depth_cutoff` value is also used during refinement to control the depth of the tree. The final decision tree will never be deeper than the `depth_cutoff` value. The default value is `100`, which means that classification may require up to 100 decisions before reaching a leaf node. Decreasing the `depth_cutoff` value will decrease the training time and most likely decrease the accuracy as well.

Controlling decisions with support_cutoff

The support_cutoff value controls how many labeled feature sets are required to refine the tree. As the DecisionTreeClassifier class refines itself, labeled feature sets are eliminated once they no longer provide value to the training process. When the number of labeled feature sets is less than or equal to support_cutoff, refinement stops, at least for that section of the tree.

Another way to look at it is that support_cutoff specifies the minimum number of instances that are required to make a decision about a feature. If support_cutoff is 20, and you have less than 20 labeled feature sets with a given feature, then you don't have enough instances to make a good decision, and refinement around that feature must come to a stop.

See also

The previous recipe covered the creation of training and test feature sets from the movie_reviews corpus. In the next recipe, we will cover training a MaxentClassifier class, and in the *Measuring precision and recall of a classifier* recipe in this chapter, we will use precision and recall to evaluate all the classifiers.

Training a maximum entropy classifier

The third classifier we will cover is the MaxentClassifier class, also known as a **conditional exponential classifier** or **logistic regression classifier**. The **maximum entropy classifier** converts labeled feature sets to vectors using encoding. This encoded vector is then used to calculate weights for each feature that can then be combined to determine the most likely label for a feature set. For more details on the math behind this, see https://en.wikipedia.org/wiki/Maximum_entropy_classifier.

Getting ready

The MaxentClassifier class requires the NumPy package. This is because the feature encodings use NumPy arrays. You can find installation details at the following link:

http://www.scipy.org/Installing_SciPy

> The MaxentClassifier class algorithms can be quite memory hungry, so you may want to quit all your other programs while training a MaxentClassifier class, just to be safe.

How to do it...

We will use the same `train_feats` and `test_feats` variables from the `movie_reviews` corpus that we constructed before, and call the `MaxentClassifier.train()` class method. Like the `DecisionTreeClassifier` class, `MaxentClassifier.train()` has its own specific parameters that I have tweaked to speed up training. These parameters will be explained in more detail later:

```
>>> from nltk.classify import MaxentClassifier
>>> me_classifier = MaxentClassifier.train(train_feats, trace=0, max_
iter=1, min_lldelta=0.5)
>>> accuracy(me_classifier, test_feats)
0.5
```

The reason this classifier has such a low accuracy is because I set the parameters such that it is unable to learn a more accurate model. This is due to the time required to train a suitable model using the default `iis` algorithm. A better algorithm is `gis`, which can be trained like this:

```
>>> me_classifier = MaxentClassifier.train(train_feats,
algorithm='gis', trace=0, max_iter=10, min_lldelta=0.5)
>>> accuracy(me_classifier, test_feats)
0.722
```

The `gis` algorithm is a bit faster and generally more accurate than the default `iis` algorithm, and can be allowed to run for up to 10 iterations in a reasonable amount of time. Both `iis` and `gis` will be explained in more detail in the next section.

If training is taking a long time, you can usually cut it off manually by hitting *Ctrl + C*. This should stop the current iteration and still return a classifier based on whatever state the model is in.

How it works...

Like the previous classifiers, `MaxentClassifier` inherits from `ClassifierI`, as shown in the following diagram:

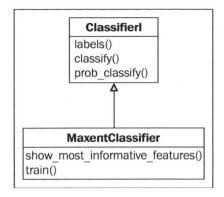

Depending on the algorithm, `MaxentClassifier.train()` calls one of the training functions in the `nltk.classify.maxent` module. The default algorithm is `iis`, and the function used is `train_maxent_classifier_with_iis()`. The other algorithm that's included is `gis`, which uses the `train_maxent_classifier_with_gis()` function. **GIS** stands for **General Iterative Scaling**, while **IIS** stands for **Improved Iterative Scaling**. The only difference between these two algorithms that really matters is that `gis` is much faster than `iis`.

If `megam` is installed and you specify the `megam` algorithm, then `train_maxent_classifier_with_megam()` is used (`megam` is covered in more detail in the next section).

 Previous versions of NLTK provided additional algorithms if SciPy was installed. These algorithms have been removed, but many other algorithms can be used in conjunction with `scikit-learn`, which we will cover in the next recipe, *Training scikit-learn classifiers*.

The basic idea behind the maximum entropy model is to build some probability distributions that fit the observed data and then choose whichever probability distribution has the highest entropy. The `gis` and `iis` algorithms do so by iteratively improving the weights used to classify features. This is where the `max_iter` and `min_lldelta` parameters come into play.

The `max_iter` variable specifies the maximum number of iterations to go through and update the weights. More iterations will generally improve accuracy, but only up to a point. Eventually, the changes from one iteration to the next will hit a plateau and further iterations are useless.

The `min_lldelta` variable specifies the minimum change in the log likelihood required to continue iteratively improving the weights. Before beginning training iterations, an instance of `nltk.classify.util.CutoffChecker` is created. When its `check()` method is called, it uses functions such as `nltk.classify.util.log_likelihood()` to decide whether the cutoff limits have been reached. The **log likelihood** is the log (using `math.log()`) of the average label probability of the training data (which is the log of the average likelihood of a label). As the log likelihood increases, the model improves. But it too will reach a plateau where further increases are so small that there is no point in continuing. Specifying the `min_lldelta` variable allows you to control how much each iteration must increase the log likelihood before stopping the iterations.

There's more...

Like the `NaiveBayesClassifier` class, you can see the most informative features by calling the `show_most_informative_features()` method:

```
>>> me_classifier.show_most_informative_features(n=4)
-0.740 worst==True and label is 'pos'

0.740 worst==True and label is 'neg'

0.715 bad==True and label is 'neg'

-0.715 bad==True and label is 'pos'
```

The numbers shown are the weights for each feature. This tells us that the word `worst` is negatively weighted towards the `pos` label, and positively weighted towards the `neg` label. In other words, if the word `worst` is found in the feature set, then there's a strong possibility that the text should be classified `neg`.

Megam algorithm

If you have installed the `megam` package, then you can use the `megam` algorithm. It's faster than the included algorithms and much more accurate, but it can also be difficult to install. Installation instructions and information can be found at the following link:

`http://www.umiacs.umd.edu/~hal/megam/`

The `nltk.classify.megam.config_megam()` function can be used to specify where the `megam` executable is found. Or, if `megam` can be found in the standard executable paths, NLTK will configure it automatically:

```
>>> me_classifier = MaxentClassifier.train(train_feats,
algorithm='megam', trace=0, max_iter=10)
[Found megam: /usr/local/bin/megam]
>>> accuracy(me_classifier, test_feats)
0.86799999999999999
```

See also

The *Bag of words feature extraction* and the *Training a Naive Bayes classifier* recipes in this chapter show how to construct the training and testing features from the `movie_reviews` corpus. The next recipe shows how to train even more accurate classifiers with `scikit-learn`. After that, we will cover how and why to evaluate a classifier using precision and recall instead of accuracy, in the *Measuring precision and recall of a classifier* recipe.

Training scikit-learn classifiers

Scikit-learn is one of the best machine learning libraries available in any programming language. It contains all sorts of machine learning algorithms for many different purposes, but they all follow the same fit/predict design pattern:

- ▸ Fit the model to the data
- ▸ Use the model to make predictions

We won't be accessing the `scikit-learn` models directly in this recipe. Instead, we'll be using NLTK's `SklearnClassifier` class, which is a wrapper class around a `scikit-learn` model to make it conform to NLTK's `ClassifierI` interface. This means that the `SklearnClassifier` class can be trained and used much like the classifiers we've used in the previous recipes in this chapter.

 I may use the terms `scikit-learn` and `sklearn` interchangeably in this recipe.

Getting ready

To use the `SklearnClassifier` class, you must have `scikit-learn` installed. Instructions are available online at `http://scikit-learn.org/stable/install.html`. If you have all the dependencies installed, such as `NumPy` and `SciPy`, you should be able to install `scikit-learn` with `pip`:

```
$ pip install scikit-learn
```

To test if everything is installed correctly, try to import the `SklearnClassifier` class:

```
>>> from nltk.classify import scikitlearn
```

If the import fails, then you are still missing `scikit-learn` and its dependencies.

How to do it...

Training an `SklearnClassifier` class has a slightly different series of steps than classifiers covered in the previous recipes of this chapter:

1. Create training features (covered in the previous recipes).

2. Choose and import an `sklearn` algorithm.

3. Construct an `SklearnClassifier` class with the chosen algorithm.

4. Train the `SklearnClassifier` class with your training features.

The main difference with NLTK classifiers is that steps 3 and 4 are usually combined. Let's put this into practice using the `MultinomialNB` classifier from `sklearn`. Refer to the earlier recipe, *Training a Naive Bayes classifier*, for details on constructing `train_feats` and `test_feats`:

```
>>> from nltk.classify.scikitlearn import SklearnClassifier
>>> from sklearn.naive_bayes import MultinomialNB
>>> sk_classifier = SklearnClassifier(MultinomialNB())
>>> sk_classifier.train(train_feats)
<SklearnClassifier(MultinomialNB(alpha=1.0, class_prior=None,
fit_prior=True))>
```

Now that we have a trained classifier, we can evaluate the accuracy:

```
>>> accuracy(sk_classifier, test_feats)
0.83
```

How it works...

The `SklearnClassifier` class is a small wrapper class whose main job is to convert NLTK feature dictionaries into `sklearn` compatible feature vectors. Here's the complete class code, minus all comments, docstrings, and most imports:

```
from sklearn.feature_extraction import DictVectorizer
from sklearn.preprocessing import LabelEncoder

class SklearnClassifier(ClassifierI):
    def __init__(self, estimator, dtype=float, sparse=True):
        self._clf = estimator
        self._encoder = LabelEncoder()
        self._vectorizer = DictVectorizer(dtype=dtype, sparse=sparse)
```

```
def batch_classify(self, featuresets):
    X = self._vectorizer.transform(featuresets)
    classes = self._encoder.classes_
    return [classes[i] for i in self._clf.predict(X)]

def batch_prob_classify(self, featuresets):
    X = self._vectorizer.transform(featuresets)
    y_proba_list = self._clf.predict_proba(X)
    return [self._make_probdist(y_proba) for y_proba in y_proba_
list]

def labels(self):
    return list(self._encoder.classes_)

def train(self, labeled_featuresets):
    X, y = list(compat.izip(*labeled_featuresets))
    X = self._vectorizer.fit_transform(X)
    y = self._encoder.fit_transform(y)
    self._clf.fit(X, y)
    return self

def _make_probdist(self, y_proba):
    classes = self._encoder.classes_
    return DictionaryProbDist(dict((classes[i], p) for i, p in
enumerate(y_proba)))
```

The class is initialized with an estimator, which is the algorithm we pass in, such as
`MultinomialNB`. It then creates a `LabelEncoder` and `DictVectorizer` object.
The `LabelEncoder` object transforms label strings to numbers. For example, the `pos` class
may be encoded as 1, and the `neg` class may be encoded as 0. The `DictVectorizer` object
is for transforming the NLTK feature dictionaries into `sklearn` compatible feature vectors.

In the `train()` method, the labeled feature sets are first encoded and transformed using the
`LabelEncoder` and `DictVectorizer` objects. Then, the model we gave as an estimator,
such as `MultinomialNB`, is fit to the data. Because the `sk_classifier` class is created
before it is trained, you might forget to train it before you try to do any classification. Luckily,
this will produce an exception with the message `'DictVectorizer' object has no
attribute 'vocabulary_'`. Since Python dictionaries are unordered (unlike vectors), the
`DictVectorizer` object must maintain a vocabulary in order to know where in the vector
a feature value belongs. This ensures that new feature dictionaries are vectorized in a manner
consistent with the training features.

To classify a feature set, it is transformed to a vector and then passed to the trained model's
`predict()` method. This is done in the `batch_classify()` method.

There's more...

The `scikit-learn` model contains many different algorithms for classification, and this recipe covers only a few. But not all the classification algorithms are compatible with the `SklearnClassifier` class, because it uses sparse vectors. Sparse vectors are more efficient because they only store the data they need, using a kind of data compression. However, some algorithms, such as sklearn's `DecisionTreeClassifier`, require dense vectors, which store every entry in the vector, even if it has no value. If you try a different algorithm with the `SklearnClassifier` class and get an exception, this is probably why.

Comparing Naive Bayes algorithms

As you saw earlier, the `MultinomialNB` algorithm got an accuracy of 83%. This is much higher than the 72.8% accuracy we got from NLTK's `NaiveBayesClassifier` class. The big difference between these two algorithms is that `MultinomialNB` can work with discrete feature values, such as word frequencies, whereas `NaiveBayesClassifier` class assumes a small set of feature values, such as strings or Booleans. There is another sklearn Naive Bayes algorithm, `BernoulliNB`, which can also work with discrete values by binarizing those values, so that the final values are 1 or 0. Our features are actually already binarized, because the feature values are `True` or `False`:

```
>>> from sklearn.naive_bayes import BernoulliNB
>>> sk_classifier = SklearnClassifier(BernoulliNB())
>>> sk_classifier.train(train_feats)
<SklearnClassifier(BernoulliNB(alpha=1.0, binarize=0.0, class_
prior=None, fit_prior=True))>
>>> accuracy(sk_classifier, test_feats)
0.812
```

Clearly, the sklearn algorithm performs better than NLTK's Naive Bayes implementation. The sklearn classifiers also have a much smaller memory footprint, and will produce much smaller pickle files on disk. Their classification speed is often slightly slower than the `NaiveBayesClassifier` class, but I think the accuracy and memory gains are quite worth it.

Training with logistic regression

Earlier in this chapter, we covered the maximum entropy classifier. This algorithm is also known as **logistic regression**, and `scikit-learn` provides a corresponding implementation.

```
>>> from sklearn.linear_model import LogisticRegression
>>> sk_classifier = SklearnClassifier(LogisticRegression())
<SklearnClassifier(LogisticRegression(C=1.0, class_weight=None,
dual=False, fit_intercept=True,
              intercept_scaling=1, penalty='l2', random_state=None,
tol=0.0001))>
>>> sk_classifier.train(train_feats)
>>> accuracy(sk_classifier, test_feats)
0.892
```

Again, we see that the sklearn algorithm has better performance than NLTK's `MaxentClassifier`, which only had 72.2% accuracy. The logistic regression algorithm also has a much faster training time than the IIS or GIS algorithms, even when those algorithms have a limited number of iterations. This can be explained by sklearn's focus on optimized numeric processing using NumPy.

Training with LinearSVC

A third family of algorithms that NLTK does not support directly is **Support Vector Machines**, or **SVM**. These algorithms have been shown to be effective at learning on high-dimensional data, such as text classification, where every word feature counts as a dimension. You can learn more about support vector machines at `https://en.wikipedia.org/wiki/Support_vector_machine`. Here are some examples of using the `sklearn` implementations:

```
>>> from sklearn.svm import SVC
>>> sk_classifier = SklearnClassifier(svm.SVC())
>>> sk_classifier.train(train_feats)
<SklearnClassifier(SVC(C=1.0, cache_size=200, class_weight=None,
coef0=0.0, degree=3, gamma=0.0,
  kernel='rbf', max_iter=-1, probability=False, random_state=None,
  shrinking=True, tol=0.001, verbose=False))>
>>> accuracy(sk_classifier, test_feats)
0.69

>>> from sklearn.svm import LinearSVC
>>> sk_classifier = SklearnClassifier(LinearSVC())
>>> sk_classifier.train(train_feats)
<SklearnClassifier(LinearSVC(C=1.0, class_weight=None, dual=True, fit_
intercept=True,
        intercept_scaling=1, loss='l2', multi_class='ovr',
penalty='l2',
        random_state=None, tol=0.0001, verbose=0))>
>>> accuracy(sk_classifier, test_feats)
0.864

>>> from sklearn.svm import NuSVC
>>> sk_classifier = SklearnClassifier(svm.NuSVC())
>>> sk_classifier.train(train_feats)
/Users/jacob/py3env/lib/python3.3/site-packages/scipy/sparse/
compressed.py:119: UserWarning: indptr array has non-integer dtype
(float64)
  % self.indptr.dtype.name)
<SklearnClassifier(NuSVC(cache_size=200, coef0=0.0, degree=3,
gamma=0.0, kernel='rbf',
    max_iter=-1, nu=0.5, probability=False, random_state=None,
    shrinking=True, tol=0.001, verbose=False))>
>>> accuracy(sk_classifier, test_feats)
0.882
```

You can see that in this case, NuSVC is the most accurate SVM classifier, just above LinearSVC, while SVC is much less accurate than either. These accuracy differences are a result of the different algorithm implementations and the default parameters. You can learn more about these specific implementations at the following link:

```
http://scikit-learn.org/stable/modules/svm.html
```

See also

If you are interested in exploring more aspects of machine learning with Python, the scikit-learn documentation is a great place to start:

```
http://scikit-learn.org/stable/documentation.html
```

Earlier in this chapter, we covered the *Training a Naive Bayes classifier* and *Training a maximum entropy classifier* recipes. We will use the LinearSVC and NuSVC classifiers again in the following recipes.

Measuring precision and recall of a classifier

In addition to accuracy, there are a number of other metrics used to evaluate classifiers. Two of the most common are **precision** and **recall**. To understand these two metrics, we must first understand **false positives** and **false negatives**. False positives happen when a classifier classifies a feature set with a label it shouldn't have gotten. False negatives happen when a classifier doesn't assign a label to a feature set that should have it. In a binary classifier, these errors happen at the same time.

Here's an example: the classifier classifies a movie review as pos when it should have been neg. This counts as a false positive for the pos label, and a false negative for the neg label. If the classifier had correctly guessed neg, then it would count as a **true positive** for the neg label, and a **true negative** for the pos label.

How does this apply to precision and recall? Precision is the *lack of false positives*, and recall is the *lack of false negatives*. As you will see, these two metrics are often in competition: the more precise a classifier is, the lower the recall, and vice versa.

How to do it...

Let's calculate the precision and recall of the NaiveBayesClassifier class we trained in the *Training a Naive Bayes classifier* recipe. The precision_recall() function in classification.py looks like this:

```
import collections
from nltk import metrics
```

```
def precision_recall(classifier, testfeats):
    refsets = collections.defaultdict(set)
    testsets = collections.defaultdict(set)

    for i, (feats, label) in enumerate(testfeats):
        refsets[label].add(i)
        observed = classifier.classify(feats)
        testsets[observed].add(i)

    precisions = {}
    recalls = {}

    for label in classifier.labels():
        precisions[label] = metrics.precision(refsets[label],
testsets[label])
        recalls[label] = metrics.recall(refsets[label], testsets[label])

    return precisions, recalls
```

This function takes two arguments:

▸   The trained classifier

▸   Labeled test features, also known as a gold standard

These are the same arguments you pass to `accuracy()`. The `precision_recall()` function returns two dictionaries; the first holds the precision for each label, and the second holds the recall for each label. Here's an example usage with `nb_classifier` and `test_feats` we created in the *Training a Naive Bayes classifier* recipe earlier:

```
>>> from classification import precision_recall
>>> nb_precisions, nb_recalls = precision_recall(nb_classifier,
test_feats)
>>> nb_precisions['pos']
0.6413612565445026
>>> nb_precisions['neg']
0.9576271186440678
>>> nb_recalls['pos']
0.98
>>> nb_recalls['neg']
0.452
```

This tells us that while the `NaiveBayesClassifier` class can correctly identify most of the `pos` feature sets (high recall), it also classifies many of the `neg` feature sets as `pos` (low precision). This behavior contributes to high precision but low recall for the `neg` label—as the `neg` label isn't given often (low recall), when it is, it's very likely to be correct (high precision). The conclusion could be that there are certain common words that are biased towards the `pos` label, but occur frequently enough in the `neg` feature sets to cause mis-classifications. To correct this behavior, we will use only the most informative words in the next recipe, *Calculating high information words*.

How it works...

To calculate precision and recall, we must build two sets for each label. The first set is known as the **reference set**, and contains all the correct values. The second set is called the **test set**, and contains the values guessed by the classifier. These two sets are compared to calculate the precision or recall for each label.

Precision is defined as the size of the intersection of both sets divided by the size of the test set. In other words, the percentage of the test set that was guessed correctly. In Python, the code is `float(len(reference.intersection(test))) / len(test)`.

Recall is the size of the intersection of both sets divided by the size of the reference set, or the percentage of the reference set that was guessed correctly. The Python code is `float(len(reference.intersection(test))) / len(reference)`.

The `precision_recall()` function in `classification.py` iterates over the labeled test features and classifies each one. We store the numeric index of the feature set (starting with 0) in the reference set for the known training label, and also store the index in the test set for the guessed label. If the classifier guesses `pos` but the training label is `neg`, then the index is stored in the reference set for `neg` and the test set for `pos`.

 We use the numeric index because the feature sets aren't hashable, and we need a unique value for each feature set.

The `nltk.metrics` package contains functions for calculating both precision and recall, so all we really have to do is build the sets and then call the appropriate function.

There's more...

Let's try it with the `MaxentClassifier` class of GIS, which we trained in the *Training a maximum entropy classifier* recipe:

```
>>> me_precisions, me_recalls = precision_recall(me_classifier,
test_feats)
>>> me_precisions['pos']
0.6456692913385826
>>> me_precisions['neg']
0.9663865546218487
>>> me_recalls['pos']
0.984
>>> me_recalls['neg']
0.46
```

This classifier is just as biased as the `NaiveBayesClassifier` class. Chances are it would be less biased if allowed to train for more iterations and/or approach a smaller log likelihood change. Now, let's try the `SklearnClassifier` class of `NuSVC` from the previous recipe, *Training scikit-learn classifiers*:

```
>>> sk_precisions, sk_recalls = precision_recall(sk_classifier,
test_feats)
>>> sk_precisions['pos']
0.9063829787234042
>>> sk_precisions['neg']
0.8603773584905661
>>> sk_recalls['pos']
0.852
>>> sk_recalls['neg']
0.912
```

In this case, the label bias is much less significant, and the reason is that the `SklearnClassifier` class of `NuSVC` weighs its features according to its own internal model. This is also true for logistic regression and many of the other `scikit-learn` algorithms. Words that are more significant are those that occur primarily in a single label, and will get higher weights in the model. Words that are common to both labels will get lower weights, as they are less significant.

F-measure

The **F-measure** is defined as the weighted harmonic mean of precision and recall. If *p* is the precision, and *r* is the recall, the formula is:

1/(alpha/p + (1-alpha)/r)

Here, *alpha* is a weighing constant that defaults to `0.5`. You can use `nltk.metrics.f_measure()` to get the F measure. It takes the same arguments as for the `precision()` and `recall()` functions: a reference set and a test set. It's often used instead of accuracy to measure a classifier, because if either precision or recall are very low, it will be reflected in the F-measure, but not necessarily in the accuracy. However, I find precision and recall to be much more useful metrics by themselves, as the F-measure can obscure the kinds of imbalances we saw with the `NaiveBayesClassifier` class.

See also

In the *Training a Naive Bayes classifier* recipe, we collected training and testing feature sets and trained the `NaiveBayesClassifier` class. The `MaxentClassifier` class was trained in the *Training a maximum entropy classifier* recipe, and the `SklearnClassifier` class was trained in the *Training scikit-learn classifiers* recipe. In the next recipe, we will explore eliminating the less significant words, and use only the high information words to create our feature sets.

Calculating high information words

A **high information** word is a word that is strongly biased towards a single classification label. These are the kinds of words we saw when we called the show_most_informative_features() method on both the NaiveBayesClassifier class and the MaxentClassifier class. Somewhat surprisingly, the top words are different for both classifiers. This discrepancy is due to how each classifier calculates the significance of each feature, and it's actually beneficial to have these different methods as they can be combined to improve accuracy, as we will see in the next recipe, *Combining classifiers with voting*.

The **low information** words are words that are common to all labels. It may be counter-intuitive, but eliminating these words from the training data can actually improve accuracy, precision, and recall. The reason this works is that using only high information words reduces the noise and confusion of a classifier's internal model. If all the words/features are highly biased one way or the other, it's much easier for the classifier to make a correct guess.

How to do it...

First, we need to calculate the high information words in the movie_review corpus. We can do this using the high_information_words() function in featx.py:

```
from nltk.metrics import BigramAssocMeasures
from nltk.probability import FreqDist, ConditionalFreqDist

def high_information_words(labelled_words, score_
fn=BigramAssocMeasures.chi_sq, min_score=5):
  word_fd = FreqDist()
  label_word_fd = ConditionalFreqDist()

  for label, words in labelled_words:
    for word in words:
      word_fd[word] += 1
      label_word_fd[label][word] += 1

  n_xx = label_word_fd.N()
  high_info_words = set()

  for label in label_word_fd.conditions():
    n_xi = label_word_fd[label].N()
    word_scores = collections.defaultdict(int)
```

```
    for word, n_ii in label_word_fd[label].items():
      n_ix = word_fd[word]
      score = score_fn(n_ii, (n_ix, n_xi), n_xx)
      word_scores[word] = score

    bestwords = [word for word, score in word_scores.items() if score
>= min_score]
    high_info_words |= set(bestwords)
  return high_info_words
```

It takes one argument from a list of two tuples of the form `[(label, words)]` where `label` is the classification label, and `words` is a list of words that occur under that label. It returns a set of the high information words.

Once we have the high information words, we use the feature detector function `bag_of_words_in_set()`, also found in `featx.py`, which will let us filter out all low information words.

```
def bag_of_words_in_set(words, goodwords):
  return bag_of_words(set(words) & set(goodwords))
```

With this new feature detector, we can call `label_feats_from_corpus()` and get a new `train_feats` and `test_feats` function using `split_label_feats()`. These two functions were covered in the *Training a Naive Bayes classifier* recipe earlier in this chapter.

```
>>> from featx import high_information_words, bag_of_words_in_set
>>> labels = movie_reviews.categories()
>>> labeled_words = [(l, movie_reviews.words(categories=[l])) for l
in labels]
>>> high_info_words = set(high_information_words(labeled_words))
>>> feat_det = lambda words: bag_of_words_in_set(words, high_info_
words)
>>> lfeats = label_feats_from_corpus(movie_reviews, feature_
detector=feat_det)
>>> train_feats, test_feats = split_label_feats(lfeats)
```

Now that we have new training and testing feature sets, let's train and evaluate a `NaiveBayesClassifier` class:

```
>>> nb_classifier = NaiveBayesClassifier.train(train_feats)
>>> accuracy(nb_classifier, test_feats)
0.91
>>> nb_precisions, nb_recalls = precision_recall(nb_classifier,
test_feats)
>>> nb_precisions['pos']
0.8988326848249028
```

```
>>> nb_precisions['neg']
0.9218106995884774
>>> nb_recalls['pos']
0.924
>>> nb_recalls['neg']
0.896
```

While the neg precision and pos recall have both decreased somewhat, neg recall and pos precision have increased drastically. Accuracy is now a little higher than the MaxentClassifier class.

How it works...

The high_information_words() function starts by counting the frequency of every word, as well as the conditional frequency for each word within each label. This is why we need the words to be labeled, so we know how often each word occurs for each label.

Once we have the FreqDist and ConditionalFreqDist variables, we can score each word on a per-label basis.

The default score_fn is nltk.metrics.BigramAssocMeasures.chi_sq(), which calculates the chi-square score for each word using the following parameters:

- n_ii: This is the frequency of the word for the label
- n_ix: This is the total frequency of the word across all labels
- n_xi: This is the total frequency of all words that occurred for the label
- n_xx: This is the total frequency for all words in all labels

The formula is n_xx * nltk.metrics.BigramAssocMeasures.phi_sq. The phi_sq() function is the squared Pearson correlation coefficient, which you can read more about at https://en.wikipedia.org/wiki/Pearson_product-moment_correlation_coefficient.

The simplest way to think about these numbers is that the closer n_ii is to n_ix, the higher the score. Or, the more often a word occurs in a label, relative to its overall occurrence, the higher the score.

Once we have the scores for each word in each label, we can filter out all words whose score is below the min_score threshold. We keep the words that meet or exceed the threshold and return all high scoring words in each label.

 It is recommended to experiment with different values of min_score to see what happens. In some cases, less words may improve the metrics even more, while in other cases more words is better.

There's more...

There are a number of other scoring functions available in the `BigramAssocMeasures` class, such as `phi_sq()` for phi-square, `pmi()` for pointwise mutual information, and `jaccard()` for using the Jaccard index. They all take the same arguments, and so can be used interchangeably with `chi_sq()`. These functions are all documented in `http://www.nltk.org/_modules/nltk/metrics/association.html` with links to the source code of the formulas.

The MaxentClassifier class with high information words

Let's evaluate the `MaxentClassifier` class using the high information words feature sets:

```
>>> me_classifier = MaxentClassifier.train(train_feats,
algorithm='gis', trace=0, max_iter=10, min_lldelta=0.5)
>>> accuracy(me_classifier, test_feats)
0.912
>>> me_precisions, me_recalls = precision_recall(me_classifier,
test_feats)
>>> me_precisions['pos']
0.8992248062015504
>>> me_precisions['neg']
0.9256198347107438
>>> me_recalls['pos']
0.928
>>> me_recalls['neg']
0.896
```

This also led to significant improvements for `MaxentClassifier`. But as we'll see, not all algorithms will benefit from high information word filtering, and in some cases, accuracy will decrease.

The DecisionTreeClassifier class with high information words

Now, let's evaluate the `DecisionTreeClassifier` class:

```
>>> dt_classifier = DecisionTreeClassifier.train(train_feats,
binary=True, depth_cutoff=20, support_cutoff=20, entropy_cutoff=0.01)
>>> accuracy(dt_classifier, test_feats)
0.68600000000000005
>>> dt_precisions, dt_recalls = precision_recall(dt_classifier, test_
feats)
>>> dt_precisions['pos']
0.6741573033707865
>>> dt_precisions['neg']
```

```
0.69957081545064381
>>> dt_recalls['pos']
0.71999999999999997
>>> dt_recalls['neg']
0.65200000000000002
```

The accuracy is about the same, even with a larger `depth_cutoff`, and smaller `support_cutoff` and `entropy_cutoff`. These results lead me to believe that the `DecisionTreeClassifier` class was already putting the high information features at the top of the tree, and it will only improve if we increase the depth significantly. But that could make training time prohibitively long and risk over-fitting the tree.

The SklearnClassifier class with high information words

Let's evaluate the `LinearSVC` `SklearnClassifier` with the same `train_feats` function:

```
>>> sk_classifier = SklearnClassifier(LinearSVC()).train(train_feats)
>>> accuracy(sk_classifier, test_feats)
0.86
>>> sk_precisions, sk_recalls = precision_recall(sk_classifier, test_feats)
>>> sk_precisions['pos']
0.871900826446281
>>> sk_precisions['neg']
0.8488372093023255
>>> sk_recalls['pos']
0.844
>>> sk_recalls['neg']
0.876
```

Its accuracy before was 86.4%, so we actually got a very slight decrease. In general, support vector machine and logistic regression-based algorithms will benefit less, or perhaps even be harmed, by pre-filtering the training features. This is because these algorithms are able to learn feature weights that correspond to the significance of each feature, whereas Naive Bayes algorithms do not.

See also

We started this chapter with the *Bag of words feature extraction* recipe. The `NaiveBayesClassifier` class was originally trained in the *Training a Naive Bayes classifier* recipe, and the `MaxentClassifier` class was trained in the *Training a maximum entropy classifier* recipe. Details on precision and recall can be found in the *Measuring precision and recall of a classifier* recipe. We will be using only high information words in the next two recipes, where we combine classifiers.

Combining classifiers with voting

One way to improve classification performance is to combine classifiers. The simplest way to combine multiple classifiers is to use voting, and choose whichever label gets the most votes. For this style of voting, it's best to have an odd number of classifiers so that there are no ties. This means combining at least three classifiers together. The individual classifiers should also use different algorithms; the idea is that multiple algorithms are better than one, and the combination of many can compensate for individual bias. However, combining a poorly performing classifier with better performing classifiers is generally not a good idea, because the poor performance of one classifier can bring the total accuracy down.

Getting ready

As we need to have at least three trained classifiers to combine, we are going to use a `NaiveBayesClassifier` class, a `DecisionTreeClassifier` class, and a `MaxentClassifier` class, all trained on the highest information words of the `movie_reviews` corpus. These were all trained in the previous recipe, so we will combine these three classifiers with voting.

How to do it...

In the `classification.py` module, there is a `MaxVoteClassifier` class:

```python
import itertools
from nltk.classify import ClassifierI
from nltk.probability import FreqDist

class MaxVoteClassifier(ClassifierI):
  def __init__(self, *classifiers):
    self._classifiers = classifiers
    self._labels = sorted(set(itertools.chain(*[c.labels() for c
in classifiers])))

  def labels(self):
    return self._labels

  def classify(self, feats):
    counts = FreqDist()

    for classifier in self._classifiers:
      counts[classifier.classify(feats)] += 1

    return counts.max()
```

To create it, you pass in a list of classifiers that you want to combine. Once created, it works just like any other classifier. Though it may take about three times longer to classify, it should generally be at least as accurate as any individual classifier.

```
>>> from classification import MaxVoteClassifier
>>> mv_classifier = MaxVoteClassifier(nb_classifier, dt_classifier,
me_classifier, sk_classifier)
>>> mv_classifier.labels()
['neg', 'pos']
>>> accuracy(mv_classifier, test_feats)
0.894
>>> mv_precisions, mv_recalls = precision_recall(mv_classifier,
test_feats)
>>> mv_precisions['pos']
0.9156118143459916
>>> mv_precisions['neg']
0.8745247148288974
>>> mv_recalls['pos']
0.868
>>> mv_recalls['neg']
0.92
```

These metrics are about on-par with the best sklearn classifiers, as well as the `MaxentClassifier` and `NaiveBayesClassifier` classes with high information features. Some numbers are slightly better, some worse. It's likely that a significant improvement to the `DecisionTreeClassifier` class could produce better numbers.

How it works...

The `MaxVoteClassifier` class extends the `nltk.classify.ClassifierI` interface, which requires the implementation of at least two methods:

- ▶ The `labels()` method must return a list of possible labels. This will be the union of the `labels()` method of each classifier passed in at initialization.

- ▶ The `classify()` method takes a single feature set and returns a label. The `MaxVoteClassifier` class iterates over its classifiers and calls `classify()` on each of them, recording their label as a vote in a `FreqDist` variable. The label with the most votes is returned using `FreqDist.max()`.

The following is the inheritance diagram:

While it doesn't check for this, the `MaxVoteClassifier` class assumes that all the classifiers passed in at initialization use the same labels. Breaking this assumption may lead to odd behavior.

See also

In the previous recipe, we trained a `NaiveBayesClassifier` class, a `MaxentClassifier` class, and a `DecisionTreeClassifier` class using only the highest information words. In the next recipe, we will use the `reuters` corpus and combine many binary classifiers in order to create a multi-label classifier.

Classifying with multiple binary classifiers

So far we have focused on **binary classifiers**, which classify with one of two possible labels. The same techniques for training a binary classifier can also be used to create a multi-class classifier, which is a classifier that can classify with one of the many possible labels. But there are also cases where you need to be able to classify with multiple labels. A classifier that can return more than one label is a **multi-label classifier**.

A common technique for creating a multi-label classifier is to combine many binary classifiers, one for each label. You train each binary classifier so that it either returns a known label or returns something else to signal that the label does not apply. Then, you can run all the binary classifiers on your feature set to collect all the applicable labels.

Getting ready

The `reuters` corpus contains multi-labeled text that we can use for training and evaluation:

```
>>> from nltk.corpus import reuters
>>> len(reuters.categories())
90
```

We will train one binary classifier per label, which means we will end up with 90 binary classifiers.

How to do it...

First, we should calculate the high information words in the `reuters` corpus. This is done with the `reuters_high_info_words()` function in `featx.py`:

```
from nltk.corpus import reuters

def reuters_high_info_words(score_fn=BigramAssocMeasures.chi_sq):
  labeled_words = []

  for label in reuters.categories():
    labeled_words.append((label, reuters.words(categories=[label])))

  return high_information_words(labeled_words, score_fn=score_fn)
```

Then, we need to get training and test feature sets based on those high information words. This is done with the `reuters_train_test_feats()` function, also found in `featx.py`. It defaults to using `bag_of_words()` as its `feature_detector`, but we will be overriding this using `bag_of_words_in_set()` to use only the high information words:

```
def reuters_train_test_feats(feature_detector=bag_of_words):
  train_feats = []
  test_feats = []
  for fileid in reuters.fileids():
    if fileid.startswith('training'):
      featlist = train_feats
    else: # fileid.startswith('test')
      featlist = test_feats
    feats = feature_detector(reuters.words(fileid))
    labels = reuters.categories(fileid)
    featlist.append((feats, labels))
  return train_feats, test_feats
```

We can use these two functions to get a list of multi-labeled training and testing feature sets.

```
>>> from featx import reuters_high_info_words, reuters_train_test_
feats
>>> rwords = reuters_high_info_words()
>>> featdet = lambda words: bag_of_words_in_set(words, rwords)
>>> multi_train_feats, multi_test_feats = reuters_train_test_
feats(featdet)
```

The `multi_train_feats` and `multi_test_feats` functions are multi-labeled feature sets. That means they have a list of labels instead of a single label, and they look like `[(featureset, [label])]`, as each feature set can have one or more labels. With this training data, we can train multiple binary classifiers. The `train_binary_classifiers()` function in `classification.py` takes a training function, a list of multi-label feature sets, and a set of possible labels to return a `dict` of `label : binary classifier`:

```
def train_binary_classifiers(trainf, labelled_feats, labelset):
  pos_feats = collections.defaultdict(list)
  neg_feats = collections.defaultdict(list)
  classifiers = {}

  for feat, labels in labelled_feats:
    for label in labels:
      pos_feats[label].append(feat)

    for label in labelset - set(labels):
      neg_feats[label].append(feat)

  for label in labelset:
    postrain = [(feat, label) for feat in pos_feats[label]]
    negtrain = [(feat, '!%s' % label) for feat in neg_feats[label]]
    classifiers[label] = trainf(postrain + negtrain)

  return classifiers
```

To use this function, we need to provide a training function that takes a single argument, which is the training data. This will be a simple lambda wrapper around a sklearn logistic regression `SklearnClassifier` class.

```
>>> from classification import train_binary_classifiers
>>> trainf = lambda train_feats: SklearnClassifier(LogisticRegressi
on()).train(train_feats)
>>> labelset = set(reuters.categories())
>>> classifiers = train_binary_classifiers(trainf, multi_train_feats,
labelset)
>>> len(classifiers)
90
```

Also in `classification.py`, we can define a `MultiBinaryClassifier` class, which takes a list of labeled classifiers of the form `[(label, classifier)]`, where the `classifier` is assumed to be a binary classifier that either returns the `label` or something else if the `label` doesn't apply.

```python
from nltk.classify import MultiClassifierI

class MultiBinaryClassifier(MultiClassifierI):
    def __init__(self, *label_classifiers):
        self._label_classifiers = dict(label_classifiers)
        self._labels = sorted(self._label_classifiers.keys())

    def labels(self):
        return self._labels

    def classify(self, feats):
        lbls = set()

        for label, classifier in self._label_classifiers.items():
            if classifier.classify(feats) == label:
                lbls.add(label)

        return lbls
```

Now we can construct this class using the binary classifiers we just created:

```python
>>> from classification import MultiBinaryClassifier
>>> multi_classifier = MultiBinaryClassifier(*classifiers.items())
```

To evaluate this classifier, we can use precision and recall, but not accuracy. That's because the accuracy function assumes single values, and doesn't take into account partial matches. For example, if the `multi_classifier` returns three labels for a feature set, and two of them are correct but the third is not, then the `accuracy()` function would mark that as incorrect. So, instead of using accuracy, we will use **masi distance**, which measures the partial overlap between two sets using the formula from this paper:

`http://citeseerx.ist.psu.edu/viewdoc/summary?doi=10.1.1.113.3752`

If the masi distance is close to 0, the better the match. But if the masi distance is close to 1, there is little or no overlap. A lower average masi distance, therefore, means more accurate partial matches. The `multi_metrics()` function in `classification.py` calculates the precision and recall of each label, along with the average masi distance.

```python
import collections
from nltk import metrics

def multi_metrics(multi_classifier, test_feats):
    mds = []
```

```
    refsets = collections.defaultdict(set)
    testsets = collections.defaultdict(set)

    for i, (feat, labels) in enumerate(test_feats):
      for label in labels:
        refsets[label].add(i)

      guessed = multi_classifier.classify(feat)

      for label in guessed:
        testsets[label].add(i)

      mds.append(metrics.masi_distance(set(labels), guessed))

    avg_md = sum(mds) / float(len(mds))
    precisions = {}
    recalls = {}

    for label in multi_classifier.labels():
        precisions[label] = metrics.precision(refsets[label],
    testsets[label])
        recalls[label] = metrics.recall(refsets[label], testsets[label])

    return precisions, recalls, avg_md
```

Using this with the `multi_classifier` function we just created gives us the following results:

```
>>> from classification import multi_metrics
>>> multi_precisions, multi_recalls, avg_md = multi_metrics
(multi_classifier, multi_test_feats)
>>> avg_md
0.23310715863026216
```

So our average masi distance isn't too bad. Lower is better, which means our multi-label classifier is only partially accurate. Let's take a look at a few precisions and recalls:

```
>>> multi_precisions['soybean']
0.7857142857142857
>>> multi_recalls['soybean']
0.3333333333333333
>>> len(reuters.fileids(categories=['soybean']))
111
```

```
>>> multi_precisions['sunseed']
1.0
>>> multi_recalls['sunseed']
2.0
>>> len(reuters.fileids(categories=['crude']))
16
```

In general, the labels that have more feature sets will have higher precision and recall, and those with less feature sets will have lower performance. Many of the categories have 0 values, because when there are not a lot of feature sets for a classifier to learn from, you can't expect it to perform well.

How it works...

The `reuters_high_info_words()` function is fairly simple; it constructs a list of `[(label, words)]` for each category of the `reuters` corpus, then passes it into the `high_information_words()` function to return a list of the most informative words in the `reuters` corpus.

With the resulting set of words, we create a feature detector function using the `bag_of_words_in_set()` function. This is then passed into the `reuters_train_test_feats()` function, which returns two lists, the first containing `[(feats, labels)]` for all the training files, and the second list has the same for all the test files.

Next, we train a binary classifier for each label using the `train_binary_classifiers()` function. This function constructs two lists for each label, one containing positive training feature sets and the other containing negative training feature sets. The **positive feature sets** are those feature sets that classify for the label. The **negative feature sets** for a label comes from the positive feature sets for all other labels. For example, a feature set that is positive for `zinc` and `sunseed` is a negative example for all the other 88 labels. Once we have positive and negative feature sets for each label, we can train a binary classifier for each label using the given training function.

With the resulting dictionary of binary classifiers, we create an instance of the `MultiBinaryClassifier` class. This class extends the `nltk.classify.MultiClassifierI` interface, which requires at least two functions:

  ▶ The `labels()` function must return a list of possible labels.

  ▶ The `classify()` function takes a single feature set and returns a set of labels. To create this set, we iterate over the binary classifiers, and any time a call to the `classify()` function returns its label, we add it to the set. If it returns something else, we continue.

The following is the inheritance diagram:

Finally, we evaluate the multi-label classifier using the `multi_metrics()` function. It is similar to the `precision_recall()` function from the *Measuring precision and recall of a classifier* recipe, but in this case, we know that the classifier is an instance of the `MultiClassifierI` interface and it can therefore return multiple labels. It also keeps track of the masi distance for each set of classification labels using the `nltk.metrics.masi_distance()` function. The `multi_metrics()` function returns three values:

- A dictionary of precisions for each label
- A dictionary of recalls for each label
- The average masi distance for each feature set

There's more...

The nature of the `reuters` corpus introduces the **class-imbalance problem**. This problem occurs when some labels have very few feature sets, and other labels have many. The binary classifiers that have few positive instances to train on, end up with far more negative instances, and are therefore strongly biased towards the negative label. There's nothing inherently wrong about this, as the bias reflects the data, but the negative instances can overwhelm the classifier to the point where it's nearly impossible to get a positive result. There are a number of advanced techniques for overcoming this problem, but they are out of the scope of this book. The paper available at `http://www.ijetae.com/files/Volume2Issue4/IJETAE_0412_07.pdf` provides a good starting reference of techniques to overcome this problem.

See also

The `SklearnClassifier` class is covered in the *Training scikit-learn classifiers* recipe in this chapter. The *Measuring precision and recall of a classifier* recipe shows how to evaluate a classifier, while the *Calculating high information words* recipe describes how to use only the best features.

Training a classifier with NLTK-Trainer

In this recipe, we'll cover the `train_classifier.py` script from NLTK-Trainer, which lets you train NLTK classifiers from the command line. NLTK-Trainer was previously introduced at the end of *Chapter 4, Part-of-speech Tagging*, and again at the end of *Chapter 5, Extracting Chunks*.

> You can find NLTK-Trainer at `https://github.com/japerk/nltk-trainer` and the online documentation at `http://nltk-trainer.readthedocs.org/`.

How to do it...

Like `train_tagger.py` and `train_chunker.py`, the only required argument for `train_classifier.py` is the name of a corpus. The corpus must have a `categories()` method, because text classification is all about learning to classify categories. Here's an example of running `train_classifier.py` on the `movie_reviews` corpus:

```
$ python train_classifier.py movie_reviews
loading movie_reviews
2 labels: ['neg', 'pos']
using bag of words feature extraction
2000 training feats, 2000 testing feats
training NaiveBayes classifier
accuracy: 0.967000
neg precision: 1.000000
neg recall: 0.934000
neg f-measure: 0.965874
pos precision: 0.938086
pos recall: 1.000000
pos f-measure: 0.968054
dumping NaiveBayesClassifier to ~/nltk_data/classifiers/movie_
reviews_NaiveBayes.pickle
```

We can use the `--no-pickle` argument to skip saving the classifier and the `--fraction` argument to limit the training set and evaluate the classifier against a test set. This example replicates what we did earlier in the *Training a Naive Bayes classifier recipe*.

```
$ python train_classifier.py movie_reviews --no-pickle --fraction 0.75
loading movie_reviews
2 labels: ['neg', 'pos']
using bag of words feature extraction
1500 training feats, 500 testing feats
training NaiveBayes classifier
accuracy: 0.726000
neg precision: 0.952000
neg recall: 0.476000
neg f-measure: 0.634667
pos precision: 0.650667
pos recall: 0.976000
pos f-measure: 0.780800
```

You can see that not only do we get accuracy, we also get the precision and recall of each class, like we covered earlier in the recipe, *Measuring precision and recall of a classifier*.

> The PYTHONHASHSEED environment variable has been omitted for clarity. This means that when you run train_classifier.py, your accuracy, precision, and recall values may vary. To get consistent values, run train_classifier.py like this:
>
> ```
> $ PYTHONHASHSEED=0 python train_classifier.py movie_
> reviews
> ```

How it works...

The train_classifier.py script goes through a series of steps to train a classifier:

1. Loads the categorized corpus.
2. Extracts features.
3. Trains the classifier.

Depending on the arguments used, there may be further steps, such as evaluating the classifier and/or saving the classifier.

The default feature extraction is a bag of words, which we covered in the first recipe of this chapter, *Bag of words feature extraction*. And the default classifier is the NaiveBayesClassifier class, which we covered earlier in the *Training a Naive Bayes classifier* recipe. You can choose a different classifier using the --classifier argument. Here's an example with DecisionTreeClassifier, replicating the same arguments we used in the *Training a decision tree classifier* recipe:

```
$ python train_classifier.py movie_reviews --no-pickle --fraction 0.75
--classifier DecisionTree --trace 0 --entropy_cutoff 0.8 --depth_cutoff 5
--support_cutoff 30 --binary
accuracy: 0.672000
neg precision: 0.683761
neg recall: 0.640000
neg f-measure: 0.661157
pos precision: 0.661654
pos recall: 0.704000
pos f-measure: 0.682171
```

There's more...

The `train_classifier.py` script supports many other arguments not shown here, all of which you can see by running the script with `--help`. Some additional arguments are presented next along with examples for other classification algorithms, followed by an introduction to another classification-related script available in `nltk-trainer`.

Saving a pickled classifier

Without the `--no-pickle` argument, `train_classifier.py` will save a pickled classifier at `~/nltk_data/classifiers/NAME.pickle`, where `NAME` is a combination of the corpus name and training algorithm. You can specify a custom filename for your classifier using the `--filename` argument like this:

```
$ python train_classifier.py movie_reviews --filename path/to/classifier.
pickle
```

Using different training instances

By default, `train_classifier.py` uses individual files as training instances. That means a single categorized file will be used as one instance. But you can instead use paragraphs or sentences as training instances. Here's an example using sentences from the `movie_reviews` corpus:

```
$ python train_classifier.py movie_reviews --no-pickle --fraction 0.75
--instances sents
loading movie_reviews
2 labels: ['neg', 'pos']
using bag of words feature extraction
50820 training feats, 16938 testing feats
training NaiveBayes classifier
accuracy: 0.638623
```

```
neg precision: 0.694942

neg recall: 0.470786

neg f-measure: 0.561313

pos precision: 0.610546

pos recall: 0.800580

pos f-measure: 0.692767
```

To use paragraphs instead of files or sentences, you can do `--instances paras`.

The most informative features

In the earlier recipe, *Training a Naive Bayes classifier*, we covered how to see the most informative features. This can also be done as an argument in `train_classifier.py`:

```
$ python train_classifier.py movie_reviews --no-pickle --fraction 0.75
--show-most-informative 5
loading movie_reviews
2 labels: ['neg', 'pos']
using bag of words feature extraction
1500 training feats, 500 testing feats
training NaiveBayes classifier
accuracy: 0.726000
neg precision: 0.952000
neg recall: 0.476000
neg f-measure: 0.634667
pos precision: 0.650667
pos recall: 0.976000
pos f-measure: 0.780800
5 most informative features


Most Informative Features
            finest = True          pos : neg    =     13.4 : 1.0
        astounding = True          pos : neg    =     11.0 : 1.0
            avoids = True          pos : neg    =     11.0 : 1.0
            inject = True          neg : pos    =     10.3 : 1.0
         strongest = True          pos : neg    =     10.3 : 1.0
```

The Maxent and LogisticRegression classifiers

In the *Training a maximum entropy classifier* recipe, we covered the `MaxentClassifier` class with the GIS algorithm. Here's how to use `train_classifier.py` to do this:

```
$ python train_classifier.py movie_reviews --no-pickle --fraction 0.75
--classifier GIS --max_iter 10 --min_lldelta 0.5
loading movie_reviews
2 labels: ['neg', 'pos']
using bag of words feature extraction
1500 training feats, 500 testing feats
training GIS classifier
  ==> Training (10 iterations)
accuracy: 0.712000
neg precision: 0.964912
neg recall: 0.440000
neg f-measure: 0.604396
pos precision: 0.637306
pos recall: 0.984000
pos f-measure: 0.773585
```

If you have `scikit-learn` installed, then you can use many different sklearn algorithms for classification. In the *Training scikit-learn classifiers* recipe, we covered the `LogisticRegression` classifier, so here's how to do it with `train_classifier.py`:

```
$ python train_classifier.py movie_reviews --no-pickle --fraction 0.75
--classifier sklearn.LogisticRegression
loading movie_reviews
2 labels: ['neg', 'pos']
using bag of words feature extraction
1500 training feats, 500 testing feats
training sklearn.LogisticRegression with {'penalty': '12', 'C': 1.0}
using dtype bool
training sklearn.LogisticRegression classifier
accuracy: 0.856000
neg precision: 0.847656
neg recall: 0.868000
neg f-measure: 0.857708
pos precision: 0.864754
pos recall: 0.844000
pos f-measure: 0.854251
```

SVMs

SVM classifiers were introduced in the *Training scikit-learn classifiers* recipe, and can also be used with `train_classifier.py`. Here's the parameters for `LinearSVC`:

```
$ python train_classifier.py movie_reviews --no-pickle --fraction 0.75
--classifier sklearn.LinearSVC
loading movie_reviews
2 labels: ['neg', 'pos']
using bag of words feature extraction
1500 training feats, 500 testing feats
training sklearn.LinearSVC with {'penalty': 'l2', 'loss': 'l2', 'C': 1.0}
using dtype bool
training sklearn.LinearSVC classifier
accuracy: 0.860000
neg precision: 0.851562
neg recall: 0.872000
neg f-measure: 0.861660
pos precision: 0.868852
pos recall: 0.848000
pos f-measure: 0.858300
```

And here's the parameters for `NuSVC`:

```
$ python train_classifier.py movie_reviews --no-pickle --fraction 0.75
--classifier sklearn.NuSVC
loading movie_reviews
2 labels: ['neg', 'pos']
using bag of words feature extraction
1500 training feats, 500 testing feats
training sklearn.NuSVC with {'kernel': 'rbf', 'nu': 0.5}
using dtype bool
training sklearn.NuSVC classifier
accuracy: 0.850000
neg precision: 0.827715
neg recall: 0.884000
neg f-measure: 0.854932
pos precision: 0.875536
pos recall: 0.816000
pos f-measure: 0.844720
```

Combining classifiers

In the *Combining classifiers with voting* recipe, we covered how to combine multiple classifiers into a single classifier using a max vote method. The `train_classifier.py` script can also combine classifiers, but it uses a slightly different algorithm. Instead of counting votes, it sums probabilities together to produce a final probability distribution, which is then used to classify each instance. Here's an example with three sklearn classifiers:

```
$ python train_classifier.py movie_reviews --no-pickle --fraction 0.75
--classifier sklearn.LogisticRegression sklearn.MultinomialNB sklearn.
NuSVC

loading movie_reviews

2 labels: ['neg', 'pos']

using bag of words feature extraction

1500 training feats, 500 testing feats

training sklearn.LogisticRegression with {'penalty': 'l2', 'C': 1.0}

using dtype bool

training sklearn.MultinomialNB with {'alpha': 1.0}

using dtype bool

training sklearn.NuSVC with {'kernel': 'rbf', 'nu': 0.5}

using dtype bool

training sklearn.LogisticRegression classifier

training sklearn.MultinomialNB classifier

training sklearn.NuSVC classifier

accuracy: 0.856000

neg precision: 0.839695

neg recall: 0.880000

neg f-measure: 0.859375

pos precision: 0.873950

pos recall: 0.832000

pos f-measure: 0.852459
```

High information words and bigrams

In the *Calculating high information words* recipe, we calculated the information gain of words, and then used only words with high information gain as features. The `train_classifier.py` script can do this too:

```
$ python train_classifier.py movie_reviews --no-pickle --fraction 0.75
--classifier NaiveBayes --min_score 5 --ngrams 1 2
```

```
loading movie_reviews

2 labels: ['neg', 'pos']

calculating word scores

using bag of words from known set feature extraction

9989 words meet min_score and/or max_feats

1500 training feats, 500 testing feats

training NaiveBayes classifier

accuracy: 0.860000

neg precision: 0.901786

neg recall: 0.808000

neg f-measure: 0.852321

pos precision: 0.826087

pos recall: 0.912000

pos f-measure: 0.866920
```

Cross-fold validation

Cross-fold validation is a method for evaluating a classification algorithm. The typical way to do it is using 10 folds, leaving one fold out for testing. What this means is that the training corpus is first split into 10 parts (or folds). Then, it is trained on nine of the folds and tested against the remaining fold. This is repeated nine more times, choosing a different fold to leave out for testing each time. By using a different set of training and testing examples each time, you can avoid any bias that might be present in the training set. Here's how to do this with train_classifier.py:

```
$ python train_classifier.py movie_reviews --classifier sklearn.
LogisticRegression --cross-fold 10

...

mean and variance across folds

-----------------------------

accuracy mean: 0.870000

accuracy variance: 0.000365

neg precision mean: 0.866884

neg precision variance: 0.000795

pos precision mean: 0.873236

pos precision variance: 0.001157

neg recall mean: 0.875482

neg recall variance: 0.000706

pos recall mean: 0.864537
```

```
pos recall variance: 0.001091

neg f_measure mean: 0.870630

neg f_measure variance: 0.000290

pos f_measure mean: 0.868246

pos f_measure variance: 0.000610
```

Most of the output has been omitted for clarity. What really matters is the final evaluation, which is the mean and variance of the results across all folds.

Analyzing a classifier

Also included in NLTK-Trainer is a script called `analyze_classifier_coverage.py`. As the name implies, you can use it to see how a classifier categorizes a given corpus. It expects the name of a corpus and a path to a pickled classifier to run on the corpus. If the corpus is categorized, you can also use the `--metrics` argument to get the accuracy, precision, and recall. The script supports many of the same corpus-related arguments as `train_classifier.py`, and also has an optional `--speed` argument, so you can see how fast the classifier is. Here's an example of analyzing a pickled `NaiveBayesClassifier` class against the `movie_reviews` corpus:

```
$ python analyze_classifier_coverage.py movie_reviews --classifier
classifiers/movie_reviews_NaiveBayes.pickle --metrics --speed

loading time: 0secs

accuracy: 0.967

neg precision: 1.000000

neg recall: 0.934000

neg f-measure: 0.965874

pos precision: 0.938086

pos recall: 1.000000

pos f-measure: 0.968054

neg 934

pos 1066

average time per classify: 3secs / 2000 feats = 1.905661 ms/feat
```

See also

NLTK-Trainer was introduced at the end of *Chapter 4, Part-of-speech Tagging*, in the *Training a tagger with NLTK-Trainer* recipe. It was also covered at the end of *Chapter 5, Extracting Chunks*, in the *Training a chunker with NLTK-Trainer* recipe. All the previous recipes in the chapter explain various aspects of how the `train_classifier.py` script works.

8

Distributed Processing and Handling Large Datasets

In this chapter, we will cover the following recipes:

- ▶ Distributed tagging with execnet
- ▶ Distributed chunking with execnet
- ▶ Parallel list processing with execnet
- ▶ Storing a frequency distribution in Redis
- ▶ Storing a conditional frequency distribution in Redis
- ▶ Storing an ordered dictionary in Redis
- ▶ Distributed word scoring with Redis and execnet

Introduction

NLTK is great for in-memory, single-processor natural language processing. However, there are times when you have a lot of data to process and want to take advantage of multiple CPUs, multicore CPUs, and even multiple computers. Or, you might want to store frequencies and probabilities in a persistent, shared database so multiple processes can access it simultaneously. For the first case, we'll be using **execnet** to do parallel and distributed processing with NLTK. For the second case, you'll learn how to use the Redis data structure server/database to store frequency distributions and more.

Distributed tagging with execnet

Execnet is a distributed execution library for Python. It allows you to create gateways and channels for remote code execution. A **gateway** is a connection from the calling process to a remote environment. The remote environment can be a local subprocess or an SSH connection to a remote node. A **channel** is created from a gateway and handles communication between the channel creator and the remote code. In this way, execnet is a kind of **Message Passing Interface** (**MPI**), where the gateway creates the connection and the channel is used to send messages back and forth.

Since many NLTK processes take 100% CPU during computation, execnet is an ideal way to distribute that computation for maximum resource usage. You can create one gateway per CPU core, and it doesn't matter whether the cores are in your local computer or spread across remote machines. In many situations, you only need to have the trained objects and data on a single machine and can send the objects and data to the remote nodes as needed.

Getting ready

You'll need to install `execnet` for this to work. It should be as simple as `sudo pip install execnet` or `sudo easy_install execnet`. The current version of `execnet`, as of this writing, is 1.2. The `execnet` home page, which has API documentation and examples, is at `http://codespeak.net/execnet/`.

How to do it...

We start by importing the required modules, as well as an additional module, `remote_tag.py`, that will be explained in the *How it works...* section. We also need to import `pickle` so we can serialize (transmit) the tagger. Execnet does not natively know how to deal with complex objects such as a part-of-speech tagger, so we must dump the tagger to a string using `pickle.dumps()`. We'll use the default tagger that's used by the `nltk.tag.pos_tag()` function, but you could use any pre-trained part-of-speech tagger as long as it implements the `TaggerI` interface.

Once we have a serialized tagger, we start execnet by making a gateway with `execnet.makegateway()`. The default gateway creates a Python subprocess, and we can call the `remote_exec()` function of the `remote_tag` module to create a channel. With an open channel, we send over the serialized tagger, followed by the first tokenized sentence of the `treebank` corpus.

 You don't have to do any special serialization of simple types such as lists and tuples, since `execnet` already knows how to handle serializing the built-in types.

Now, if we call `channel.receive()`, we get back a tagged sentence that is equivalent to the first tagged sentence in the `treebank` corpus, so we know the tagging worked. We end by exiting the gateway, which closes the channel and kills the subprocess.

```
>>> import execnet, remote_tag, nltk.tag, nltk.data
>>> from nltk.corpus import treebank
>>> import pickle
>>> pickled_tagger = pickle.dumps(nltk.data.load(nltk.tag._POS_
TAGGER))
>>> gw = execnet.makegateway()
>>> channel = gw.remote_exec(remote_tag)

>>> channel.send(pickled_tagger)
>>> channel.send(treebank.sents()[0])

>>> tagged_sentence = channel.receive()
>>> tagged_sentence == treebank.tagged_sents()[0]
True
>>> gw.exit()
```

Visually, the communication process looks like this:

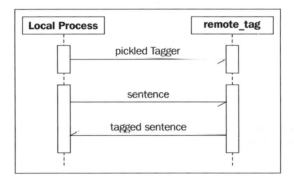

How it works...

The gateway's `remote_exec()` method takes a single argument that can be one of the following three types:

- ▸ A string of code to execute remotely
- ▸ The name of a **pure function** that will be serialized and executed remotely
- ▸ The name of a **pure module** whose source will be executed remotely

We use option three with the `remote_tag.py` module, which is defined as follows:

```
import pickle

if __name__ == '__channelexec__':
    tagger = pickle.loads(channel.receive())

    for sentence in channel:
        channel.send(tagger.tag(sentence))
```

A **pure module** is a module that is self-contained: it can only access Python modules that are available where it executes, and does not have access to any variables or states that exist wherever the gateway is initially created. Similarly, a **pure function** is a self-contained function, with no external dependencies. To detect that the module is being executed by `execnet`, you can look at the __name__ variable. If it's equal to '__channelexec__', then it is being used to create a remote channel. This is similar to doing if __name__ == '__main__' to check if a module is being executed on the command line.

The first thing we do is call `channel.receive()` to get the serialized tagger, which we load using `pickle.loads()`. You may notice that `channel` is not imported anywhere—that's because it is included in the global namespace of the module. Any module that `execnet` executes remotely has access to the `channel` variable in order to communicate with the `channel` creator.

Once we have the `tagger`, we iteratively `tag()` each tokenized sentence that we receive from the channel. This allows us to tag as many sentences as the sender wants to send, as iteration will not stop until the channel is closed. What we've essentially created is a compute node for part-of-speech tagging that dedicates 100% of its resources to tagging whatever sentences it receives. As long as the channel remains open, the node is available for processing.

There's more...

This is a simple example that opens a single gateway and channel. But `execnet` can do a lot more, such as opening multiple channels to increase parallel processing, as well as opening gateways to remote hosts over SSH to do distributed processing.

Creating multiple channels

We can create multiple channels, one per gateway, to make the processing more parallel. Each gateway creates a new subprocess (or remote interpreter if using an SSH gateway), and we use one channel per gateway for communication. Once we've created two channels, we can combine them using the `MultiChannel` class, which allows us to iterate over the channels and make a receive queue to receive messages from each channel.

After creating each channel and sending the tagger, we cycle through the channels to send an even number of sentences to each channel for tagging. Then, we collect all the responses from the queue. A call to `queue.get()` will return a 2-tuple of `(channel, message)` in case you need to know which channel the message came from.

 If you don't want to wait forever, you can also pass a `timeout` keyword argument with the maximum number of seconds you want to wait, as in `queue.get(timeout=4)`. This can be a good way to handle network errors.

Once all the tagged sentences have been collected, we can exit the gateways. Here's the code:

```
>>> import itertools
>>> gw1 = execnet.makegateway()
>>> gw2 = execnet.makegateway()
>>> ch1 = gw1.remote_exec(remote_tag)
>>> ch1.send(pickled_tagger)
>>> ch2 = gw2.remote_exec(remote_tag)
>>> ch2.send(pickled_tagger)
>>> mch = execnet.MultiChannel([ch1, ch2])
>>> queue = mch.make_receive_queue()
>>> channels = itertools.cycle(mch)
>>> for sentence in treebank.sents()[:4]:
...         channel - next(channels)
...         channel.send(sentence)
>>> tagged_sentences = []
>>> for i in range(4):
...         channel, tagged_sentence = queue.get()
...         tagged_sentences.append(tagged_sentence)
>>> len(tagged_sentences)
4
>>> gw1.exit()
>>> gw2.exit()
```

In the example code, we're only sending four sentences, but in real-life, you'd want to send thousands. A single computer can tag four sentences very quickly, but when thousands, or hundreds of thousands of sentences need to be tagged, sending sentences to multiple computers can be much faster than waiting for a single computer to do it all.

Local versus remote gateways

The default gateway spec is `popen`, which creates a Python subprocess on the local machine. This means `execnet.makegateway()` is equivalent to `execnet.makegateway('popen')`. If you have password-less SSH access to a remote machine, then you can create a remote gateway using `execnet.makegateway('ssh=remotehost')`, where `remotehost` should be the hostname of the machine. An SSH gateway spawns a new Python interpreter for executing the code remotely. As long as the code you're using for remote execution is **pure**, you only need a Python interpreter on the remote machine.

Channels work exactly the same no matter what kind of gateway is used; the only difference will be communication time. This means you can mix and match local subprocesses with remote interpreters to distribute your computations across many machines in a network. There are many more details on gateways in the API documentation at `http://codespeak.net/execnet/basics.html`.

See also

Part-of-speech tagging and taggers are covered in detail in *Chapter 4, Part-of-speech Tagging*. In the next recipe, we'll use `execnet` to do distributed chunk extraction.

Distributed chunking with execnet

In this recipe, we'll do chunking and tagging over an `execnet` gateway. This will be very similar to the tagging in the previous recipe, but we'll be sending two objects instead of one, and we will be receiving a `Tree` instead of a list, which requires pickling and unpickling for serialization.

Getting ready

As in the previous recipe, you must have `execnet` installed.

How to do it...

The setup code is very similar to the last recipe, and we'll use the same pickled `tagger` as well. First, we'll pickle the default `chunker` used by `nltk.chunk.ne_chunk()`, though any chunker would do. Next, we make a gateway for the `remote_chunk` module, get a channel, and send the pickled `tagger` and `chunker` over. Then, we receive a pickled `Tree`, which we can unpickle and inspect to see the result. Finally, we exit the gateway:

```
>>> import execnet, remote_chunk
>>> import nltk.data, nltk.tag, nltk.chunk
>>> import pickle
>>> from nltk.corpus import treebank_chunk
```

```
>>> tagger = pickle.dumps(nltk.data.load(nltk.tag._POS_TAGGER))
>>> chunker = pickle.dumps(nltk.data.load(nltk.chunk._MULTICLASS_NE_
CHUNKER))
>>> gw = execnet.makegateway()
>>> channel = gw.remote_exec(remote_chunk)
>>> channel.send(tagger)
>>> channel.send(chunker)
>>> channel.send(treebank_chunk.sents()[0])
>>> chunk_tree = pickle.loads(channel.receive())
>>> chunk_tree
Tree('S', [Tree('PERSON', [('Pierre', 'NNP')]), Tree('ORGANIZATION',
[('Vinken', 'NNP')]), (',', ','), ('61', 'CD'), ('years', 'NNS'),
('old', 'JJ'), (',', ','), ('will', 'MD'), ('join', 'VB'), ('the',
'DT'), ('board', 'NN'), ('as', 'IN'), ('a', 'DT'), ('nonexecutive',
'JJ'), ('director', 'NN'), ('Nov.', 'NNP'), ('29', 'CD'), ('.', '.')]])
>>> gw.exit()
```

The communication this time is slightly different, as shown in the following diagram:

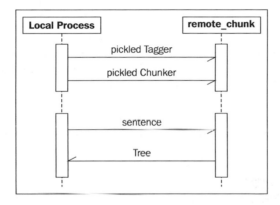

How it works...

The `remote_chunk.py` module is just a little bit more complicated than the `remote_tag.py` module from the previous recipe. In addition to receiving a pickled `tagger`, it also expects to receive a pickled `chunker` that implements the `ChunkerI` interface. Once it has both a `tagger` and a `chunker`, it expects to receive any number of tokenized sentences, which it tags and parses into a `Tree`. This `Tree` is then pickled and sent back over the channel:

```
import pickle

if __name__ == '__channelexec__':
    tagger = pickle.loads(channel.receive())
    chunker = pickle.loads(channel.receive())
```

```
for sentence in channel:
  chunk_tree = chunker.parse(tagger.tag(sent))
  channel.send(pickle.dumps(chunk_tree))
```

 The Tree must be pickled because it is not a simple built-in type.

There's more...

Note that the remote_chunk module is pure. Its only external dependency is the pickle module, which is part of the Python standard library. It doesn't need to import any NLTK modules in order to use the tagger or chunker, because all the necessary data is pickled and sent over the channel. As long as you structure your remote code like this, with no external dependencies, you only need NLTK to be installed on a single machine—the one that starts the gateway and sends the objects over the channel.

Python subprocesses

If you look at your task/system monitor (or top on *nix) while running the execnet code, you may notice a few extra Python processes. Every gateway spawns a new, self-contained, shared-nothing Python interpreter process, which is killed when you call the exit() method. Unlike with threads, there is no shared memory to worry about, and no global interpreter lock to slow things down. All you have are separate communicating processes. This is true whether the processes are local or remote. Instead of locking and synchronization, all you have to worry about is the order in which the messages are sent and received.

See also

The previous recipe explains execnet gateways and channels in detail. In the next recipe, we'll use execnet to process a list in parallel.

Parallel list processing with execnet

This recipe presents a pattern for using execnet to process a list in parallel. It's a function pattern for mapping each element in the list to a new value, using execnet to do the mapping in parallel.

How to do it...

First, we need to decide exactly what we want to do. In this example, we'll just double integers, but we could do any pure computation. Following is the `remote_double.py` module, which will be executed by `execnet`. It receives a 2-tuple of `(i, arg)`, assumes `arg` is a number, and sends back `(i, arg*2)`. The need for `i` will be explained in the next section.

```
if __name__ == '__channelexec__':
  for (i, arg) in channel:
    channel.send((i, arg * 2))
```

To use this module to double every element in a list, we import the `plists` module (explained in the *How it works...* section) and call `plists.map()` with the `remote_double` module, and a list of integers to double.

```
>>> import plists, remote_double
>>> plists.map(remote_double, range(10))
[0, 2, 4, 6, 8, 10, 12, 14, 16, 18]
```

Communication between channels is very simple, as shown in the following diagram:

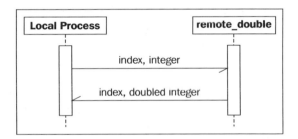

How it works...

The `map()` function is defined in `plists.py`. It takes a pure module, a list of arguments, and an optional list of 2-tuples consisting of `(spec, count)`. The default specs are `[('popen', 2)]`, which means we'll open two local gateways and channels. Once these channels are opened, we put them into an `itertools` cycle, which creates an infinite iterator that cycles back to the beginning once it hits the end.

Now we can send each argument in `args` to a `channel` for processing, and since the channels are cycled, each channel gets an almost even distribution of arguments. This is where `i` comes in—we don't know in what order we'll get the results back, so `i`, as the index of each `arg` in the list, is passed to the channel and back so we can combine the results in the original order. We then wait for the results with a `MultiChannel` receive queue and insert them into a prefilled list that's the same length as the original `args`. Once we have all the expected results, we can exit the gateways and return the results:

```
import itertools, execnet

def map(mod, args, specs=[('popen', 2)]):

    gateways = []
    channels = []


    for spec, count in specs:
      for i in range(count):
        gw = execnet.makegateway(spec)
        gateways.append(gw)
        channels.append(gw.remote_exec(mod))

    cyc = itertools.cycle(channels)

    for i, arg in enumerate(args):
      channel = next(cyc)
      channel.send((i, arg))

    mch = execnet.MultiChannel(channels)
    queue = mch.make_receive_queue()
    l = len(args)
    results = [None] * l # creates a list of length l, where every
element is None

    for i in range(l):
      channel, (i, result) = queue.get()
      results[i] = result

    for gw in gateways:
      gw.exit()

    return results
```

There's more...

You can increase the parallelization by modifying the specs, as follows:

```
>>> plists.map(remote_double, range(10), [('popen', 4)])
[0, 2, 4, 6, 8, 10, 12, 14, 16, 18]
```

However, more parallelization does not necessarily mean faster processing. It depends on the available resources, and the more gateways and channels you have open, the more overhead is required. Ideally, there should be one gateway and channel per CPU core to get maximum resource utilization.

You can use `plists.map()` with any pure module as long as it receives and sends back 2-tuples where `i` is the first element. This pattern is most useful when you have a bunch of numbers to crunch and want to process them as quickly as possible.

See also

The previous two recipes cover `execnet` features in greater detail.

Storing a frequency distribution in Redis

The `nltk.probability.FreqDist` class is used in many classes throughout NLTK for storing and managing frequency distributions. It's quite useful, but it's all in-memory, and doesn't provide a way to persist the data. A single `FreqDist` is also not accessible to multiple processes. We can change all that by building a `FreqDist` on top of Redis.

Redis is a **data structure server** that is one of the more popular *NoSQL* databases. Among other things, it provides a network-accessible database for storing dictionaries (also known as **hash maps**). Building a `FreqDist` interface to a Redis hash map will allow us to create a persistent `FreqDist` that is accessible to multiple local and remote processes at the same time.

 Most Redis operations are **atomic**, so it's even possible to have multiple processes write to the `FreqDist` concurrently.

Getting ready

For this and the subsequent recipes, we need to install both `Redis` and `redis-py`. The Redis website is at `http://redis.io/` and includes many documentation resources. To use hash maps, you should install the latest version, which at the time of this writing is 2.8.9.

The Redis Python driver, `redis-py`, can be installed using `pip install redis` or `easy_install redis`. The latest version at this time is 2.9.1. The `redis-py` home page is at `http://github.com/andymccurdy/redis-py/`.

Once both are installed and a `redis-server` process is running, you're ready to go. Let's assume `redis-server` is running on localhost on port `6379` (the default host and port).

How to do it...

The `FreqDist` class extends the standard library `collections.Counter` class, which makes a `FreqDist` a small wrapper with a few extra methods, such as `N()`. The `N()` method returns the number of sample outcomes, which is the sum of all the values in the frequency distribution.

We can create an API-compatible class on top of Redis by extending a `RedisHashMap` (which will be explained in the next section) and then implementing the `N()` method. Since the `FreqDist` only stores integers, we also override a few other methods to ensure values are always integers. This `RedisHashFreqDist` (defined in `redisprob.py`) sums all the values in the hash map for the `N()` method:

```
from rediscollections import RedisHashMap

class RedisHashFreqDist(RedisHashMap):
  def N(self):
    return int(sum(self.values()))

  def __missing__(self, key):
    return 0

  def __getitem__(self, key):
    return int(RedisHashMap.__getitem__(self, key) or 0)

  def values(self):
    return [int(v) for v in RedisHashMap.values(self)]

  def items(self):
    return [(k, int(v)) for (k, v) in RedisHashMap.items(self)]
```

We can use this class just like a `FreqDist`. To instantiate it, we must pass a `Redis` connection and the name of our hash map. The name should be a unique reference to this particular `FreqDist` so that it doesn't clash with any other keys in `Redis`.

```
>>> from redis import Redis
>>> from redisprob import RedisHashFreqDist
>>> r = Redis()
>>> rhfd = RedisHashFreqDist(r, 'test')
```

```
>>> len(rhfd)
0
>>> rhfd['foo'] += 1
>>> rhfd['foo']
1
>>> rhfd.items()
>>> len(rhfd)
1
```

The name of the hash map and the sample keys will be encoded to replace whitespace and & characters with _. This is because the Redis protocol uses these characters for communication. It's best if the name and keys don't include whitespace to begin with.

How it works...

Most of the work is done in the RedisHashMap class, found in rediscollections.py, which extends collections.MutableMapping and then overrides all methods that require Redis-specific commands. Here's an outline of each method that uses a specific Redis command:

- __len__(): This uses the hlen command to get the number of elements in the hash map

- __contains__(): This uses the hexists command to check if an element exists in the hash map

- __getitem__(): This uses the hget command to get a value from the hash map

- __setitem__(): This uses the hset command to set a value in the hash map

- __delitem__(): This uses the hdel command to remove a value from the hash map

- keys(): This uses the hkeys command to get all the keys in the hash map

- values(): This uses the hvals command to get all the values in the hash map

- items(): This uses the hgetall command to get a dictionary containing all the keys and values in the hash map

- clear(): This uses the delete command to remove the entire hash map from Redis

Extending collections.MutableMapping provides a number of other dict compatible methods based on the previous methods, such as update() and setdefault(), so we don't have to implement them ourselves.

The initialization used for `RedisHashFreqDist` is actually implemented here, and requires a `Redis` connection and a name for the hash map. The connection and name are both stored internally to use with all the subsequent commands. As mentioned earlier, whitespace is replaced by an underscore in the name and all keys for compatibility with the Redis network protocol.

```
import collections, re

white = re.compile('[\s&]+')

def encode_key(key):
  return white.sub('_', key.strip())

class RedisHashMap(collections.MutableMapping):
  def __init__(self, r, name):
    self._r = r
    self._name = encode_key(name)

  def __iter__(self):
    return self.items()

  def __len__(self):
    return self._r.hlen(self._name)

  def __contains__(self, key):
    return self._r.hexists(self._name, encode_key(key))

  def __getitem__(self, key):
    return self._r.hget(self._name, encode_key(key))

  def __setitem__(self, key, val):
    self._r.hset(self._name, encode_key(key), val)

  def __delitem__(self, key):
    self._r.hdel(self._name, encode_key(key))

  def keys(self):
    return self._r.hkeys(self._name)

  def values(self):
    return self._r.hvals(self._name)

  def items(self):
    return self._r.hgetall(self._name).items()

  def get(self, key, default=0):
    return self[key] or default

  def clear(self):
    self._r.delete(self._name)
```

There's more...

The RedisHashMap can be used by itself as a persistent key-value dictionary. However, while the hash map can support a large number of keys and arbitrary string values, its storage structure is more optimal for integer values and smaller numbers of keys. However, don't let that stop you from taking full advantage of Redis. It's very fast (for a network server) and does its best to efficiently encode whatever data you throw at it.

> While Redis is quite fast for a network database, it will be significantly slower than the in-memory FreqDist. There's no way around this, but while you sacrifice speed, you gain persistence and the ability to do concurrent processing.

See also

In the next recipe, we'll create a conditional frequency distribution based on the Redis frequency distribution created here.

Storing a conditional frequency distribution in Redis

The nltk.probability.ConditionalFreqDist class is a container for FreqDist instances, with one FreqDist per condition. It is used to count frequencies that are dependent on another condition, such as another word or a class label. We used this class in the *Calculating high information words* recipe in *Chapter 7, Text Classification*. Here, we'll create an API-compatible class on top of Redis using the RedisHashFreqDist from the previous recipe.

Getting ready

As in the previous recipe, you'll need to have Redis and redis-py installed with an instance of redis-server running.

How to do it...

We define a RedisConditionalHashFreqDist class in redisprob.py that extends nltk.probability.ConditionalFreqDist and overrides the __getitem__() method. We override __getitem__() so we can create an instance of RedisHashFreqDist instead of a FreqDist:

```
from nltk.probability import ConditionalFreqDist
from rediscollections import encode_key
```

```
class RedisConditionalHashFreqDist(ConditionalFreqDist):
  def __init__(self, r, name, cond_samples=None):
    self._r = r
    self._name = name
    ConditionalFreqDist.__init__(self, cond_samples)

    for key in self._r.keys(encode_key('%s:*' % name)):
      condition = key.split(':')[1]
      self[condition] # calls self.__getitem__(condition)

  def __getitem__(self, condition):
    if condition not in self._fdists:
      key = '%s:%s' % (self._name, condition)
      val = RedisHashFreqDist(self._r, key)
      super(RedisConditionalHashFreqDist, self).__setitem__(condition,
val)

    return super(RedisConditionalHashFreqDist, self).__getitem__
(condition)

  def clear(self):
    for fdist in self.values():
      fdist.clear()
```

An instance of this class can be created by passing in a Redis connection and a **base name**. After that, it works just like a ConditionalFreqDist:

```
>>> from redis import Redis
>>> from redisprob import RedisConditionalHashFreqDist
>>> r = Redis()
>>> rchfd = RedisConditionalHashFreqDist(r, 'condhash')
>>> rchfd.N()
0
>>> rchfd.conditions()
[]

>>> rchfd['cond1']['foo'] += 1
>>> rchfd.N()
1
>>> rchfd['cond1']['foo']
1
>>> rchfd.conditions()
['cond1']
>>> rchfd.clear()
```

How it works...

The `RedisConditionalHashFreqDist` uses name prefixes to reference `RedisHashFreqDist` instances. The name passed into the `RedisConditionalHashFreqDist` is a base name that is combined with each condition to create a unique name for each `RedisHashFreqDist`. For example, if the base name of the `RedisConditionalHashFreqDist` is `'condhash'`, and the condition is `'cond1'`, then the final name for the `RedisHashFreqDist` is `'condhash:cond1'`. This naming pattern is used at initialization to find all the existing hash maps using the `keys` command. By searching for all keys matching `'condhash:*'`, we can identify all the existing conditions and create an instance of `RedisHashFreqDist` for each.

Combining strings with colons is a common naming convention for `Redis` keys as a way to define namespaces. In our case, each `RedisConditionalHashFreqDist` instance defines a single namespace of hash maps.

There's more...

`RedisConditionalHashFreqDist` also defines a `clear()` method. This is a helper method that calls `clear()` on all the internal `RedisHashFreqDist` instances. The `clear()` method is not defined in `ConditionalFreqDist`.

See also

The previous recipe covers `RedisHashFreqDist` in detail. Also, see the *Calculating high information words* recipe in *Chapter 7, Text Classification*, for example usage of `ConditionalFreqDist`.

Storing an ordered dictionary in Redis

An ordered dictionary is like a normal `dict`, but the keys are ordered by an ordering function. In the case of Redis, it supports ordered dictionaries whose keys are strings and whose values are floating point scores. This structure can come in handy in cases where we need to calculate the information gain (covered in the *Calculating high information words* recipe in *Chapter 7, Text Classification*), and when you want to store all the words and scores for later use.

Getting ready

Again, you'll need `Redis` and `redis-py` installed with an instance of `redis-server` running, as explained in the earlier recipe, *Storing a frequency distribution in Redis*.

How to do it...

The `RedisOrderedDict` class in `rediscollections.py` extends
`collections.MutableMapping` to get a number of `dict` compatible
methods for free. Then, it implements all the key methods that require `Redis`
ordered set (also known as **Zset**) commands:

```python
class RedisOrderedDict(collections.MutableMapping):
    def __init__(self, r, name):
        self._r = r
        self._name = encode_key(name)

    def __iter__(self):
        return iter(self.items())

    def __len__(self):
        return self._r.zcard(self._name)

    def __getitem__(self, key):
        return self._r.zscore(self._name, encode_key(key))

    def __setitem__(self, key, score):
        self._r.zadd(self._name, encode_key(key), score)

    def __delitem__(self, key):
        self._r.zrem(self._name, encode_key(key))

    def keys(self, start=0, end=-1):
        # we use zrevrange to get keys sorted by high value instead of by
lowest
        return self._r.zrevrange(self._name, start, end)

    def values(self, start=0, end=-1):
        return [v for (k, v) in self.items(start=start, end=end)]

    def items(self, start=0, end=-1):
        return self._r.zrevrange(self._name, start, end, withscores=True)

    def get(self, key, default=0):
        return self[key] or default

    def iteritems(self):
        return iter(self)

    def clear(self):
        self._r.delete(self._name)
```

You can create an instance of `RedisOrderedDict` by passing in a `Redis` connection and a unique name:

```
>>> from redis import Redis
>>> from rediscollections import RedisOrderedDict
>>> r = Redis()
>>> rod = RedisOrderedDict(r, 'test')
>>> rod.get('bar')
>>> len(rod)
0
>>> rod['bar'] = 5.2
>>> rod['bar']
5.2000000000000002
>>> len(rod)
1
>>> rod.items()
[(b'bar', 5.2)]
>>> rod.clear()
```

 By default, keys are returned as binary strings. If you want a plain string, you can convert the keys using `key.decode()`. You can always look up values with normal strings.

How it works...

Much of the code may look similar to the `RedisHashMap`, which is to be expected since they both extend `collections.MutableMapping`. The main difference here is that `RedisOrderedSet` orders keys by floating point values, and so it is not suited for arbitrary key-value storage like the `RedisHashMap`. Here's an outline explaining each key method and how they work with Redis:

- `__len__()`: This uses the `zcard` command to get the number of elements in the ordered set.
- `__getitem__()`: This uses the `zscore` command to get the score of a key, and returns 0 if the key does not exist.
- `__setitem__()`: This uses the `zadd` command to add a key to the ordered set with the given score, or updates the score if the key already exists.
- `__delitem__()`: This uses the `zrem` command to remove a key from the ordered set.
- `keys()`: This uses the `zrevrange` command to get all the keys in the ordered set, sorted by the highest score. It takes two optional keyword arguments, `start` and `end`, to more efficiently get a slice of the ordered keys.

- ▶ `values()`: This extracts all the scores from the `items()` method.
- ▶ `items()`: This uses the `zrevrange` command to get the scores of each key in order to return a list of 2-tuples ordered by the highest score. Like `keys()`, it takes `start` and `end` keyword arguments to efficiently get a slice.
- ▶ `clear()`: This uses the `delete` command to remove the entire ordered set from `Redis`.

The default ordering of items in a `Redis` ordered set is low-to-high, so that the key with the lowest score comes first. This is the same as Python's default list ordering when you call `sort()` or `sorted()`, but this is not what we want when it comes to scoring. For storing scores, we expect items to be sorted from high-to-low, which is why `keys()` and `items()` use `zrevrange` instead of `zrange`.

All the Redis commands are documented at `http://redis.io/commands`.

There's more...

As mentioned previously, the `keys()` and `items()` methods take optional `start` and `end` keyword arguments to get a slice of the results. This makes `RedisOrderedDict` optimal for storing scores and getting the top *N* keys.

The `start` and `end` keyword arguments are inclusive, so if you use `start=0` and `end=2`, you will get up to three elements.

Here's a simple example where we assign three word scores and get the top two:

```
>>> from redis import Redis
>>> from rediscollections import RedisOrderedDict
>>> r = Redis()
>>> rod = RedisOrderedDict(r, 'scores')
>>> rod['best'] = 10
>>> rod['worst'] = 0.1
>>> rod['middle'] = 5
>>> rod.keys()
[b'best', b'middle', b'worst']
>>> rod.keys(start=0, end=1)
[b'best', b'middle']
>>> rod.clear()
```

The *Calculating high information words* recipe in *Chapter 7, Text Classification*, describes how to calculate information gain, which is a good case for storing word scores in a `RedisOrderedDict`. The *Storing a frequency distribution in Redis* recipe introduces `Redis` and the `RedisHashMap`.

Distributed word scoring with Redis and execnet

We can use `Redis` and `execnet` together to do distributed word scoring. In the *Calculating high information words* recipe in *Chapter 7, Text Classification*, we calculated the information gain of each word in the `movie_reviews` corpus using a `FreqDist` and `ConditionalFreqDist`. Now that we have `Redis`, we can do the same thing using a `RedisHashFreqDist` and a `RedisConditionalHashFreqDist`, and then store the scores in a `RedisOrderedDict`. We can use `execnet` to distribute the counting in order to get a better performance out of `Redis`.

Getting ready

`Redis`, `redis-py`, and `execnet` must be installed, and an instance of `redis-server` must be running on localhost.

How to do it...

We start by getting a list of (`label, words`) tuples for each label in the `movie_reviews` corpus (which only has pos and neg labels). Then, we get the `word_scores` using `score_words()` from the `dist_featx` module. The `word_scores` function is an instance of `RedisOrderedDict`, and we can see that the total number of words is 39,764. Using the `keys()` method, we can then get the top 1,000 words and inspect the top five, just to see what they are. Once we've gotten all we want from `word_scores`, we can delete the keys in `Redis`, as we no longer need the data.

```
>>> from dist_featx import score_words
>>> from nltk.corpus import movie_reviews
>>> labels = movie_reviews.categories()
>>> labelled_words = [(l, movie_reviews.words(categories=[l])) for l
in labels]
>>> word_scores = score_words(labelled_words)
>>> len(word_scores)
39767
>>> topn_words = word_scores.keys(end=1000)
```

```
>>> topn_words[0:5]
[b'bad', b',', b'and', b'?', b'movie']
>>> from redis import Redis
>>> r = Redis()
>>> [r.delete(key) for key in ['word_fd', 'label_word_fd:neg',
'label_word_fd:pos', 'word_scores']]
[1, 1, 1, 1]
```

The `score_words()` function from `dist_featx` can take a while to complete, so expect to wait a couple of minutes. The overhead of using `execnet` and `Redis` means it will take significantly longer than a nondistributed, in-memory version of the function.

How it works...

The `dist_featx.py` module contains the `score_words()` function, which does the following:

- ▸ Opens gateways and channels, sending initialization data to each channel
- ▸ Sends each `(label, words)` tuple over a channel for counting
- ▸ Sends a `done` message to each channel, waits for a `done` reply back, then closes the channels and gateways
- ▸ Calculates the score of each word based on the counts and stores in a `RedisOrderedDict`

In our case of counting words in the `movie_reviews` corpus, calling `score_words()` opens two gateways and channels, one for counting the `pos` words and the other for counting the `neg` words. The communication looks like the following diagram:

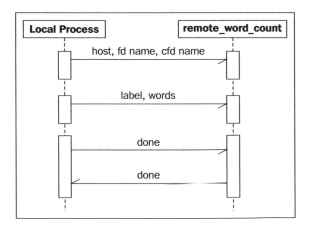

Once the counting is finished, we can score all the words and store the results. The code itself is as follows:

```
import itertools, execnet, remote_word_count
from nltk.metrics import BigramAssocMeasures
from redis import Redis
from redisprob import RedisHashFreqDist, RedisConditionalHashFreqDist
from rediscollections import RedisOrderedDict

def score_words(labelled_words, score_fn=BigramAssocMeasures.chi_sq,
host='localhost', specs=[('popen', 2)]):
  gateways = []
  channels = []

  for spec, count in specs:
    for i in range(count):
      gw = execnet.makegateway(spec)
      gateways.append(gw)
      channel = gw.remote_exec(remote_word_count)
      channel.send((host, 'word_fd', 'label_word_fd'))
      channels.append(channel)

  cyc = itertools.cycle(channels)

  for label, words in labelled_words:
    channel = next(cyc)
    channel.send((label, list(words)))

  for channel in channels:
    channel.send('done')
    assert 'done' == channel.receive()
    channel.waitclose(5)

  for gateway in gateways:
    gateway.exit()

  r = Redis(host)
  fd = RedisHashFreqDist(r, 'word_fd')
  cfd = RedisConditionalHashFreqDist(r, 'label_word_fd')
  word_scores = RedisOrderedDict(r, 'word_scores')
  n_xx = cfd.N()

  for label in cfd.conditions():
    n_xi = cfd[label].N()
```

```
      for word, n_ii in cfd[label].iteritems():
        word = word.decode()
        n_ix = fd[word]

        if n_ii and n_ix and n_xi and n_xx:
          score = score_fn(n_ii, (n_ix, n_xi), n_xx)
          word_scores[word] = score

    return word_scores
```

 Note that this scoring method will only be accurate for comparing two labels. If there are more than two labels, a different scoring method should be used, and its requirements will dictate how you store word scores.

The remote_word_count.py module looks like the following code:

```
from redis import Redis
from redisprob import RedisHashFreqDist, RedisConditionalHashFreqDist

if __name__ == '__channelexec__':
  host, fd_name, cfd_name = channel.receive()
  r = Redis(host)
  fd = RedisHashFreqDist(r, fd_name)
  cfd = RedisConditionalHashFreqDist(r, cfd_name)

  for data in channel:
    if data == 'done':
      channel.send('done')
      break

    label, words = data

    for word in words:
      fd[word] += 1
      cfd[label][word] += 1
```

You'll notice that this is not a pure module, as it requires being able to import both `redis` and `redisprob`. The reason is that instances of `RedisHashFreqDist` and `RedisConditionalHashFreqDist` cannot be pickled and sent over the `channel`. Instead, we send the hostname and key names over the channel so we can create the instances in the remote module. Once we have the instances, there are two kinds of data we can receive over the `channel`:

- ▶ A `done` message, which signals that there is no more data coming in over the channel. We reply back with another `done` message, then exit the loop to close the channel.

- ▶ A 2-tuple of `(label, words)`, which we then iterate over to increment counts in both the `RedisHashFreqDist` and `RedisConditionalHashFreqDist`.

There's more...

In this particular case, it would be faster to compute the scores without using `Redis` or `execnet`. However, by using `Redis`, we can store the scores persistently for later examination and usage. Being able to inspect all the word counts and scores manually is a great way to learn about your data. We can also tweak feature extraction without having to re-compute the scores. For example, you could use `featx.bag_of_words_in_set()` (found in *Chapter 7, Text Classification*) with the top N words from the `RedisOrderedDict`, where N could be 1,000, 2,000, or whatever number you want. If our data size is much greater, the benefits of `execnet` will be much more apparent. Horizontal scalability using `execnet` or some other method to distribute computations across many nodes becomes more valuable as the size of the data you need to process increases. This method of word scoring is much slower than if we weren't using `Redis`, but the benefit is that the numbers are stored persistently.

See also

The *Calculating high information words* recipe in *Chapter 7, Text Classification*, introduces information gain scoring of words for feature extraction and classification. The first three recipes of this chapter show how to use `execnet`, while the next three recipes describe `RedisHashFreqDist`, `RedisConditionalHashFreqDist`, and `RedisOrderedDict`, respectively.

9

Parsing Specific Data Types

In this chapter, we will cover the following recipes:

- ▶ Parsing dates and times with dateutil
- ▶ Timezone lookup and conversion
- ▶ Extracting URLs from HTML with lxml
- ▶ Cleaning and stripping HTML
- ▶ Converting HTML entities with BeautifulSoup
- ▶ Detecting and converting character encodings

Introduction

This chapter covers parsing specific kinds of data, focusing primarily on dates, times, and HTML. Luckily, there are a number of useful libraries to accomplish this, so we don't have to delve into tricky and overly complicated regular expressions. These libraries can be great complements to NLTK:

- ▶ `dateutil` provides datetime parsing and timezone conversion
- ▶ `lxml` and `BeautifulSoup` can parse, clean, and convert HTML
- ▶ `charade` and `UnicodeDammit` can detect and convert text character encoding

These libraries can be useful for preprocessing text before passing it to an NLTK object, or postprocessing text that has been processed and extracted using NLTK. Coming up is an example that ties many of these tools together.

Let's say you need to parse a blog article about a restaurant. You can use `lxml` or `BeautifulSoup` to extract the article text, outbound links, and the date and time when the article was written. The date and time can then be parsed to a Python `datetime` object with `dateutil`. Once you have the article text, you can use `charade` to ensure it's `utf-8` before cleaning out the HTML and running it through NLTK-based part-of-speech tagging, chunk extraction, and/or text classification to create additional metadata about the article. Real-world text processing often requires more than just NLTK-based natural language processing, and the functionality covered in this chapter can help with those additional requirements.

Parsing dates and times with dateutil

If you need to parse dates and times in Python, there is no better library than `dateutil`. The `parser` module can parse `datetime` strings in many more formats than can be shown here, while the `tz` module provides everything you need for looking up timezones. When combined, these modules make it quite easy to parse strings into timezone-aware `datetime` objects.

Getting ready

You can install `dateutil` using `pip` or `easy_install`, that is, `sudo pip install dateutil==2.0` or `sudo easy_install dateutil==2.0`. You need the 2.0 version for Python 3 compatibility. The complete documentation can be found at `http://labix.org/python-dateutil`.

How to do it...

Let's dive into a few parsing examples:

```
>>> from dateutil import parser
>>> parser.parse('Thu Sep 25 10:36:28 2010')
datetime.datetime(2010, 9, 25, 10, 36, 28)
>>> parser.parse('Thursday, 25. September 2010 10:36AM')
datetime.datetime(2010, 9, 25, 10, 36)
>>> parser.parse('9/25/2010 10:36:28')
datetime.datetime(2010, 9, 25, 10, 36, 28)
>>> parser.parse('9/25/2010')
datetime.datetime(2010, 9, 25, 0, 0)
>>> parser.parse('2010-09-25T10:36:28Z')
datetime.datetime(2010, 9, 25, 10, 36, 28, tzinfo=tzutc())
```

As you can see, all it takes is importing the parser module and calling the `parse()` function with a datetime string. The parser will do its best to return a sensible `datetime` object, but if it cannot parse the string, it will raise a `ValueError`.

How it works...

The parser does not use regular expressions. Instead, it looks for recognizable tokens and does its best to guess what those tokens refer to. The order of these tokens matters; for example, some cultures use a date format that looks like *Month/Day/Year* (the default order), while others use a *Day/Month/Year* format. To deal with this, the `parse()` function takes an optional keyword argument, `dayfirst`, which defaults to `False`. If you set it to `True`, it can correctly parse dates in the latter format.

```
>>> parser.parse('25/9/2010', dayfirst=True)
datetime.datetime(2010, 9, 25, 0, 0)
```

Another ordering issue can occur with two-digit years. For example, `'10-9-25'` is ambiguous. Since `dateutil` defaults to the *Month-Day-Year* format, `'10-9-25'` is parsed to the year 2025. But if you pass `yearfirst=True` into `parse()`, it will be parsed to the year 2010:

```
>>> parser.parse('10-9-25')
datetime.datetime(2025, 10, 9, 0, 0)
>>> parser.parse('10-9-25', yearfirst=True)
datetime.datetime(2010, 9, 25, 0, 0)
```

There's more...

The `dateutil` parser can also do fuzzy parsing, which allows it to ignore extraneous characters in a datetime string. With the default value of `False`, `parse()` will raise a `ValueError` when it encounters unknown tokens. But if `fuzzy=True`, then a `datetime` object can usually be returned:

```
>>> try:
...     parser.parse('9/25/2010 at about 10:36AM')
... except ValueError:
...     'cannot parse'
'cannot parse'
>>> parser.parse('9/25/2010 at about 10:36AM', fuzzy=True)
datetime.datetime(2010, 9, 25, 10, 36)
```

See also

In the next recipe, we'll use the `tz` module of `dateutil` to do timezone lookup and conversion.

Timezone lookup and conversion

Most datetime objects returned from the dateutil parser are naïve, meaning they don't have an explicit tzinfo, which specifies the timezone and UTC offset. In the previous recipe, only one of the examples had a tzinfo, and that's because it's in the standard ISO format for UTC datetime strings. UTC is the coordinated universal time, and is basically the same as GMT. **ISO** is the **International Standards Organization**, which among other things, specifies standard datetime formatting.

Python datetime objects can either be naïve or aware. If a datetime object has a tzinfo, then it is aware. Otherwise, the datetime is naïve. To make a naïve datetime object timezone aware, you must give it an explicit tzinfo. However, the Python datetime library only defines an abstract baseclass for tzinfo, and leaves it up to others to actually implement tzinfo creation. This is where the tz module of dateutil comes in—it provides everything you need to look up timezones from your OS timezone data.

Getting ready

dateutil should be installed using pip or easy_install. You should also make sure your operating system has timezone data. On Linux, this is usually found in /usr/share/zoneinfo, and the Ubuntu package is called tzdata. If you have a number of files and directories in /usr/share/zoneinfo, such as America/ and Europe/, then you should be ready to proceed. The upcoming examples show directory paths for Ubuntu Linux.

How to do it...

Let's start by getting a UTC tzinfo object. This can be done by calling tz.tzutc(), and you can check that the offset is 0 by calling the utcoffset() method with a UTC datetime object:

```
>>> from dateutil import tz
>>> tz.tzutc()
tzutc()
>>> import datetime
>>> tz.tzutc().utcoffset(datetime.datetime.utcnow())
datetime.timedelta(0)
```

To get `tzinfo` objects for other timezones, you can pass in a timezone file path to the `gettz()` function:

```
>>> tz.gettz('US/Pacific')
tzfile('/usr/share/zoneinfo/US/Pacific')
>>> tz.gettz('US/Pacific').utcoffset(datetime.datetime.utcnow())
datetime.timedelta(-1, 61200)
>>> tz.gettz('Europe/Paris')
tzfile('/usr/share/zoneinfo/Europe/Paris')
>>> tz.gettz('Europe/Paris').utcoffset(datetime.datetime.utcnow())
datetime.timedelta(0, 7200)
```

You can see that the UTC offsets are `timedelta` objects, where the first number is days and the second number is seconds.

> If you're storing datetimes in a database, it's a good idea to store them all in UTC to eliminate any timezone ambiguity. Even if the database can recognize timezones, it's still good practice.

To convert a non-UTC `datetime` object to UTC, it must be made timezone aware. If you try to convert a naïve `datetime` to UTC, you'll get a `ValueError` exception. To make a naïve `datetime` timezone aware, you simply call the `replace()` method with the correct `tzinfo`. Once a `datetime` object has a `tzinfo`, then UTC conversion can be performed by calling the `astimezone()` method with `tz.tzutc()`.

```
>>> pst = tz.gettz('US/Pacific')
Y
>>> dt = datetime.datetime(2010, 9, 25, 10, 36)
>>> dt.tzinfo
>>> dt.astimezone(tz.tzutc())
Traceback (most recent call last):
  File "/usr/lib/python2.6/doctest.py", line 1248, in __run
  compileflags, 1) in test.globs
  File "<doctest __main__[22]>", line 1, in <module>
  dt.astimezone(tz.tzutc())
ValueError: astimezone() cannot be applied to a naive datetime
>>> dt.replace(tzinfo=pst)
datetime.datetime(2010, 9, 25, 10, 36, tzinfo=tzfile('/usr/share/
zoneinfo/US/Pacific'))
>>> dt.replace(tzinfo=pst).astimezone(tz.tzutc())
datetime.datetime(2010, 9, 25, 17, 36, tzinfo=tzutc())
```

> The `tzfile` paths vary across operating systems, so your `tzfile` paths may differ from the examples. There is no cause for concern, unless you are getting different `datetime` values.

How it works...

The `tzutc` and `tzfile` objects are both subclasses of `tzinfo`. As such, they know the correct UTC offset for timezone conversion (which is 0 for `tzutc`). A `tzfile` object knows how to read your operating system's `zoneinfo` files to get the necessary offset data. The `replace()` method of a `datetime` object does what the name implies—it replaces attributes. Once a `datetime` has a `tzinfo`, the `astimezone()` method will be able to convert the time using the UTC offsets, and then replace the current `tzinfo` with the new `tzinfo`.

> Note that both `replace()` and `astimezone()` return new `datetime` objects. They do not modify the current object.

There's more...

You can pass a `tzinfos` keyword argument into the `dateutil` parser to detect the otherwise unrecognized timezones:

```
>>> parser.parse('Wednesday, Aug 4, 2010 at 6:30 p.m. (CDT)',
fuzzy=True)
datetime.datetime(2010, 8, 4, 18, 30)
>>> tzinfos = {'CDT': tz.gettz('US/Central')}
>>> parser.parse('Wednesday, Aug 4, 2010 at 6:30 p.m. (CDT)',
fuzzy=True, tzinfos=tzinfos)
datetime.datetime(2010, 8, 4, 18, 30, tzinfo=tzfile('/usr/share/
zoneinfo/US/Central'))
```

In the first instance, we get a naïve `datetime` since the timezone is not recognized. But when we pass in the `tzinfos` mapping, we get a timezone-aware `datetime`.

Local timezone

If you want to look up your local timezone, you can call `tz.tzlocal()`, which will use whatever your operating system thinks is the local timezone. In Ubuntu Linux, this is usually specified in the `/etc/timezone` file.

Custom offsets

You can create your own `tzinfo` object with a custom UTC offset using the `tzoffset` object. A custom offset of 1 hour could be created as follows:

```
>>> tz.tzoffset('custom', 3600)
tzoffset('custom', 3600)
```

You must provide a name as the first argument and the offset time in seconds as the second argument.

The previous recipe, *Parsing dates and times with dateutil*, covers parsing datetime strings with dateutil.parser.

Extracting URLs from HTML with lxml

A common task when parsing HTML is extracting links. This is one of the core functions of every general web crawler. There are a number of Python libraries for parsing HTML, and lxml is one of the best. As you'll see, it comes with some great helper functions geared specifically towards link extraction.

Getting ready

lxml is a Python binding for the C libraries libxml2 and libxslt. This makes it a very fast XML and HTML parsing library, while still being Pythonic. But that also means you need to install the C libraries for it to work. Installation instructions are available at http://lxml.de/installation.html. But if you're running Ubuntu Linux, installation is as easy as sudo apt-get install python-lxml. You can also try doing pip install lxml. The latest version as of this writing is 3.3.5.

How to do it...

lxml comes with an html module designed specifically for parsing HTML. Using the fromstring() function, we can parse an HTML string and get a list of all the links. The iterlinks() method generates 4-tuples of the form (element, attr, link, pos):

- ▸ element: This is the parsed node of the anchor tag from which the link is extracted. If you're just interested in the link, you can ignore this.
- ▸ attr: This is the attribute the link came from, which is usually 'href'.
- ▸ link: This is the actual URL extracted from the anchor tag.
- ▸ pos: This is the numeric index of the anchor tag in the document. The first tag has a pos of 0, the second has a pos of 1, and so on.

Here's some code to demonstrate:

```
>>> from lxml import html
>>> doc = html.fromstring('Hello <a href="/world">world</a>')
>>> links = list(doc.iterlinks())
>>> len(links)
1
```

```
>>> (el, attr, link, pos) = links[0]
>>> attr
'href'
>>> link
'/world'
>>> pos
0
```

How it works...

lxml parses the HTML into an `ElementTree`. This is a tree structure of parent nodes and child nodes, where each node represents an HTML tag and contains all the corresponding attributes of that tag. Once the tree is created, it can be iterated on to find elements, such as the **a** or **anchor** tag. The core tree handling code is in the `lxml.etree` module, while the `lxml.html` module contains only HTML-specific functions for creating and iterating a tree. For complete documentation, see the lxml tutorial at `http://lxml.de/tutorial.html`.

There's more...

You'll notice that the link mentioned earlier is **relative**, meaning it's not an absolute URL. We can make it **absolute** by calling the `make_links_absolute()` method with a base URL before extracting the links:

```
>>> doc.make_links_absolute('http://hello')
>>> abslinks = list(doc.iterlinks())
>>> (el, attr, link, pos) = abslinks[0]
>>> link
'http://hello/world'
```

Extracting links directly

If you don't want to do anything other than extract links, you can call the `iterlinks()` function with an HTML string:

```
>>> links = list(html.iterlinks('Hello <a href="/world">world</a>'))
>>> links[0][2]
'/world'
```

Parsing HTML from URLs or files

Instead of parsing an HTML string using the `fromstring()` function, you can call the `parse()` function with a URL or filename; for example, `html.parse('http://my/url')` or `html.parse('/path/to/file')`. The result will be the same as if you loaded the URL or file into a string yourself and then called `fromstring()`.

Extracting links with XPaths

Instead of using the `iterlinks()` method, you can also get links using the `xpath()` method, which is a general way to extract whatever you want from HTML or XML parse trees:

```
>>> doc.xpath('//a/@href')[0]
'http://hello/world'
```

For more on XPath syntax, see `http://www.w3schools.com/XPath/xpath_syntax.asp`.

See also

In the next recipe, we'll cover cleaning and stripping HTML.

Cleaning and stripping HTML

Cleaning up text is one of the unfortunate but entirely necessary aspects of text processing. When it comes to parsing HTML, you probably don't want to deal with any embedded JavaScript or CSS, and are only interested in the tags and text.

Getting ready

You'll need to install `lxml`. See the previous recipe or `http://lxml.de/installation.html` for installation instructions.

How to do it...

We can use the `clean_html()` function in the `lxml.html.clean` module to remove unnecessary HTML tags and embedded JavaScript from an HTML string:

```
>>> import lxml.html.clean
>>> lxml.html.clean.clean_html('<html><head></head><body
onload=loadfunc()>my text</body></html>')
'<div><body>my text</body></div>'
```

The result is much cleaner and easier to deal with.

How it works...

The `lxml.html.clean_html()` function parses the HTML string into a tree and then iterates over and removes all nodes that should be removed. It also cleans nodes of unnecessary attributes (such as embedded JavaScript) using regular expression matching and substitution.

There's more...

The `lxml.html.clean` module defines a default `Cleaner` class that's used when you call `clean_html()`. You can customize the behavior of this class by creating your own instance and calling its `clean_html()` method. For more details on this class, see `http://lxml.de/lxmlhtml.html#cleaning-up-html`.

See also

The `lxml.html` module was introduced in the previous recipe for parsing HTML and extracting links. In the next recipe, we'll cover unescaping HTML entities.

Converting HTML entities with BeautifulSoup

HTML entities are strings such as "`&amp;`" or "`&lt;`". These are encodings of normal ASCII characters that have special uses in HTML. For example, "`&lt;`" is the entity for "`<`", but you can't just have "`<`" within HTML tags because it is the beginning character for an HTML tag, hence the need to escape it and define the "`&lt;`" entity. "`&amp;`" is the entity code for "`&`", which as we've just seen is the beginning character for an entity code. If you need to process the text within an HTML document, then you'll want to convert these entities back to their normal characters so you can recognize them and handle them appropriately.

Getting ready

You'll need to install `BeautifulSoup`, which you should be able to do with `sudo pip install beautifulsoup4` or `sudo easy_install beautifulsoup4`. You can read more about `BeautifulSoup` at `http://www.crummy.com/software/BeautifulSoup/`.

How to do it...

`BeautifulSoup` is an HTML parser library that can also be used for entity conversion. It's quite simple: create an instance of `BeautifulSoup` given a string containing HTML entities, then get the `string` attribute:

```
>>> from bs4 import BeautifulSoup
>>> BeautifulSoup('&lt;').string
'<'
>>> BeautifulSoup('&amp;').string
'&'
```

However, the reverse is not true. If you try to do `BeautifulSoup('<')`, you will get a `None` result because that is not valid in HTML.

How it works...

To convert the HTML entities, `BeautifulSoup` looks for tokens that look like an entity and replaces them with their corresponding value in the `htmlentitydefs.name2codepoint` dictionary from the Python standard library. It can do this if the entity token is within an HTML tag, or when it's in a normal string.

There's more...

`BeautifulSoup` is an excellent HTML and XML parser in its own right, and can be a great alternative to `lxml`. It's particularly good at handling malformed HTML. You can read more about how to use it at `http://www.crummy.com/software/BeautifulSoup/bs4/doc/`.

Extracting URLs with BeautifulSoup

Here's an example of using `BeautifulSoup` to extract URLs, like we did in the *Extracting URLs from HTML with lxml* recipe. You first create the `soup` with an HTML string, call the `findAll()` method with `'a'` to get all anchor tags, and pull out the `'href'` attribute to get the URLs:

```
>>> from bs4 import BeautifulSoup
>>> soup = BeautifulSoup('Hello <a href="/world">world</a>')
>>> [a['href'] for a in soup.findAll('a')]
['/world']
```

See also

In the *Extracting URLs from HTML with lxml* recipe, we covered how to use `lxml` to extract URLs from an HTML string, and we also covered the *Cleaning and stripping HTML* recipe after that.

Detecting and converting character encodings

A common occurrence with text processing is finding text that has nonstandard character encoding. Ideally, all text would be ASCII or utf-8, but that's just not the reality. In cases when you have non-ASCII or non-utf-8 text and you don't know what the character encoding is, you'll need to detect it and convert the text to a standard encoding before doing further processing.

Getting ready

You'll need to install the `charade` module using `sudo pip install charade` or `sudo easy_install charade`. You can learn more about `charade` at `https://pypi.python.org/pypi/charade`.

How to do it...

Encoding detection and conversion functions are provided in `encoding.py`. These are simple wrapper functions around the `charade` module. To detect the encoding of a string, call `encoding.detect(string)`. You'll get back a `dict` containing two attributes: `confidence` and `encoding`. The `confidence` attribute is a probability of how confident `charade` is that the value for `encoding` is correct.

```
# -*- coding: utf-8 -*-
import charade

def detect(s):
  try:
    if isinstance(s, str):
      return charade.detect(s.encode())
    else:
      return charade.detect(s)
  except UnicodeDecodeError:
    return charade.detect(s.encode('utf-8'))

def convert(s):
  if isinstance(s, str):
    s = s.encode()

  encoding = detect(s)['encoding']

  if encoding == 'utf-8':
    return s.decode()
  else:
    return s.decode(encoding)
```

And here's some example code using `detect()` to determine character encoding:

```
>>> import encoding
>>> encoding.detect('ascii')
{'confidence': 1.0, 'encoding': 'ascii'}
>>> encoding.detect('abcdé')
{'confidence': 0.505, 'encoding': 'utf-8'}
>>> encoding.detect(bytes('\222\222\223\225', 'latin-1'))
{'confidence': 0.5, 'encoding': 'windows-1252'}
```

To convert a string to a standard `unicode` encoding, call `encoding.convert()`. This will decode the string from its original encoding and then re-encode it as utf-8.

```
>>> encoding.convert('ascii')
'ascii'
>>> encoding.convert('abcdé')
'abcdé'
>>> encoding.convert((bytes('\222\222\223\225', 'latin-1'))
'\u2019\u2019\u201c\u2022'
```

How it works...

The `detect()` function is a wrapper around `charade.detect()` that can encode strings and handle `UnicodeDecodeError` exceptions. The `charade.detect()` method expects a `bytes` object, not a string, so in these cases, the string is encoded before trying to detect the encoding.

The `convert()` function first calls `detect()` to get the encoding and, then returns a decoded string.

There's more...

The comment at the top of the module, `# -*- coding: utf-8 -*-`, is a hint to the Python interpreter that tells which encoding to use for the strings in the code. This is helpful for when you have non-ASCII strings in your source code, and is documented in detail at `http://www.python.org/dev/peps/pep-0263/`.

Converting to ASCII

If you want pure ASCII text, with non-ASCII characters converted to ASCII equivalents or dropped if there is no equivalent character, then you can use the `unicodedata.normalize()` function:

```
>>> import unicodedata
>>> unicodedata.normalize('NFKD', 'abcd\xe9').encode('ascii',
'ignore')
b'abcde'
```

Specifying `'NFKD'` as the first argument ensures that the non-ASCII characters are replaced with their equivalent ASCII versions, and the final call to `encode()` with `'ignore'` as the second argument will remove any extraneous unicode characters. This returns a `bytes` object, which you can call `decode()` on to get a string.

UnicodeDammit conversion

The `BeautifulSoup` library contains a helper class called `UnicodeDammit`, which can do automatic conversion to unicode. Its usage is very simple:

```
>>> from bs4 import UnicodeDammit
>>> UnicodeDammit('abcd\xe9').unicode_markup
'abcdé'
```

Installing `BeautifulSoup` is covered in the previous recipe, *Converting HTML entities with BeautifulSoup*.

See also

Encoding detection and conversion is a recommended first step before doing HTML processing with `lxml` or `BeautifulSoup`, covered in the *Extracting URLs from HTML with lxml* and *Converting HTML entities with BeautifulSoup* recipes.

Penn Treebank
Part-of-speech Tags

The following is a table of all the part-of-speech tags that occur in the `treebank` corpus distributed with NLTK. The tags and counts shown here were acquired using the following code:

```
>>> from nltk.probability import FreqDist
>>> from nltk.corpus import treebank
>>> fd = FreqDist()
>>> for word, tag in treebank.tagged_words():
...     fd[tag] += 1
>>> fd.items()
```

The `FreqDist fd` contains all the counts shown here for every tag in the `treebank` corpus. You can inspect each tag count individually, by doing `fd[tag]`, for example, `fd['DT']`. Punctuation tags are also shown, along with special tags such as `-NONE-`, which signifies that the part-of-speech tag is unknown. Descriptions of most of the tags can be found at the following link:
`http://www.ling.upenn.edu/courses/Fall_2003/ling001/penn_treebank_pos.html`

Part-of-speech tag	Frequency of occurrence
#	16
$	724
''	694
,	4886
-LRB-	120
-NONE-	6592
-RRB-	126
.	384

Part-of-speech tag	Frequency of occurrence
:	563
' '	712
CC	2265
CD	3546
DT	8165
EX	88
FW	4
IN	9857
JJ	5834
JJR	381
JJS	182
LS	13
MD	927
NN	13166
NNP	9410
NNPS	244
NNS	6047
PDT	27
POS	824
PRP	1716
PRP$	766
RB	2822
RBR	136
RBS	35
RP	216
SYM	1
TO	2179
UH	3
VB	2554
VBD	3043
VBG	1460
VBN	2134
VBP	1321
VBZ	2125
WDT	445
WP	241
WP$	14
WRB	178

Index

National Institute of Standards
and Technology (NIST) 147
Natural Language ToolKit. *See* NLTK
ne_chunk() method 147
negations
replacing, with antonyms 46, 47
negative feature sets 226
ngram 94
NgramTagger class 96
ngram taggers
combining 94, 95
training 94, 95
n_ii parameter 216
n_ix parameter 216
NLTK
about 7, 237
URL, for data installation 8
URL, for installation instructions 8
URL, for starting Python console 8
nltk.chunk functions 141
nltk.corpus
treebank corpora, defining 75
nltk.corpus.treebank_chunk corpus 63
nltk.data.load() function 51
NLTK functionality
URL, for demos 7
nltk.metrics package 212
NLTK-Trainer
about 114
classifier, analyzing 236
classifiers, combining 234
cross-fold validation 235
high information words 234
LogisticRegression classifier 232
Maxent classifier 232
pickled classifier, saving 230
pickled tagger, saving 119
SVM classifiers 233
tagger, training with 114-119
training instances, using 230, 231
training, on custom corpus 120
URL, for documentation 114
URL, for installation instructions 114
used, for training chunker 156-158
used, for training classifier 228, 229
noun cardinals
swapping 170, 171

Noun Phrase (NP) 59
NumPy package
URL 201
n_xi parameter 216
n_xx parameter 216

O

ordered dictionary
storing, in Redis 253-257

P

paragraph block reader
customizing 57
parallel list processing
using, with execnet 244-247
parsed_docs() method 155
parse trees
training 160
partial parsing
about 123
performing, with regular
expressions 136, 137
part-of-speech tag. *See* POS tag
part-of-speech tagged word corpus
creating 55, 56
part-of-speech tagging 55, 85, 86
Path and Leacock Chordorow (LCH)
similarity 24
pattern creation 128
Penn Treebank corpus
about 124
URL 12
personal word lists 42
PersonChunker class 150
P(features | label) parameter 191
P(features) parameter 191
phi_sq() function 216, 217
phrases 123
pickle corpus view 79
pickled chunker
saving 159
pickled tagger
saving 119
trained tagger, loading with 93
pivot point 169
P(label | features) parameter 191

WordNetTagger class 109
WordPunctTokenizer 12
WordReplacer class 43
words
  lemmatizing, with WordNet 32, 33
  replacing, with synonyms 43, 44
  sentences, tokenizing into 10, 11
  stemming 30
  tagging, with regular expressions 99, 100
  replacing, with regular expressions 34-36
word_tag_model() function 98
word_tokenize() function 10
word tokenizer
  customizing 57
wup_similarity method 23

X

xpath() method
  reference link 271
  used, for extracting URLs 271

Y

YAML file
  loading 52
YAML synonym replacement 45

Z

Zset 254

Thank you for buying
Python 3 Text Processing
with NLTK 3 Cookbook

About Packt Publishing

Packt, pronounced 'packed', published its first book "*Mastering phpMyAdmin for Effective MySQL Management*" in April 2004 and subsequently continued to specialize in publishing highly focused books on specific technologies and solutions.

Our books and publications share the experiences of your fellow IT professionals in adapting and customizing today's systems, applications, and frameworks. Our solution based books give you the knowledge and power to customize the software and technologies you're using to get the job done. Packt books are more specific and less general than the IT books you have seen in the past. Our unique business model allows us to bring you more focused information, giving you more of what you need to know, and less of what you don't.

Packt is a modern, yet unique publishing company, which focuses on producing quality, cutting-edge books for communities of developers, administrators, and newbies alike. For more information, please visit our website: www.packtpub.com.

About Packt Open Source

In 2010, Packt launched two new brands, Packt Open Source and Packt Enterprise, in order to continue its focus on specialization. This book is part of the Packt Open Source brand, home to books published on software built around Open Source licenses, and offering information to anybody from advanced developers to budding web designers. The Open Source brand also runs Packt's Open Source Royalty Scheme, by which Packt gives a royalty to each Open Source project about whose software a book is sold.

Writing for Packt

We welcome all inquiries from people who are interested in authoring. Book proposals should be sent to author@packtpub.com. If your book idea is still at an early stage and you would like to discuss it first before writing a formal book proposal, contact us; one of our commissioning editors will get in touch with you.

We're not just looking for published authors; if you have strong technical skills but no writing experience, our experienced editors can help you develop a writing career, or simply get some additional reward for your expertise.

PUBLISHING

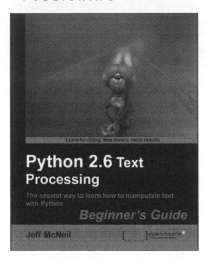

Python 2.6 Text Processing Beginners Guide

ISBN: 978-1-84951-212-1   Paperback: 380 pages

The easiest way to learn how to manipulate text with Python

1. The easiest way to learn text processing with Python.

2. Deals with the most important textual data formats that you will encounter.

3. Learn to use the most popular text processing libraries available for Python.

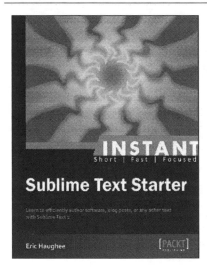

Instant Sublime Text Starter

ISBN: 978-1-84969-392-9   Paperback: 46 pages

Learn to efficiently author software, blog posts, or any other text with Sublime Text 2

1. Learn something new in an Instant! A short, fast, focused guide delivering immediate results.

2. Reduce redundant typing with contextual auto-complete.

3. Get a visual overview of, and move around in, your document with the preview pane.

4. Efficiently edit many lines of text with multiple cursors.

Please check **www.PacktPub.com** for information on our titles